Selected Lectures on
the Gosho

Daisaku Ikeda

Selected Lectures on the Gosho

Vol. I

Nichiren Shoshu International Center

First Edition, 1979
Fifth Printing, 1990

Copyright © 1979 by Nichiren Shoshu International
Center. All rights reserved
Published by
Nichiren Shoshu International Center
1-33-11 Sendagaya, Shibuya-ku, Tokyo 151

Library of Congress Catalog Card Number: 80-474224

ISBN4-88872-003-7   C1315
Printed in Japan

Contents

Contents

Foreword

The wisdom of Buddhism pervades every writing of Nichiren Daishonin, even his personal letters to his lay believers. It is our hope to convey this wisdom to the peoples of the world, and thus we are working steadily on the translation of Nichiren Daishonin's writings. *The Major Writings of Nichiren Daishonin*, vol. 1, was the first product of this continuing endeavor.

Now, in order to make his works more accessible to those who are interested in Buddhism and to those who share in the ideal of Buddhism—the sanctity of every single human life—we are publishing this volume, *Selected Lectures on the Gosho*, by Daisaku Ikeda, the third president of the Nichiren Shoshu Soka Gakkai. (The *Gosho* is the generic title given to Nichiren Daishonin's works.)

The Gosho entitled "Requital for the Buddha's Favor" (*Hō-on Shō*) reads, "The deeper the root, the more flourishing the branches. The deeper the spring, the longer the flow." This holds true for any religion and especially for Nichiren Daishonin's Buddhism. After a span of seven hundred years it has found its way into almost every country of the world, breaking the deadlock which had long prevented its spread.

Ironically, because of its universal and humanistic nature, Nichiren Daishonin's Buddhism had found the going rough in the pre-democratic religious conditions of Japan. During the second world war, even freedom of religion was suppressed by the military government. Under these circumstances Tsunesaburo Makiguchi, the founder and first president of the Soka Gakkai, opposed the government's efforts to impose faith in Shintoism on the whole nation and, together with his disciple, Josei Toda, was imprisoned as a result. He died, a martyr to his belief, in the prison infirmary.

Mr. Toda, on his release from prison, set about to reorganize the group and in so doing called the members' attention to the wisdom in Nichiren Daishonin's writings. In 1952, seven years after his release, Mr. Toda published *Nichiren Daishonin Gosho Zenshū* (Complete Works of Nichiren Daishonin) under the editorial supervision of Nichikō Hori, the fifty-ninth High Priest of Nichiren Shoshu.

In an age seemingly bereft of direction, the glory of Buddhism is that it sheds new light on the current predicament of humanity. And it does this by taking a penetrating look at the inner life of each human being. This is why we now see the spread of Nichiren Daishonin's Buddhism on a global scale.

The Gosho are an indispensable guideline for the practice of faith for all Nichiren Shoshu followers. The successive presidents of the Soka Gakkai have shown people how to apply the Gosho to their daily lives by urging them to follow the Daishonin's exhortation in "The True Entity of Life": "Exert yourself in the two ways of practice and study. Without practice and study, there can be no Buddhism."

Thus, there are myriad examples of people who, supported by a Gosho passage, have changed the course of their lives, as if transforming a harsh winter into a joyful spring. Today, hundreds of thousands, even millions, of people, young and old, from all walks of life, commit themselves to the study of Nichiren Daishonin's Buddhism, striving to deepen their faith and cultivate their characters.

The Soka Gakkai named both 1977 and 1978 the "Year of Study" and promoted study of the Gosho. A powerful thrust in this direction was given by third President Ikeda's lectures on several important writings of Nichiren Daishonin. Out of them, three relatively lengthy lectures are included in this volume of *Selected Lectures on the Gosho*.

Mr. Ikeda's lectures on "The True Entity of Life" and the "Heritage of the Ultimate Law of Life" appeared in the *Seikyo Shimbun*, the Soka Gakkai's newspaper, at the beginning of 1977 and in April 1977, respectively. His lecture on a portion of "The True Object of Worship" was carried in the January and February issues of the *Daibyakurenge*, the monthly study magazine of the Soka Gakkai. Translated into English, the three were serialized in the monthly *Seikyo Times*: "The True Entity of Life" between March and May of 1977, the "Heritage of the Ultimate Law of Life" between July and September of 1977, and "The True Object of Worship" between March and June of 1978. The editors have since revised the *Seikyo Times'* translations, to accord with Mr. Ikeda's desires and to further clarify them for English-speaking audiences.

The Gosho were written by Nichiren Daishonin with thirteenth century Japanese society as their setting. However, everywhere within and between the lines is the immutable truth of Buddhism, shining like a glistening jewel—here is the core of true Buddhism. In his lectures, Mr. Ikeda gave considerable thought to many Buddhist principles, looking at them from various angles, and attempted to apply them to every facet of society and modern life. We hope the reader will use this volume, *Selected Lectures on the Gosho*, as further nourishment for his growth in faith and human revolution.

Nichiren Shoshu International Center
Editorial Department

ONE

The True Entity of Life

Gosho Text

Question: In the *Hōben* chapter of Volume One of the Lotus Sutra is the passage: "The true entity of all phenomena can only be understood and shared between Buddhas. This reality consists of appearance, nature . . . and their consistency from beginning to end." What does this passage mean?

Answer: It means that all beings and their environments in any of the Ten Worlds, from Hell at the lowest to Buddhahood at the highest, are, without exception, the manifestations of Myoho-renge-kyo. Where there is an environment, there is life within it. Miao-lo states, "Both life (*shōhō*) and its environment (*ehō*) always manifest Myoho-renge-kyo." He also states, "The true entity is invariably revealed in all phenomena, and all phenomena invariably possess the Ten Factors. The Ten Factors invariably function within the Ten Worlds, and the Ten Worlds invariably entail both life and its environment." And, "Both the life and environment of Hell exist within the life of Buddha. On the other hand, the life and environment of Buddha do not transcend the lives of common mortals." Such precise explanations leave no room for doubt. Thus, all life in the universe is clearly Myoho-renge-kyo. Even the two Buddhas, Shakyamuni and Tahō, are the functions of Myoho-renge-kyo who appeared to bestow its blessings upon mankind. They manifested themselves as the two Buddhas and, seated together in the Treasure Tower, nodded in mutual agreement.

No one but Nichiren has ever revealed these teachings. T'ien-t'ai, Miao-lo and Dengyō knew in their hearts but did not declare them aloud. There was reason for their silence: The Buddha had not entrusted them with this mission, the time had not yet come, and they had not been the Buddha's disciples from ages past. No one but Jōgyō, Muhengyō and the other leaders of the Bodhisattvas of the Earth can appear during the first five hundred years of the Latter Day to spread the Law of Myoho-renge-kyo. Only they are qualified to inscribe the object of worship which physically manifests the ceremony of the two Buddhas seated together in the Treasure Tower. This is because both the Law and the object of worship are the reality of *ichinen sanzen* revealed in the *Juryō* chapter of the essential teaching.

The two Buddhas, Shakyamuni and Tahō, are merely functions of the true Buddha, while Myoho-renge-kyo actually is the true Buddha. The sutra explains this as "the Tathagata's secret and his mystic power." The "secret" refers to the entity of the Buddha's three properties and the "mystic power" to their functions. The entity is the true Buddha and the function, a provisional Buddha. The common mortal is the entity of the three properties, or the true Buddha. The Buddha is the function of the three properties, or a provisional Buddha. Shakyamuni is thought to have possessed the three virtues of sovereign, teacher and parent for the sake of us common mortals, but on the contrary, it is the common mortal who endowed him with the three virtues.

T'ien-t'ai explains the Tathagata as follows: "*Nyorai* is the title of the Buddhas of the ten directions and three existences, of the two Buddhas and the three Buddhas, and of all the Buddhas, true and provisional." Here the "true Buddha" is the common mortal, whereas "provisional Buddhas" means the Buddha. Nevertheless, there is a clear distinction between a Buddha and a common mortal, in that a common mortal is deluded while a Buddha is enlightened. The common mortal fails to realize that he himself possesses both the entity and the function of the Buddha's three properties.

"All phenomena" in the sutra refers to the Ten Worlds, and the "true entity" is what permeates the Ten Worlds. Reality is another expression for Myoho-renge-kyo; hence Myoho-renge-kyo is manifest in all phenomena. Hell appears hellish; that is the reality of Hell. When Hunger emerges, the reality of Hell is no longer present. A Buddha exhibits the reality of a Buddha, and a common mortal, that of a common mortal. All phenomena are themselves manifestations of Myoho-renge-kyo. This is the meaning of "all phenomena reveal the true entity." T'ien-t'ai states, "The profound principle of 'true entity' is the original law of Myoho-renge-kyo," thus identifying the phrase "true entity" with the theoretical teaching and "the original law of Myoho-renge-kyo" with the essential teaching. You should ponder this passage deep in your heart.

Although not worthy of the honor, Nichiren was nevertheless the first to spread the Mystic Law entrusted to Bodhisattva Jōgyō for propagation in the Latter Day of the Law. Nichiren was also the first to inscribe the Gohonzon, which is the embodiment of the Buddha from the remote past as revealed in the *Juryō* chapter of the essential teaching, of Tahō Buddha who appeared when the *Hōtō* chapter of the theoretical teaching was preached, and the Bodhisattvas of the Earth who emerged with the *Yujutsu* chapter. No matter how people may hate Nichiren, they cannot possibly alter the fact of his enlightenment.

To have exiled Nichiren to this remote island is therefore a sin that can never be expiated, even with the passing of countless aeons. A passage from the *Hiyu* chapter reads, "Not even an aeon would be time enough to explain the full gravity of this sin." On the other hand, not even the wisdom of the Buddha can fathom the blessings one will obtain by giving alms to Nichiren and by becoming his disciple. The *Yakuō* chapter reads, "Not even with the Buddha's wisdom can one measure these benefits."

Nichiren alone began to carry out the task of the

Bodhisattvas of the Earth. He may even be one of them. If Nichiren should be a Bodhisattva of the Earth, then so must his disciples. The *Hosshi* chapter states, "If there is someone, whether man or woman, who secretly teaches to one person even a single phrase of the Lotus Sutra, let it be known that he is the envoy of the Buddha, sent to carry out the Buddha's work." Who else but us can this possibly refer to?

When one is praised highly by others, he feels there is no hardship he cannot bear. Such is the courage which springs from words of praise. The votary born in the Latter Day of the Law who propagates the Lotus Sutra will encounter the three powerful enemies, who will cause him to be exiled and even sentence him to death. Yet Shakyamuni Buddha will enfold in his robe of mercy those who nonetheless persevere in propagating. All gods will make them offerings, support them with their shoulders and carry them on their backs. They possess supreme good fortune and qualify as leaders of all mankind. Thus extolled by Shakyamuni Buddha, Tahō Buddha and all of the other Buddhas and bodhisattvas, the seven ranks of heavenly gods and five ranks of earthly gods, Kishimojin and her ten daughters, the Four Heavenly Kings, Bonten, Taishaku, King Emma, the gods of the waters and winds, the gods of the seas and mountains, Dainichi Buddha, Bodhisattvas Fugen and Monju and the gods of the sun and the moon, Nichiren has been able to endure countless harsh trials.

When praised, one does not consider his personal risk, and when criticized, he can recklessly cause his own ruin. Such is the way of common mortals.

No matter what, maintain your faith as a votary of the Lotus Sutra, and forever exert yourself as Nichiren's disciple. If you are of the same mind as Nichiren, you must be a Bodhisattva of the Earth. And since you are a Bodhisattva of the Earth, there is not the slightest doubt that you have been a disciple of the Buddha from the remotest past. The *Yujutsu* chapter states, "I have taught these people since the remotest past." There should be no discrimination among those who propagate the five characters of Myoho-renge-kyo in the Latter Day of the Law, be they men or women. Were they not Bodhisattvas of the Earth, they could not chant the daimoku. Only I, Nichiren, at first chanted Nam-myoho-renge-kyo, but then two, three and a hundred followed, chanting and teaching others. Likewise, propagation will unfold this way in the future. Doesn't this signify "emerging from the earth"? At the time of *kōsen-rufu*, the entire Japanese nation will chant Nam-myoho-renge-kyo, as surely as an arrow aimed at the earth cannot miss the target.

But now you must build your reputation as a votary of the Lotus Sutra and devote yourself to it. Shakyamuni Buddha and Tahō Buddha, seated in the Treasure Tower in the air, surrounded by all other Buddhas and bodhisattvas, nodded in agreement. What they decided upon was solely for the perpetuation of the True Law throughout the Latter Day. Tahō Buddha had offered Shakyamuni Buddha a place beside him, and when they unfurled the banner of Myoho-renge-kyo, the two leaders of the entire multitude made their decision together. Could there have been anything false in their decision? Their ultimate purpose in meeting was to provide a way for all of us ordinary people to attain Buddhahood.

Although I was not at that ceremony, in looking at the sutra, this is crystal-clear. On the other hand, I may have been at the ceremony, but since I am a common mortal, it is beyond my power to know the past. There is no doubt, however, that in the present life I am the votary of the Lotus Sutra, and that in the future I will therefore reach the seat of enlightenment. Judging the past from this point of view, I must have been at the ceremony in the air. There can be no discontinuity between past, present and future.

Because I view things this way, I feel immeasurable delight even though I am now an exile. Joy as well as sorrow brings us to tears. Tears express our feeling for both blessings and misfortune. The one thousand arhats shed tears in memory of the Buddha, and in tears Bodhisattva Monju chanted Myoho-renge-kyo. From among those one thousand arhats, the venerable Ananda replied in tears, "Thus I heard." Thereupon the tears of all the others fell, wetting their inkstones, and they wrote "Myoho-renge-kyo" followed by "Thus I heard." I, Nichiren, now feel exactly as they did. I am now in exile because I spread the teaching of Myoho-renge-kyo. I spread this teaching because I, too, "heard thus": Shakyamuni Buddha and Tahō Buddha left Myoho-renge-kyo for the Japanese and all people in the future.

I cannot hold back my tears when I think of the great persecution confronting me now, or when I think of the joy of attaining Buddhahood in the future. Birds cry, but never shed tears. I, Nichiren, do not cry, but my tears flow ceaselessly. I shed my tears not for worldly affairs but solely for the sake of the Lotus Sutra. So indeed, they must be tears of *amrita*. The Nirvana Sutra states that while the tears one sheds throughout his many existences on the death of his parents, brothers, sisters, wives, children and followers may surpass the quantity of water in all the seas, he weeps not a drop for Buddhism. One becomes a votary of the Lotus Sutra by virtue of his practice in past existences. It is karmic relationships that determine which among so many of the same kind of trees are made into images of Buddha. It is also because of karma that some Buddhas are born as provisional ones.

In this letter, I have written my most important teachings. Grasp their meaning and make them part of your life. Believe in the Gohonzon, the supreme object of worship in the world. Forge strong faith and receive the protection of Shakyamuni, Tahō and all the other Buddhas. Exert yourself in the two ways of practice and study. Without practice and study, there can be no Buddhism. You must not only persevere yourself; you must also teach others. Both practice and study arise from faith. Teach others to the best of your ability, even if only a single sentence or phrase. Nam-myoho-renge-kyo, Nam-myoho-renge-kyo.

With my deep respect,
Nichiren

The seventeenth day of the fifth month

Postscript:

I have already passed on to you many of my important teachings. Those I have revealed to you in this letter are especially important. Is there not a mystic bond between us? Are you not the embodiment of one of the Four Bodhisattvas of the Earth headed by Jōgyō who led bodhisattvas equal in number to the sands of the sixty thousand Ganges Rivers? There must be some profound reason for our relationship. I have given you some of the most important teachings relating to my own life and practice. Nichiren may be one of the countless Bodhisattvas of the Earth, for I have been chanting Nam-myoho-renge-kyo out of my desire to guide all the men and women in Japan. Hence the phrase of the sutra: "Among the bodhisattvas are four who led the entire multitude: The first is called Jōgyō; [the second, Muhengyō; the third, Jyōgyō; and the fourth, Anryūgyō.] They are the four highest leaders." Our deep relationship in the past has made you one of my disciples. By all means keep these matters to yourself. Nichiren has herein committed to writing the teachings of his own enlightenment. I will end here.

Lecture

Spirit of Buddhist Study

Seeing the sun of Nichiren Daishonin's Buddhism rise among each of us, I would like to speak to you about *Shohō Jissō Shō* (The True Entity of Life) with prayers for the good health of each of you. First, let me recount a story that relates to the Soka Gakkai's study movement as it opens the way for the "religion of man." It concerns Kumarajiva (344–409 A.D.) of Kucha in Central Asia. He was responsible for great waves of Buddhist thought which flowed across China over a thousand years ago. As you know, he was a priest who completed the unexcelled translation of the Lotus Sutra from Sanskrit into Chinese, and he rendered the sutra's title and essence as *Myoho-renge-kyo*. However, what moves me more than his work is the passion with which he went to China and dedicated his entire life to the transmission of the true spirit of Buddhism. It is said that Kumarajiva was over fifty when he entered Ch'angan, after long years of hardship. That was the starting point of his struggle to fulfill the purpose he had long cherished. From then on, the hard work of passing on the Buddhist teachings started. He carried out his translation work at a great pace, as if all the power pent up within him were released all at once. Hearing of his arrival, priests came from every district in China to form a great religious order under him.

It is said that he ended his days eight or twelve years later, and that during this period more than three hundred volumes of sutras were translated at the tremendous speed of two or three a month. His enterprise was a vivid movement of Buddhist study that went far beyond translation. According to the prefaces of various scriptures he translated, a large number of capable people—eight hundred on one occasion and two thousand on another—gathered around him to engage in the translation effort. Carrying the translated sutras with him, Kumarajiva unfolded his interpretation of Buddhism before these audiences. He elucidated each teaching clearly and thoroughly, explaining why the wording of a sutra had been rendered in such a way and wherein the true meaning lay. He patiently answered many questions from the people assembled under him until they truly understood the meaning of each sutra. One would think he had devoted decades to these difficult translations, confined to his study with nothing but dictionaries around him, but that was not the way he worked. He worked with the people, acutely sensing their innermost feelings as he carried on discussions about Buddhism with them. His translation of the Lotus Sutra was the fruit of this broad and sensitive approach. I am convinced this is why Kumarajiva was able to produce such a smooth and still accurate rendition of the sutra's original meaning. No matter how important or valuable the teachings of Buddhism may be, if they cannot be correctly understood, they will never become part of the lives of the people. Philosophy's true value can only shine through communication between people and in their daily experience. Without the work of Kumarajiva and his group to propagate the sutras, the development of Buddhism and its flowering with T'ien-t'ai in China and Dengyō in Japan could never have taken place.

I do not want simply to praise the greatness of Kumarajiva and his mission, but to suggest what we can learn from the way he approached his mission and apply it to our own study of Buddhism. He devoted himself to dialogue with the people, always remaining among them. In a sense we are the Kumarajivas of today. He helped introduce the Buddhist scriptures from India to China through translation, and the Kumarajivas of this day must bring to life the seven-hundred-year-old scripture of the Latter Day of the Law by introducing it and propagating it to people of modern times. Our study movement follows the same pattern as Kumarajiva's. With the Gosho as our sutra, we use the forms each occasion requires—lectures, questions and answers, and personal guidance. And we unfold Buddhism through dialogue, keeping in direct touch with the hearts of the people.

Shakyamuni Buddha also expounded his teachings among the people, sharing their joys and sorrows until he passed away. The teachings he left still shine, filled with the understanding that comes from direct confrontation with the suffering that is an inseparable part of every man's existence. One extremist Buddhist scholar goes so far as to say that Shakyamuni did not expound Buddhism. Of course there can be no question that Shakyamuni gave birth to Buddhism, but there is something significant in what that scholar said. When someone speaks of the many sutras taught by Shakyamuni or their classification by T'ien-t'ai into five periods and eight teachings,* it sounds as though Shakyamuni

---

*T'ien-t'ai's classification of Shakyamuni's teachings according to the order and content of their preaching. The five periods are the Kegon, Agon, Hōdō, Hannya and Hokke-Nehan periods. During the last period Shakyamuni expounded the Lotus Sutra, fully revealing his enlightenment. The eight teachings are subdivided into two groups: four teachings of *kehō* (doctrine) and four teachings of *kegi* (method). The first are: 1) *zōkyō*, Hinayana teachings; 2) *tsūgyō*, lower provisional Mahayana teachings; 3) *bekkyō*, higher provisional Mahayana teachings; and 4) *engyō*, or true Mahayana, that is, the Lotus Sutra. The second, a division by method of teaching, are: 1) *tonkyō*, to reveal the teaching of enlightenment directly; 2) *zenkyō*, to reveal the teaching gradually; 3) *himitsukyō*, to teach so that everyone, unknowingly, receives a different benefit according to his capacity; and 4) *fujōkyō*, to teach so that everyone knowingly receives a different benefit.

preached according to some detailed, prearranged system. The truth is that Shakyamuni taught in the form of encouragement to poverty-stricken people—to an old woman afflicted with illness, as if he felt her pain as his own and carried her on his back, or warm encouragement to a youth in the grip of deep spiritual suffering. All his sutras were the natural result of his lifelong devotion to the people, the accumulation of every compassionate word he spoke to alleviate the pain of people oppressed by the cruel caste system. That is why the sutras consist of questions and answers throughout. The teachings of Shakyamuni sprang from his disciples' memories and records of his talks with the people and his behavior among them. These are what were finally compiled in the form of the sutras we have today.

The same is true with Nichiren Daishonin. He carried on in the same spirit as Shakyamuni. The voluminous Gosho we study is the crystallization of the Daishonin's continuous struggle to save the people through hundreds of letters and thousands of dialogues. He did not confine himself to a library to write the Gosho but talked and wrote right at the site of his battle—among the people. He fought for the people, talking with them and writing them individual letters of encouragement. To think of Buddhism as a placid teaching expounded in a bucolic setting under the shade of a tree is a totally false image. Buddhism is intensely practical, not escapist. It lives in human society and has been handed down among the people—this is the true flow of Buddhism.

The True Entity of Life is a comparatively short Gosho, but it contains important elements of the Daishonin's Buddhism. In the postscript Nichiren Daishonin wrote, "Those I have revealed to you in this letter are especially important. . . . By all means keep these matters to yourself. Nichiren has herein committed to writing the teachings of his own enlightenment." Nichiren Daishonin wrote this Gosho on May 17, 1273, a month after he wrote *The True Object of*

Worship (April 25). In the latter, he revealed the core of Buddhist practice in the Latter Day of the Law by explaining the Dai-Gohonzon, the supreme object of worship, in terms of the Law (Nam-myoho-renge-kyo), and the way for all people to attain enlightenment. *The True Entity of Life* begins with a passage from the *Hōben* chapter—the heart of the theoretical teaching (*shakumon*) of the Lotus Sutra—which reads, "The true entity of all phenomena can only be understood and shared between Buddhas. This reality consists of appearance, nature . . . and their consistency from beginning to end." It then reveals the essence of the Lotus Sutra—Myoho-renge-kyo and its embodiment, the Gohonzon. Nichiren Daishonin, in other words, clarified the significance of *hō-honzon*, explaining the Gohonzon from the viewpoint of the Law.

After elucidating the ultimate teaching of the Lotus Sutra the Daishonin declares that only Bodhisattva Jōgyō, the leader of the Bodhisattvas of the Earth, can propagate it, and that the Daishonin himself was carrying out the mission entrusted to Bodhisattva Jōgyō. Superficially, Nichiren Daishonin suggests that he is the incarnation of Bodhisattva Jōgyō. But a deeper understanding lets us know that the Daishonin is the Buddha who is to establish the Dai-Gohonzon for the salvation of the people of the Latter Day and the original Buddha of *kuon ganjo*. Thus, in this Gosho the Daishonin also reveals *nin-honzon*, explaining the Gohonzon in terms of the Person. In terms of both the Person and Law, Nichiren Daishonin reveals the prime object of reverence to the people of the Latter Day. Thus, this Gosho contains the main points expounded in *The Opening of the Eyes* (*nin-honzon*) and elaborated on in *The True Object of Worship* (*hō-honzon*).

In the latter half of this Gosho, moreover, the Daishonin predicts that *kōsen-rufu* will be attained in the future, and concludes by setting down the core of Buddhist practice throughout the Latter Day on into eternity—the way of faith, practice and study. In the final analysis, this Gosho reveals clearly and concisely the profound essence and practice of Buddhism for the Latter Day of the Law.

Because we in the Soka Gakkai stress the need for people to return to the teachings of Nichiren Daishonin as the prime point in their lives, this Gosho has continued to have special importance in deepening the members' faith, giving them guidance and working as the guideline for our activities. I have heard that our first president, Tsunesaburo Makiguchi, constantly gave guidance to people by referring to this Gosho. Then too, apart from his lectures on the Lotus Sutra, the first Gosho on which President Josei Toda lectured before a small group of disciples was *The True Entity of Life*. I was one of those present at that time.

I myself have given frequent lectures on *The True Entity of Life* to the high school division and selected members of the headquarters staff. But every time I read this Gosho, I am always impressed and moved anew at the strength and depth of Nichiren Daishonin's conviction. In commemoration of the 46th anniversary of the Soka Gakkai's founding, I revised my many lectures on this Gosho and set them in the context of our era. With these comments as a brief introduction, let us go on to explore *The True Entity of Life* in greater depth.

All Phenomena Manifest the True Entity

Question: In the *Hōben* chapter of Volume One of the Lotus Sutra is the passage: "The true entity of all phenomena can only be understood and shared between Buddhas. This reality consists of the appearance, nature, ... and their consistency from beginning to end." What does this passage mean?

The passage, "The true entity of all phenomena...," is the

essence of the theoretical teaching of the Lotus Sutra, and in T'ien-t'ai's Buddhism it is the core of all of Shakyamuni's teachings as well as the foundation on which to expound the principle of *ichinen sanzen* (three thousand conditions in a momentary existence of life). Sairenbō Nichijō, who received this letter containing that passage, is said to have been a priest of the Tendai sect before he became a follower of Nichiren Daishonin. We can presume, therefore, that he knew about "the true entity of all phenomena" as the basic teaching of the Tendai school. He could not, however, thoroughly understand it through T'ien-t'ai's theory, and so he asked the Daishonin to explain the exact meaning of the passage.

Answer: It means that all beings and their environments in any of the Ten Worlds, from Hell at the lowest to Buddhahood at the highest, are, without exception, the manifestations of Myoho-renge-kyo.

Through this passage Nichiren Daishonin gives a clear-cut explanation of "the true entity of all phenomena," saying that, of all phenomena (*shohō*), none is any different from the true entity of life (*jissō*). In other words, the innumerable forms and appearances in the great universe are all manifestations of Myoho-renge-kyo, and both the environment (*ehō*) of the world of Hell and the people (*shohō*) who suffer in Hell are ultimately Myoho-renge-kyo. Both *ehō* and *shohō* of the world of Hunger are also Myoho-renge-kyo. This holds true with the rest of the Ten Worlds including Bodhisattva and Buddhahood.

"The true entity" (*jissō*) of "all phenomena" (*shohō*) does not, however, mean that the true entity is contained within all phenomena or vice versa, nor does it assume the existence of some being that exists beyond all universal phenomena and governs them. Western philosophers and other non-Buddhist thinkers and systems of thought have long sought some truth or essence either beyond or behind phenomena. The Christian idea of an absolute God as the creator of the world is a good example of how these other philosophies removed the ultimate truth from all real phenomena. The inevitable result was a split between God and man or between Creator and creature. Churches and priests took over as the "authorized" intermediaries between the two, and they grew so powerful that the people were treated like vassals.

Buddhism is totally different. The Buddhist finds truth in reality itself; he discovers the underlying truth by steadily and carefully observing man and the things around him. "The true entity of all phenomena" is, therefore, a philosophy that sees into the real aspect of every reality in the universe, especially human life. All phenomena and the true entity are "two but not two," for one cannot exist without the other. This is what binds the true entity and all phenomena together, making them one and the same, even though they may seem to be different. All phenomena—the sun and the moon as they rise and set, the ebb and flow of the seas, the bending of trees before the wind—in the eye of Buddhism all appear as the action of Myoho-renge-kyo. Unlike the Lotus Sutra, which gives careful, deep treatment of this principle, all the other sutras deal solely with the phenomena themselves and point out only differences among them. The Lotus Sutra sees beyond the superficial differences and discovers the Mystic Law equally permeating the depths of all. This is what sets the "perfect and all-embracing Lotus Sutra" above the "provisional teachings of discrimination." The principle of equality meant by "the true entity of all phenomena" is an expression of the Buddha's great and impartial wisdom, which recognizes the potential for Buddhahood in all people alike. Nonetheless, the first half of the Lotus Sutra (theoretical teaching) only explains this theoretically, while the second half (essential teaching) gives practical meaning to the theory.

Take for instance Newton's law of gravitation. It is a law of physics and, even if it is not directly parallel to this Buddhist principle, we know that it operates throughout the universe. Regardless of who discovered it or whether it was "discovered" at all, the law of gravitation has always existed, and all things move according to it. To the eye of physics, the movement of the sun, moon, and stars, the changes in the tides, an apple falling from a tree—all these are understood in terms of the law of physics. Without understanding gravity, people merely see an apple ripening and falling to the earth, yet a physicist recognizes the law behind this phenomenon, that gravity is working between two objects, the earth and the apple. This law keeps on working whether one is aware of it or not, but he cannot apply it to anything if he cannot first identify and analyze it. Then again, to know about gravity and not do anything with that knowledge may be a serious waste. Only when we translate this knowledge into some practical use by creating an airplane, spaceship or something else of value to man, can we enjoy the benefits of the knowledge we have gained from the law of gravity.

In Buddhism, the true entity of all the movements of the universe is Myoho-renge-kyo. Common mortals see nothing but the trees waving in the wind, yet the Buddha sees the mystic rhythm of Myoho-renge-kyo pulsing within. To him the sun's radiance is the harmonious manifestation of the Mystic Law that fosters all kinds of life on earth. Every aspect of our life is made up according to the Mystic Law, and we always act in rhythm with it. Merely to realize this fact is, however, still a theoretical understanding. Anyone who does not know how to bring his life into oneness with the Mystic Law would be like someone falling in an attempt to fly, ignorant of the law of gravitation. He would fall into one suffering and then another, only getting more and more deeply confused.

Likewise, if we grasp the principle of "the true entity of all phenomena" only philosophically, we are none the better for it. Nichiren Daishonin inscribed the Gohonzon to enable us to apply its principle to the creation of happy and hopeful lives. The principle was embodied in the Gohonzon by the Daishonin when he put his life and soul into it. By inscribing the Gohonzon, he gave us the entity of value creation. It is not mere philosophy any more. It is the true entity—the very life of Nichiren Daishonin, his life of *ichinen sanzen*. This is why the Gohonzon is called the entity of *ichinen sanzen*.

"The true entity of all phenomena" is a philosophy that sees all universal phenomena as manifestations of Myoho-renge-kyo. Yet, in its essential meaning, it points to the Gohonzon as the ultimate crystallization of all phenomena in the universe. In the Daishonin's Buddhism, "the true entity of all phenomena" therefore means the Gohonzon.

Life and the Environment

Where there is an environment, there is life within it. Miao-lo states, "Both life (*shōhō*) and its environment (*ehō*) always manifest Myoho-renge-kyo."

Does the order of these words puzzle you? "Where there is an environment, there is life within it." We learned, after all, from the Lotus Sutra that life is like the body, and the environment like the shadow. Should it not read, "Where there is life, there is an environment surrounding it," reversing it completely?

To explain this briefly, all the pre-Lotus Sutra teachings expounded the Ten Worlds as ten different places. As you may already know, the world of Hell (*jigoku*) was said to be one thousand *yujun* underground; the world of Hunger (*gaki*) five hundred *yujun* underground; the world of Animality (*chikushō*) in the water, on land, and in the sky; the world of Anger (*shura*) on the coast and in the depths of the sea; the world of Humanity or Tranquillity (*nin*) on the earth; and the world of Heaven or Rapture (*ten*) in a palace or from the middle of Mount Sumeru upward. The four noble worlds were explained similarly: the world of two vehicles (Learning and Realization) was one of transience (*hōben-do*); the world of Bodhisattva (*bosatsu*) was one of actual rewards (*jippō-do*); and the world of Buddhahood (*butsu*) was the Buddha land (*jakkō-do*). Since these environments were thought to exist in different places, it naturally followed that the people dwelling in them were also different. The truth is, however, that the people (*shohō*) and their environments (*ehō*) are inseparable. This is the way life exists. The Lotus Sutra, the true philosophy of life, was the first to state that an environment can only be explained in relationship with the living things in it.

Miao-lo of China states in his *Hokke Mongu Ki* (Annotations on the Words and Phrases of the Lotus Sutra) that all of the ten states of environment and life manifest Myoho-renge-kyo. He explains that the essence of environment and that of life are in perfect oneness. An environment is the entity of Myoho-renge-kyo and life is also. Both are aspects of the Law of Myoho-renge-kyo, for the original Law, Myoho-renge-kyo, manifests itself simultaneously as living things and their environments. They are united on the level of life. Thus we can see the powerful principle in Buddhism that a revolution within life (*shohō*) always leads to one in the environment (*ehō*).

I want to mention an article by Dr. Hisayuki Omodaka, in which he writes: "Men tend to think in terms of one large environment in which all living things exist. However, human beings, fish, birds, etc., each have their own particular environments. For each individual the environment differs. Hence there are actually countless environments. No environment exists apart from living things. Just as living things gradually reproduce themselves and develop specific features and qualities, the environment also gradually departs from living things and develops into the form that corresponds with each unique being." Dr. Omodaka insists that living things and their environments adapt to each other and that the origin of both is "primitive existence." His observation of the world of living things conforms with the principle of *eshō funi* (oneness of life and the environment).

Buddha Is Not an Abstract Being

He also states, "The true entity is invariably revealed in all phenomena, and all phenomena invariably possess the Ten Factors. The Ten Factors invariably function within the Ten Worlds, and the Ten Worlds invariably entail both life and its environment."

This is a passage from the *Kompeiron*, Miao-lo's thesis on the Buddha nature inherent in all things, living and non-living. It explains the structure of *ichinen sanzen*. As mentioned earlier, the true entity refers to Myoho-renge-kyo and represents *ichinen* (the life-moment) of *ichinen sanzen*. "The true entity is invariably revealed in all phenomena" means that the *ichinen* or Myoho-renge-kyo is eternally manifested in phenomena. In the following passage, Miao-lo states the true entity by analyzing all phenomena into the Ten Factors, the Ten Worlds, and life and its environment.

First of all, the Ten Factors represent the ten aspects common to all phenomena. They are appearance (*nyoze-sō*), nature (*nyoze-shō*), entity (*nyoze-tai*), power (*nyoze-riki*), influence (*nyoze-sa*), internal cause (*nyoze-in*), relation (*nyoze-en*), latent effect (*nyoze-ka*), manifest effect (*nyoze-hō*), and consistency from beginning to end (*nyoze-honmatsu-*

kukyō-tō). All phenomena have these Ten Factors and all of them manifest one or another of the Ten Worlds. The Ten Factors are inherent in each of the Ten Worlds—even in Hell and Buddhahood. This is what is meant by the reality of all phenomena.

"The Ten Worlds invariably entail both life and its environment," means that each of the Ten Worlds is certainly seen in both a living thing and its surroundings. This is the working of the principle of *eshō funi*, the oneness of life and its environment.

Concretely, Myoho-renge-kyo exists nowhere outside our daily activities. That is what Miao-lo meant by, "The true entity is invariably revealed in all phenomena."

"All phenomena invariably possess the Ten Factors" is another way of saying that life as it changes moment by moment never loses its Ten Factors. No one can say, "I have no *nyoze-sō* (appearance)." Everyone has a face and figure. He has also *nyoze-shō* (mind or nature). He cannot just exist like a stone. Actually, even a stone has its *nyoze-shō*. The same is true for *nyoze-tai* (entity).

Also, everyone has his own specific power, influence, internal cause, relation, latent effect, and manifest effect. A person's life-condition, whatever it is, as it is, is reflected simultaneously in all the nine factors, from the first, "appearance," to the last, "manifest effect." This is "their consistency from beginning to end," of the *Hōben* chapter.

The true entity, if it were not to exist as phenomena or possess the Ten Factors, could not be true any more. For example, such Buddhas as Dainichi (Skt., Mahavairochana), who appear in the pre-Lotus Sutra teachings, do not possess the Ten Factors. They do not even have *nyoze-sō* (form or appearance). Who on earth has ever seen Dainichi Buddha? Buddhas who are not endowed with appearance, nature and entity have no power to save people.

The Judeo-Christian religions may assert that their su-

preme beings do not appear in any real form, but the Lotus
Sutra proclaims that there is no true entity outside of phenomena or the Ten Factors. Shakyamuni Buddha was a
real person, and Nichiren Daishonin also plunged into the
midst of actual society, shared the people's sufferings and
gave his enlightenment equally to all mankind. I insist that
the Buddha is not an imaginary or an abstract being but one
who clearly expresses himself in real behavior through the
function of his Ten Factors.

"The Ten Factors invariably function within the Ten
Worlds"—the Ten Factors are not indifferent to suffering
and joy. Each factor represents a facet of the same momentary life-condition, and for that reason, all the Ten Factors
are involved in any one of the Ten Worlds. The Ten Factors
reflect Buddhahood just as easily as they reflect Hell. When
you did not know about the Gohonzon, you created the
causes for and received the effects of suffering. Your power
and influence were weak. When filled with joy, it is impossible for you to look fierce; when overcome by sorrow, you
cannot laugh with joy. When you suffered, all of your Ten
Factors at one time reflected Hell or other lower conditions.
But now you embrace the Gohonzon and are changing your
life, so that you appear blessed with good fortune, with a
gentle and generous nature, and you develop great power and
influence to support your family and direct all your causes
and effects toward creating a happier life. I hope that all of
you will keep your Ten Factors this way throughout your
lives.

Lastly, "the Ten Worlds invariably entail both life and its
environment"—the Ten Worlds we experience become
apparent both within ourselves and our environment. When
a person is in the state of Hell, he finds his environment in
Hell, too. Conversely, a man whose life-condition is Buddhahood makes his place the Buddha land. This is what
we can attain by human revolution. Even if you enshrine

the Gohonzon at home, if you leave your home untidy and remain inconsiderate to your neighbors, you are not practicing what the above passage tells you. Only when you each make a golden castle of your own home, fill it with pleasant laughter and contribute to the prosperity of your community can you advance toward making the whole world the Buddha land. I hope you do so. Then you are truly making this passage part of your life.

The deepest meaning of this passage of Miao-lo comes out when we think about it in terms of Nichiren Daishonin's Buddhism. It exactly represents the Gohonzon of the Three Great Secret Laws. Phenomena are composed of three thousand conditions including the Ten Worlds, and all are perfectly represented in the Gohonzon. All of the Ten Worlds are contained in the one Law, Nam-myoho-renge-kyo. This is the Gohonzon. To be more specific, "Nam-myoho-renge-kyo, Nichiren" written down the center of the Gohonzon represents the true entity of all phenomena of the Ten Worlds, while the representatives of the Ten Worlds on both sides are the Ten Worlds of the Daishonin's life, the ten differing activities of life illuminated by the eternal light of Nam-myoho-renge-kyo.

In the upper part on both sides of Nam-myoho-renge-kyo are the names of Shakyamuni and Tahō Buddhas. Sitting on each side of the original Buddha, they represent the state of Buddhahood. Further to their left and right are inscribed the names of the four leaders of the Bodhisattvas of the Earth: Jōgyō, Muhengyō, Jyōgyō and Anryūgyō. They represent the state of Bodhisattva. Lower down Shariputra and Mahakashyapa represent the two vehicles (Learning and Realization); Bonten and Taishaku, the gods of the sun and the moon, and the Devil of the Sixth Heaven represent the state of Heaven or Rapture; the wheel-rolling king represents the state of Humanity or Tranquillity; King Ashura represents the state of Anger; the Dragon King's daughter represents the state of Animality; Kishimojin and her ten daughters (Jūrasetsunyo) represent the state of Hunger; and Devadatta represents the state of Hell. All these representatives of the Ten Worlds "consist of the Ten Factors."

The statement that the Ten Worlds are manifest in life and its environment can be interpreted to mean that the Daishonin's life is manifest in the scroll of the Gohonzon and its environment is the Buddhist altar.

And, "Both the life and environment of Hell exist within the life of Buddha. On the other hand, the life and environment of Buddha do not transcend the lives of common mortals."

This also comes from the *Kompeiron*. Even the world of Hell and the people in it are entirely within the supreme life of the Buddha himself. On the other hand, the supreme life and land of the Buddha exist within the lives of common mortals. In short, this reveals the principle of the mutual possession of the Ten Worlds through the examples of Hell and Buddhahood.

If we look deeper into this passage, we see that because both the supreme life of the Buddha and the life of common mortals are entities of Myoho-renge-kyo, even a Buddha has the potential to manifest the state of Hell, and common mortals equally have the potential to manifest Buddhahood.

Such precise explanations leave no room for doubt. Thus, all life in the universe is clearly Myoho-renge-kyo. Even the two Buddhas, Shakyamuni and Tahō, are the functions of Myoho-renge-kyo who appeared to bestow its blessings upon mankind. They manifested themselves as the two Buddhas and, seated together in the Treasure Tower, nodded in mutual agreement.

Nichiren Daishonin says that the phrase, "the true entity

of all phenomena," reveals that all life in the universe is Myoho-renge-kyo. In the Lotus Sutra Shakyamuni preached the truth using principles, parables, or by explaining the relationship between himself and his disciples in past existences. In these three ways he enabled his disciples of *shōmon* to attain enlightenment. The subsequent appearance of the Treasure Tower was for the benefit of those to come after Shakyamuni Buddha's passing. With it, the magnificent ceremony in the air* began, centering on the Treasure Tower with Shakyamuni and Tahō Buddhas seated side by side. The sentence, "Even the two Buddhas, Shakyamuni and Tahō, . . . ," means that the ceremony ultimately revealed Myoho-renge-kyo. This sentence also has another meaning. It signifies that the Law of Myoho-renge-kyo started working to bless the people through the actions of Shakyamuni and Tahō. The two Buddhas are the functions of the Mystic Law, as is mentioned later: "The function is a provisional Buddha." All the magnificent Buddhas mentioned in various sutras are, in the final analysis, functions of Myoho-renge-kyo or the Buddhahood which pervades the universe. Myoho-renge-kyo functions in all life of the Ten Worlds including Buddhahood.

"They . . . in the Treasure Tower, nodded in mutual agreement" means that the Law which Shakyamuni and Tahō Buddhas unveiled at the ceremony in the air is Myoho-renge-kyo. "Nodded in mutual agreement" symbolizes that Shakyamuni gave the teaching and that Tahō agreed to it and testified to the validity of the Law. President Toda once lectured about the significance of the ceremony of the Treasure Tower:

*The ceremony in which the entire assembly floats in space, and one of the three assemblies described in the Lotus Sutra, extending from the *Hōtō* (11th) to the *Zokurui* (22nd) chapter. In this ceremony, Shakyamuni clarifies his original enlightenment in the remote past and transfers the essence of the sutra to the Bodhisattvas of the Earth led by Bodhisattva Jōgyō, entrusting them with the mission to propagate it in the Latter Day of the Law.

With the ceremony of the Treasure Tower Shakyamuni revealed the mutual possession of the Ten Worlds and *ichinen sanzen* inherent in his life. In the same way, Nichiren Daishonin made use of the ceremony when he embodied on the scroll of the Gohonzon the ultimate teaching of enlightenment hidden within the *Juryō* chapter. The Gohonzon, therefore, depicts Shakyamuni's ceremony of the Treasure Tower only to reveal the mutual possession of the Ten Worlds and *ichinen sanzen* in the Daishonin's own life—the life of the original Buddha. Since the Gohonzon is the expression of the eternal life of the original Buddha, it is the only object of worship that has the power to enable the people of the Latter Day to attain Buddhahood.

The True Envoys

No one but Nichiren has ever revealed these teachings. T'ien-t'ai, Miao-lo and Dengyō knew in their hearts but did not declare them aloud. There was reason for their silence: The Buddha had not entrusted them with this mission, the time had not yet come, and they had not been the Buddha's disciples from ages past. No one but Jōgyō, Muhengyō and the other leaders of the Bodhisattvas of the Earth can appear during the first five hundred years of the Latter Day to spread the Law of Myoho-renge-kyo. Only they are qualified to inscribe the object of worship which physically manifests the ceremony of the two Buddhas seated together in the Treasure Tower. This is because both the Law and the object of worship are the reality of *ichinen sanzen* revealed in the *Juryō* chapter of the essential teaching.

Nichiren Daishonin was the first person ever to reveal that "the true entity of all phenomena" taught in the *Hōben* chapter and the ceremony in the air that takes place in the essential teaching both express Myoho-renge-kyo. However, since the true aim of the Lotus Sutra is to reveal Myoho-renge-kyo, T'ien-t'ai, Miao-lo and Dengyō, who so thoroughly mastered the Lotus Sutra, must have known this truth in their hearts. This is why the Daishonin was able to say, "T'ien-t'ai, Miao-lo and Dengyō knew in their hearts but did not declare them aloud."

"Declare them aloud" of course means to teach what they knew to others, but why didn't T'ien-t'ai, Miao-lo and Dengyō teach anyone else what they had realized within their own hearts? The Daishonin gives us three reasons: One is that the Buddha did not direct them to carry out the mission. During the ceremony of the Lotus Sutra Shakyamuni Buddha singled out his original disciples, the Bodhisattvas of the Earth, for the mission of propagating the sutra's most important teaching. In comparison, T'ien-t'ai, Miao-lo and Dengyō were bodhisattvas of the theoretical teaching, whom the Buddha had excluded from this mission.

The second reason is that the time was not yet right. For in the *Yakuō* (23rd) chapter of the Lotus Sutra it is stated, "In the fifth five hundred years after my death, accomplish worldwide *kōsen-rufu*." The time to commence propagation of the ultimate teaching of the Lotus Sutra, he said, would be the fifth half-millennium after Shakyamuni's death—the first five hundred years of the Latter Day of the Law. "The time" is the most important condition for the spreading of the Law. Only a Buddha who thoroughly understands the three existences of life can know when the time is right for propagation. That is why the Buddha himself clearly set the time for the teaching of the Mystic Law. The age when T'ien-t'ai, Miao-lo and Dengyō made their advent in this world fell in the fourth half-millennium, and that is why they did not "declare aloud" the Mystic Law to the people of their day.

The third reason is that they were not among the original

disciples of the Buddha. The original disciples of the Buddha are those totally in one mind with the Buddha and sharing his enlightenment. The Bodhisattvas of the Earth are the disciples of the original Buddha himself. They temporarily appeared in the ceremony of the sutra to receive the mission of propagating the Mystic Law. Only those who have attained the same level of enlightenment as the Buddha and are in every way equal to the Buddha can teach and propagate the Mystic Law. To propagate the Mystic Law is, as the sutra states, "to carry out the Buddha's work as the envoy of the Buddha."

At this point, let me say a few words about the relationship between the original Buddha's disciples, the Bodhisattvas of the Earth, and the bodhisattvas of the theoretical teaching. As to where the Bodhisattvas of the Earth live, the Lotus Sutra says it is "the space below the earth," and T'ien-t'ai, "the ultimate depth of life, that being the absolute reality." Nichiren Daishonin defined it simply as "Nam-myoho-renge-kyo." It is Bodhisattvas of the Earth who realize Nam-myoho-renge-kyo as their very life and take on the propagation of Nam-myoho-renge-kyo as their mission and life's work.

In contrast, the bodhisattvas of the theoretical teaching work to benefit the people through their various capacities—Kannon with the ability to recognize the trends of society, Myō'on by soothing people with beautiful music, Miroku with a merciful heart, and Yakuō by relieving people of their illness with medicine. Using their special skills, these bodhisattvas contribute to the welfare of the people. Those today who serve others and contribute to society with all the talents at their command and a truly benevolent heart are considered to correspond to these bodhisattvas. However, we are the only ones in the world who devote their lives to the people by propagating the supreme law, Nam-myoho-renge-kyo. In this sense, we are Bodhisattvas of the Earth.

According to the Lotus Sutra, Shakyamuni did not allow the transient bodhisattvas to propagate the teaching after his death. He said, "Desist, men of good faith!" and then pointedly summoned clouds of bodhisattvas from under the ground. He entrusted these Bodhisattvas of the Earth with the task of spreading the ultimate teaching. Only the Bodhisattvas of the Earth, disciples of the original Buddha, can devote their lives to benefiting the people and society of our day by propagating the supreme teaching of Nam-myoho-renge-kyo. And that is the fundamental practice in the Latter Day of the Law.

We know our religious activities befit bodhisattvas who fulfill the Buddha's mission, but what about our secular activities? Although our social activities are just like those of transient bodhisattvas, who use their skills for the people, when we understand that it is our life's work to live only by Nam-myoho-renge-kyo and propagate it to society, we are following the way of Bodhisattvas of the Earth. To put it another way, we are bodhisattvas who contribute to society in two ways: religious or essential, and secular or phenomenal. But if we forget that our mission is to propagate and live by the Law of Nam-myoho-renge-kyo, we will be unable to carry out the benevolent acts of transient bodhisattvas. We would become too involved in the pursuit of fame or power, lose control of ourselves in daily life, and finally fall into the four evil paths (Hell, Hunger, Animality and Anger). Those who devote themselves to *kōsen-rufu*, be they students, housewives, scholars or working men, are all Bodhisattvas of the Earth, which is what we must all strive to become. If a housewife or a student thinks of faith only as something to help in overcoming personal troubles, that person will be lost in a very shallow view of his or her mission. We must get to the core of our true identity as Bodhisattvas of the Earth and root our entire being in the Gohonzon, the Soka Gakkai, and work for *kōsen-rufu*.

Because T'ien-t'ai, Miao-lo and Dengyō lacked the three requirements that were specified for propagation, they were unable to spread the ultimate teaching of the Lotus Sutra. Only the Bodhisattvas of the Earth—the original Buddha, Nichiren Daishonin, and his disciples—can propagate this teaching. "No one but Jōgyō, Muhengyō and the other leaders of the Bodhisattvas of the Earth can . . . spread the Law of Myoho-renge-kyo" corresponds to the words: "the Buddha had not entrusted them [T'ien-t'ai, Miao-lo and Dengyō] with this mission." Further, the Buddha's statement in the *Yujutsu* (15th) chapter, "I have taught these people [the Bodhisattvas of the Earth] since the remotest past" verifies the passage in the Gosho, "[T'ien-t'ai, Miao-lo and Dengyō] had not been the Buddha's disciples from ages past." Certainly, "No one but Jōgyō . . . can appear during the first five hundred years of the Latter Day" states very clearly the meaning of "the time had not yet come." Nichiren Daishonin is the very person who fulfills all of the above-mentioned three conditions.

"No one but Jōgyō . . . can appear . . . to spread the Law of Myoho-renge-kyo" is saying that the Daishonin first propagated the daimoku of true Buddhism. "No one but Jōgyō . . . are qualified to inscribe the object of worship which physically manifests the ceremony of the two Buddhas seated together in the Treasure Tower" signifies that the Daishonin established the object of worship of true Buddhism. If the only purpose of the Daishonin's advent was to propagate the daimoku, he would not have stated that he would also embody the ceremony of the Treasure Tower. Therefore, there can be no question that the purpose of Nichiren Daishonin's advent was to inscribe the Dai-Gohonzon.

Why is it that no one but the leaders of Bodhisattvas of the Earth can spread the daimoku and inscribe the Gohonzon? The Gosho says, "This is because both the Law and the object of worship are the reality of *ichinen sanzen* revealed in the *Juryō* chapter of the essential teaching." As you know, *ichinen sanzen* was explained by T'ien-t'ai in his perfect analysis of life. But a theory is not enough to help all people make the truth of life their own. This is why Nichiren Daishonin embodied his own life of *ichinen sanzen* in the form of the Gohonzon to enable everyone to attain enlightenment by chanting daimoku to the Gohonzon. The four leaders of those bodhisattvas—Jōgyō, Muhengyō, Jyōgyō and Anryūgyō—represent the four virtues of the original Buddha, the integrity, freedom, purity and happiness of Nichiren Daishonin's life. Then, "Jōgyō and the other leaders of the Bodhisattvas of the Earth" indicates a single person, Nichiren Daishonin, who possesses all their virtues in his own life. The original Buddha is the object of worship as the Person, and *ichinen sanzen* the object of worship as the Law. Because the original Buddha's life is *ichinen sanzen* itself, they are not two different things but one. That is the oneness of the Person and the Law. Whereas the Bodhisattvas of the Earth can propagate the teaching, the other bodhisattvas cannot; they spread only the theoretical teaching in the former half of the Lotus Sutra.

I think you can see that *ichinen sanzen* as used in the passage quoted does not indicate the theory T'ien-t'ai expounded. Rather, seen in the light of the Daishonin's enlightenment, it refers to the Law of Nam-myoho-renge-kyo, the core of the *Juryō* chapter in the latter half (essential teaching) of the Lotus Sutra.

Shakyamuni, T'ien-t'ai and Dengyō all attained Buddhahood by realizing the Mystic Law. They appeared among people to prepare the way for Nichiren Daishonin. The Law which they sought for their entire lives is embodied in the Gohonzon. We embrace the Daishonin's philosophy—the supreme philosophy of life. Let us renew our determination to carry out our great mission in this world.

Entity and Function

The two Buddhas, Shakyamuni and Tahō, are merely functions of the true Buddha, while Myoho-renge-kyo actually is the true Buddha. The sutra explains this as "the Tathagata's secret and his mystic power." The "secret" refers to the entity of the Buddha's three properties and the "mystic power" to their functions. The entity is the true Buddha and the function, a provisional Buddha.

The Daishonin says here that Myoho-renge-kyo or Nam-myoho-renge-kyo is the eternal and indestructible basis of the Buddha's life, and that Shakyamuni and Tahō Buddhas are functions of Nam-myoho-renge-kyo. The relationship between entity and function appears clearly in the Gohonzon. Written in the center of the Gohonzon is "Nam-myoho-renge-kyo, Nichiren," while Shakyamuni and Tahō Buddhas are inscribed on the left and right sides. In other words, the two Buddhas are situated in positions to express the intrinsic functions of the Mystic Law. Not only Shakyamuni and Tahō but all other Buddhas in the universe as well are functions of the Mystic Law. Nam-myoho-renge-kyo is Nichiren Daishonin's life itself; therefore, the Daishonin can move all other Buddhas in the universe. By embracing the Gohonzon we too can stir these Buddhas and bodhisattvas at our command. What a great ocean of life we can discover! When we really develop our powers of faith and practice, the life of the Daishonin wells up from our depths, just as stated in Nichikan Shonin's annotation of the *Tōtaigi Shō* (The Entity of the Mystic Law), "As the result of embracing and believing in the Mystic Law we can manifest ourselves as Nichiren Daishonin."

The difference between "true" and "provisional" is that the former means the actual self of our life, while the latter is the temporal reflection or image of that self. To explain in easier language, T'ien-t'ai compares the relationship between "true" and "provisional" to that between the moon in the sky and its reflection on the surface of a pond. The moon shining in the nocturnal sky is "true" and its reflection on the surface of a pond, "provisional."

The moon is of course reflected in many surfaces—the sea, a pond or even a glass of water. Reflections appear on any smooth reflective surface. A movie screen is also a good surface for reflecting light. In the latter half, or essential teaching, of the Lotus Sutra, Shakyamuni revealed that he had attained enlightenment in the distant past. When the Buddha taught he had attained enlightenment long ago in *gohyaku-jintengō*, he revealed his true identity, but in all the earlier teachings when he taught that his enlightenment came for the first time in India, he was only revealing the image projected on the screen of ancient Indian society. The same can be said of Bodhisattvas of the Earth. Their true identity is the original Buddha. Therefore, it follows that they are images which the original Buddha projected on the screen of the ceremony of the Lotus Sutra. In addition, Shakyamuni and Tahō Buddhas are also images which Nam-myoho-renge-kyo or the entity of the original Buddha projected on the screen of the ceremony in the air.

Let us apply this to our life. We project our various images on the screens of society: the image of father on the screen of the family; a director on the screen of the company; a block chief on the screen of the Soka Gakkai organization; a Japanese on the screen of international society; and a human being on the screen of the biological world. When these screens shake, their images also shake. Some images disappear, even though the screens themselves do not change. The image as a student disappears with graduation. Students sometimes seem to want to erase their images on the screen of school as soon as possible and project a new image on the screen of society, but find themselves in a bind because they cannot graduate.

What then is the "true" and unchangeable thing that produces and transcends these ever-changing images? It is the eternal source, Nam-myoho-renge-kyo. People tend to regard their fleeting images projected on various screens of endeavor as being "true" and constant, and herein lies the main source of human misery. Each of us is a human being, which is an image relatively close to this "true" and eternal thing. As long as we live and breathe, this should not be forgotten, but even life as a human being is a "provisional" existence which is eventually subject to death. That is why Buddhism always stresses the continual flux of human existence—birth, old age, sickness and death—piercing into the eternal unchanging entity that goes beyond life and death. Buddhism arrived at the truth that Nam-myoho-renge-kyo itself is eternal and indestructible, the true entity of our life and all things in the universe. Thus the Daishonin declares that Myoho-renge-kyo is the true Buddha and that Shakyamuni and Tahō are its functions, or provisional Buddhas.

The Daishonin next cites a passage in the *Juryō* chapter, "the Tathagata's secret and his mystic power." He defines the Tathagata's secret as the entity of the three properties of life, or the true Buddha. Furthermore, he defines "the Tathagata's mystic power" as the function, or a provisional Buddha. T'ien-t'ai defines the "secret" as the truth that the Buddha's life manifests the three enlightened properties, and that these are always inherent in the Buddha's life. The Daishonin used the term "the Buddha's three properties" in that sense. On the deepest level, "the Tathagata" in the sutra is the Buddha of Nam-myoho-renge-kyo, and the word "secret" is not just something that the Buddha keeps to himself. Here, as in *On the Three Great Secret Laws*, it indicates the Dai-Gohonzon which is hidden in the depths of the *Juryō* chapter. The "mystic power" is the function of the

Gohonzon—the Buddha of Nam-myoho-renge-kyo. T'ien-t'ai defines the "mystic power" as the function of the entity of the three properties of life. He says in the *Hokke Mongu* (Words and Phrases of the Lotus Sutra), "*Jinzū shi riki* (the mystic power) indicates the function of the three properties of life. *Jin* indicates the unchangeable law in the universe and corresponds to *hosshin* or the property of the Law. *Zū* indicates the boundless mystic wisdom or *hōshin*, the property of wisdom. *Riki* means unlimited power or *ōjin*, the property of action." *Jinzū shi riki* then indicates the function of all three properties of life.

Man Is the True Buddha

The common mortal is the entity of the three properties, or the true Buddha. The Buddha is the function of the three properties, or a provisional Buddha. Shakyamuni is thought to have possessed the three virtues of sovereign, teacher and parent for the sake of us common mortals, but on the contrary, it is the common mortal who endowed him with the three virtues.

The entity of life and its environment in the Ten Worlds is Myoho-renge-kyo, which in turn is "the true Buddha." The common mortal in the Ten Worlds of life is therefore "the true Buddha." In contrast, all the Buddhas mentioned in the sutras, including Shakyamuni, are "provisional Buddhas." This conclusion is derived from the principle of "the true entity of all phenomena" and the other teachings of the Lotus Sutra. No one but Nichiren Daishonin, however, so clearly declared that it is the common mortal who is the true Buddha. Because of this his teaching possesses the never-fading power to benefit mankind in the Latter Day, for ten thousand years and on into eternity.

"The common mortal" specifically refers to Nichiren Daishonin as the original Buddha. This is endorsed by the *Ongi Kuden*, which states, "The Buddha in the Latter Day is the common mortal, the common priest. . . . He is called a Buddha, and he is called a common priest." In more general terms, "the common mortal" refers to each one of us. Nichiren Daishonin taught us that the common mortal is the greatest and most valuable existence by his own appearance and behavior as a common mortal.

Nichiren Daishonin's Buddhism, from beginning to end, focuses on man. In explaining the true purpose of the Buddha's advent as described in the *Hōben* chapter of the Lotus Sutra, the *Ongi Kuden* quotes the following passage from T'ien-t'ai's *Hokke Mongu*: "People develop the seeking spirit to desire the Buddha's advent; that is the inherent cause [for the Buddha's advent]. The Buddha perceives that spirit and responds to it; that is the external cause." Thus it is clear that because there were suffering people the Daishonin came into the world. The power and blessings of the Gohonzon are all intended for the benefit of common mortals. The Daishonin's Buddhism, furthermore, is propagated through the efforts of courageous people fighting through storms of life.

All religions in the past regarded God or Buddha as a sacred, superhuman being. Man's dignity was recognized only as long as he was enveloped in God's grace or the Buddha's mercy. Therefore, most of these religions considered those who directly served God or Buddha to be a privileged class, and regarded laymen—the general public—as contemptible. People in power, however, were considered to have God's special grace, which justified, for example, the so-called divine right of kings. Under this theory different classes of people were accorded different degrees of religious authority, and this eventually became a fixed system.

In every society, therefore, democratization could only be accomplished by denying the secular authority of religious institutions and rendering them politically powerless. However, the weakening of religious bodies and loss of faith in some established sects only upset the balance of the human spirit and rotted the bonds of human trust. As it is, voices are rising, calling for the people to regain spiritual richness in life. However, it is clear that a revival of past religions will not answer current needs. I believe Nichiren Daishonin's Buddhism—the religion which teaches that man himself is the entity of the Mystic Law and as such is innately endowed with ultimate sanctity—can provide a clear-cut answer to the questions man asks himself.

The Bible states that God created man. But how many modern thinkers have cried that man created God? Nichiren Daishonin declared, "Shakyamuni is thought to have possessed the three virtues of sovereign, teacher and parent for the sake of us common mortals, but on the contrary, it is the common mortal who endowed him with the three virtues." Isn't this declaration even more to the point than the remark, "man created God"? Nichiren Daishonin's Buddhism is a humanistic religion that clearly stands out from such theistic religions. Whereas many religions lapsed to hierarchies, Nichiren Daishonin's Buddhism binds all people together in equality. It is therefore the very religion that man has been seeking for his spiritual renaissance.

T'ien-t'ai explains the Tathagata as follows: "*Nyorai* is the title of the Buddhas of the ten directions and three existences, of the two Buddhas and the three Buddhas, and of all the Buddhas, true and provisional."

Here the "true Buddha" is the common mortal, whereas "provisional Buddhas" means the Buddha. Nevertheless, there is a clear distinction between a

**Buddha and a common mortal, in that a common
mortal is deluded while a Buddha is enlightened. The
common mortal fails to realize that he himself possesses both the entity and the function of the Buddha's
three properties.**

Here the Daishonin quotes a passage from T'ien-t'ai's
Hokke Mongu which interprets *nyorai* (tathagata) of *Nyorai-
juryō-hon*, the title of the sixteenth chapter of the Lotus
Sutra. "The two Buddhas" indicate a Buddha in his true
and original state and a Buddha in a form he assumes when
he comes into the world to save the people. "The three
Buddhas" are the Buddha of *hosshin* (the essential property
of his life), the Buddha of *hōshin* (the spiritual property of
his life), and the Buddha of *ōjin* (the physical property of his
life).

Nyorai indicates Buddha. Philosophically, *nyorai* means
to "appear from the truth moment by moment." The
state of life at each passing moment is called either *nyorai*,
tathagata, or Buddha. Tathagata is neither a statue nor a
picture of the Buddha. Life that is fully active, the rhythm
of cosmic life condensed into a single entity—this is tathagata. The Tathagata of Nam-myoho-renge-kyo is the
Buddha who, at each and every moment, brings forth the
life of Nam-myoho-renge-kyo, the life that has existed since
time without beginning.

Tathagata is the common title of all Buddhas; it is not
limited to Shakyamuni alone. The sutras mention a number
of Buddhas, such as Kashō Buddha and Ashuku Buddha.
But specifically it indicates *jijuyūshin nyorai* of *kuon ganjo*, the
tathagata who embodies the fundamental law by which all
Buddhas attain enlightenment.

The Daishonin quoted T'ien-t'ai's interpretation prin-
cipally in order to explain the difference between the true
Buddha and a provisional Buddha. As the passage says, the

common mortal is the true Buddha, whereas the Buddhas mentioned in the scriptures are nothing but provisional Buddhas. The meaning of this line is self-explanatory when we consider the true Buddha and a provisional Buddha in the light of the *Juryō* chapter of the Lotus Sutra.

The *Juryō* chapter dispels the belief that Shakyamuni attained enlightenment for the first time in India, and reveals that in reality he had become a Buddha much earlier—in the remote past called *gohyaku-jintengō*. As you know, this Buddha of *gohyaku-jintengō* is considered "the true Buddha" in the *Juryō* chapter. This means that Shakyamuni had been a Buddha since long before he was born in India and attained enlightenment at the age of thirty. He was a Buddha even while he lived as a common mortal. It follows, therefore, that the Buddhahood he attained when he was thirty was tentative or "provisional" Buddhahood. Furthermore, according to the deepest meaning of the *Juryō* chapter, even the Buddha who attained enlightenment in *gohyaku-jintengō* is a provisional Buddha.

In the section "On Chapter Sixteen, Nam-myoho-renge-kyo *Nyorai-juryō-hon*," the *Ongi Kuden* states: "All in all, the deepest significance of the *Juryō* chapter does not lie in subjugating delusions one by one in order to attain enlightenment. You should realize that its significance is to gain enlightenment as you are, remaining as the entity of a common mortal. What is the behavior of the Buddha enlightened in the three properties of life? It is Nam-myoho-renge-kyo." As this teaching says, the true Buddha is the one who, without changing his identity as a common mortal, manifests himself as the Tathagata of Nam-myoho-renge-kyo. That is why the Daishonin says, "The 'true Buddha' is the common mortal, whereas 'provisional Buddhas' means the Buddha."

Both the Buddha and man are common mortals, but there is a distinct difference. It lies in whether one is enlightened or deluded. As the Gosho states, "One who is enlightened is a Buddha; one who is deluded is a common mortal." A common mortal who is enlightened is a Buddha; a common mortal who is deluded is an ordinary human. Nichiren Daishonin is enlightened to the truth that he himself is the entity of Nam-myoho-renge-kyo. We are common mortals still bound by delusion. What is it that can transform delusion into enlightenment? It is faith, and faith alone.

The sentence, "the common mortal fails to realize that he himself possesses both the entity and the function of the Buddha's three properties," relates to the earlier statement, "The entity is the true Buddha and the function, a provisional Buddha. The common mortal is the entity of the three properties, or the true Buddha. The Buddha is the function of the three properties, or a provisional Buddha." A deluded common mortal does not realize that he himself is a true Buddha; he believes only that the Buddhas mentioned in the scriptures are true Buddhas. Therefore, he understands neither that it is the common mortal who is the entity and the true Buddha, nor that a Buddha is the function, a provisional Buddha. He cannot understand, therefore, that Nam-myoho-renge-kyo is the entity and that Shakyamuni and Tahō Buddhas are the function.

Let me briefly explain the relation between entity and function. The entity is always accompanied by its function, and the function manifests itself wherever and whenever there is an entity.

"Entity," as the term is used in Buddhism, does not exist by itself. It is always accompanied by its "function." The two are impossible to separate. For instance, we can perceive the "entity" of General Director Hiroshi Hōjō only in his behavior; all of his behavior is the function of his "entity."

The "entity" of Nam-myoho-renge-kyo is accompanied by the "function" of all phenomena. Therefore, when we manifest the life of Nam-myoho-renge-kyo in ourselves, we will be able to make everything in the universe function for our benefit. In the phrase, "the true entity of all phenomena," "the true entity" indicates the entity and "all phenomena" the function.

All Are Manifestations of Myoho-renge-kyo

"All phenomena" in the sutra refers to the Ten Worlds, and the "true entity" is what permeates the Ten Worlds. Reality is another expression for Myoho-renge-kyo; hence Myoho-renge-kyo is manifest in all phenomena.

The entity of a common mortal is Myoho-renge-kyo. Miao-lo uses the words "all phenomena" to indicate the Ten Worlds and explains that all phenomena—all life and its environment in the Ten Worlds—are themselves the true entity. The true entity is another expression for Myoho-renge-kyo. It follows, therefore, that all life and its environment in any of the Ten Worlds is without exception the manifestation of Myoho-renge-kyo.

Hell appears hellish; that is the reality of Hell. When Hunger emerges, the reality of Hell is no longer present. A Buddha exhibits the reality of a Buddha, and a common mortal, that of a common mortal. All phenomena are themselves manifestations of Myoho-renge-kyo. This is the meaning of "all phenomena reveal the true entity."

The entity of Myoho-renge-kyo is found in all phenomena, whether of Hell, Hunger, a common mortal or a Buddha. This is what "the true entity of all phenomena" signifies. This teaching refutes all the views previously held in Buddhism. According to conventional Buddhist thought, only Buddhas, bodhisattvas and those in the two vehicles (Learning and Realization) were considered respectable. All other people, especially those in Hell, Hunger and Animality, were regarded as despicable and detestable. This is exactly why the Japanese words meaning Hunger and Animality have been used to insult and abuse others. The conventional Buddhist concepts exerted an even more harmful influence upon society: they gave rise to the cruel tendency to despise and shun people who are forced to live in poverty and suffering.

The principle of "the true entity of all phenomena" completely demolished such concepts. It declared that all people, whether in the world of Hell, Hunger or Animality, are just as much entities of the Mystic Law as are Buddhas and bodhisattvas, and that all are equally worthy of respect. Furthermore, in Buddhist teaching life in the nine worlds can transform itself into the highest of life-states, Buddhahood. In the Gohonzon all beings in the nine worlds are bathed in the brilliant light of the Mystic Law and manifest their intrinsic enlightened nature. When our lives become one and in perfect harmony with the Gohonzon, even Hell and Hunger will come to reveal their inherent Buddhahood. We will therefore be able to direct our lives in the nine worlds toward any goal we wish. Of course we will have sorrows, agonies and desires, but all these will be as but the waves rising and falling on the surface of the great sea of Buddhahood; they will work to give spice to the highest state of life man can live. The principle of "the true entity of all phenomena" can only be put into action through the Buddhism of Nichiren Daishonin, the Buddha who established the Gohonzon.

The Ultimate Law of Nam-myoho-renge-kyo

T'ien-t'ai states, "The profound principle of 'true entity' is the original law of Myoho-renge-kyo," thus

identifying the phrase "true entity" with the theoretical teaching and "the original law of Myoho-renge-kyo" with the essential teaching. You should ponder this passage deep in your heart.

What is the substance of the "true entity" as expounded in the *Hōben* chapter, one of the theoretical teachings? The Daishonin teaches us that it is Myoho-renge-kyo itself, and corroborates this with T'ien-t'ai's interpretation of the Lotus Sutra. He says, "You should ponder this passage deep in your heart," because it is a profound teaching that concerns the fundamental principle of the Lotus Sutra. T'ien-t'ai does not make his statement explicit enough, but from the Daishonin's perspective, the true entity ultimately means Nam-myoho-renge-kyo concealed in the depths of the *Juryō* chapter.

Now let us look over the whole system of the Lotus Sutra. The Lotus Sutra aims at clarifying the Law to which all Buddhas are enlightened and which is the key to all people attaining Buddhahood. It is the Law suggested by the phrase, "The wisdom of all Buddhas is infinitely profound and immeasurable," in the beginning of the *Hōben* chapter. This description of the Law is revealed in the same chapter as the true entity of all phenomena and the Ten Factors of Life. Shariputra, one of Shakyamuni's ten major disciples who was reputed to have the highest wisdom, was immediately able to attain enlightenment when he heard this teaching about the true entity of all phenomena. The other major disciples, who understood only some or little of what they were taught, also attained enlightenment one after another when, as stated in the chapters that followed, they heard the parables or learned of their past relationship with Shakyamuni.

When Shakyamuni finished preaching for his disciples, he began to expound the *Hosshi* (tenth), *Hōtō* (eleventh) and other chapters. In these chapters, he first asks if there are any who are willing to propagate Myoho-renge-kyo after his death. The bodhisattvas of the theoretical teaching respond to his call and volunteer for the task. But Shakyamuni turns them down, summons the Bodhisattvas of the Earth from underground and entrusts them with the propagation of the Law. It is evident from the sentences in the *Hosshi* chapter and those which follow that Shakyamuni was selecting those who would propagate the Law after his death. But that is not all; within those sentences is revealed the Law itself—the Law to be propagated after Shakyamuni's passing. This is the original law of Myoho-renge-kyo.

Shakyamuni's disciples received the seed of Buddhahood and formed a relationship with him in the past. They were therefore able to understand that the seed actually existed in them when, in the ceremony of the Lotus Sutra, they heard Shakyamuni's preaching of the true entity of all phenomena, the parable of the three carts and the burning mansion, or of the relationship they had formed with him in the distant past called *sanzen-jintengo*.

Each of them could be likened to a man who has gotten lost on a road he has walked before because his memory has grown dim. He remembers most of the way except the corner where he should turn. If someone tells him where to turn, he can get to his destination without any trouble. Thus Shariputra immediately attained enlightenment when he heard the teaching of the true entity of all phenomena.

On the other hand, the people in the ages after Shakyamuni's demise, especially those in the Latter Day, have neither received the seed of Buddhahood nor formed a relationship with him in the past. They are like travelers who find themselves on a road they have never traveled before. Even if someone tells them where to turn, they will be lost because they don't know what their destination is. They need to be directed to the destination itself. This destination is the original law of Myoho-renge-kyo.

The *Hōtō* chapter and the chapters that follow describe the ceremony in the air. First, the Treasure Tower appears. Shakyamuni and Tahō Buddhas seat themselves side by side in the tower. All the Buddhas in the universe then come and assemble around the two. Next, the bodhisattvas who were taught by the original Buddha emerge from underground. The ceremony in the air, whose essence is given in the *Juryō* chapter, depicts the Law of Myoho-renge-kyo. However, all twenty-eight chapters of Shakyamuni's Lotus Sutra, even the essential teaching in the latter half, are only a map showing the road to the original law of Myoho-renge-kyo. It is Nichiren Daishonin who gave concrete form to the original Mystic Law that the benighted common mortals in the Latter Day would need to embrace.

So "the true entity of all phenomena" takes on different meaning according to how it is seen: in light of the theoretical teaching, the essential teaching, or Nichiren Daishonin's standpoint. From the Daishonin's standpoint, the true entity of all phenomena is the Gohonzon itself. Therefore, when we dedicate ourselves heart and soul to the Gohonzon, the life of the Mystic Law will well up within us. The principle of the true entity of all phenomena will manifest itself as our happiness and human revolution in a process that continually strengthens our lives.

Inscription of the Gohonzon

Although not worthy of the honor, Nichiren was nevertheless the first to spread the Mystic Law entrusted to Bodhisattva Jōgyō for propagation in the Latter Day of the Law. Nichiren was also the first to inscribe the Gohonzon, which is the embodiment of the Buddha from the remote past as revealed in the *Juryō* chapter of the essential teaching, of Tahō Buddha who appeared when the *Hōtō* chapter of the theoretical

teaching was preached, and the Bodhisattvas of the Earth who emerged with the *Yujutsu* chapter. No matter how people may hate Nichiren, they cannot possibly alter the fact of his enlightenment.

The core of this passage is that Nichiren Daishonin spread faith in the daimoku and the Gohonzon of the Three Great Secret Laws, which are to be propagated in the Latter Day. According to the Lotus Sutra, this task was entrusted to Bodhisattva Jōgyō, leader of the Buddha's original disciples, the Bodhisattvas of the Earth. However, since the Daishonin was a common priest, he dared not state that he was the incarnation of Jōgyō. Instead, he used the phrases "Nichiren was ... the first to spread ..." and "[he] was also the first to inscribe ... " The meaning of this passage becomes clear when we compare it with the previous statement that T'ien-t'ai, Miao-lo and Dengyō could neither spread the daimoku nor establish the Gohonzon because they were not Bodhisattvas of the Earth.

Although the Daishonin qualified his statement with the phrase, "Nichiren was the first ... ," he could have neither spread the daimoku nor inscribed the Gohonzon if he had not been eligible. With respect to the Lotus Sutra, therefore, the Daishonin is the incarnation of Jōgyō, leader of the Bodhisattvas of the Earth, who appeared in the Latter Day and established the supreme Buddhism. But this still is not the true identity of Nichiren Daishonin. To know his true identity, we must delve into the Daishonin's inscription of the Gohonzon, which the above passage says "is the embodiment of the Buddha from the remote past." If he embodies the Buddhahood attained by Shakyamuni and Tahō as well as Nam-myoho-renge-kyo, the life of the original Buddha from time without beginning, he must possess that Buddhahood within himself. In fact, he himself states in the Gosho, "I, Nichiren, have inscribed my life in *sumi*, so believe in the Gohonzon with your whole heart." Since the Law he taught was embodied in his own existence, Nichiren Daishonin was able to inscribe the Gohonzon, the crystallization of the Person and the Law in a single entity. This is, as the passage says, "his enlightenment." "No matter how people may hate Nichiren, they cannot possibly alter the fact of his enlightenment." This means that no matter how people hated and persecuted the Daishonin, they could in no way affect his enlightenment as the Buddha in the Latter Day of the Law.

To have exiled Nichiren to this remote island is therefore a sin that can never be expiated, even with the passing of countless aeons. A passage from the *Hiyu* chapter reads, "Not even an aeon would be time enough to explain the full gravity of this sin." On the other hand, not even the wisdom of the Buddha can fathom the blessings one will obtain by giving alms to Nichiren and by becoming his disciple. The *Yakuō* chapter reads, "Not even with the Buddha's wisdom can one measure these benefits."

Here the Daishonin contrasts the terrible effects of hating or persecuting him with the blessings one obtains by giving him support and becoming his disciple. The passage brings out his conviction that he is the original Buddha and the Buddha of the Latter Day of the Law. "A passage from the *Hiyu* chapter" refers to the sentence which reads, "If a person slanders this sutra, not even an aeon would be time enough to explain the full gravity of this sin." The passage in the *Yakuō* chapter describing the immeasurable benefits reads, "Suppose a person has had the opportunity to hear this sutra, and copies it himself or lets others copy it. The benefits he thus obtains cannot be measured even with the Buddha's wisdom."

The Envoy of the Buddha

Nichiren alone began to carry out the task of the Bodhisattvas of the Earth. He may even be one of them. If Nichiren should be a Bodhisattva of the Earth, then so must his disciples. The *Hosshi* chapter states, "If there is someone, whether man or woman, who secretly teaches to one person even a single phrase of the Lotus Sutra, let it be known that he is the envoy of the Buddha, sent to carry out the Buddha's work." Who else but us can this possibly refer to?

Nichiren Daishonin says that if he is indeed to be included among the Bodhisattvas of the Earth, then, according to the principle of the oneness of master and disciple, his disciples must certainly be Bodhisattvas of the Earth. A Bodhisattva of the Earth does not act only when he is told to. He bases his life entirely on the Mystic Law which is immanent in cosmic life. Therefore, just as grass or a tree grows of itself from the earth, so does he, of his own accord, chant daimoku and contribute toward the well-being of his society and peace in the world.

The Daishonin cites a passage from the *Hosshi* chapter in order to assure his disciples that they are Bodhisattvas of the Earth. Quoted in full, it reads, "Suppose there be a man or woman of devout faith after my passing, who secretly teaches to one person even a single phrase of the Lotus Sutra. Let it be known that he or she is the envoy of the Buddha, sent to carry out the Buddha's work. All the more so are those who teach the sutra widely among the people."

As I have already said, Shakyamuni preached the *Hosshi* chapter to exhort the assembly to propagate the Lotus Sutra after his demise. The above passage is the very one which carries these words of encouragement. Bodhisattvas of the theoretical teaching responded to Shakyamuni's call. But

he declined their offer, and instead entrusted the Bodhisattvas of the Earth with the propagation of the Lotus Sutra
because he knew that only they were able to shoulder the
task. Therefore, according to the *Hosshi* chapter, those now
in the Latter Day who teach the Mystic Law and fight for
kōsen-rufu are Bodhisattvas of the Earth. The Daishonin
says that this is exactly what his disciples are doing.

To go a step further, the phrase, "he is the envoy of the
Buddha, sent to carry out the Buddha's work," implies that
he is equal to the Buddha, that he himself is the Buddha from
time without beginning. Let me explain why this is so.
The word "envoy," as it is used in a general sense, means a
person who speaks for and acts in the same capacity as his
superior. Suppose two countries want to conclude a peace
treaty between them. Each country sends an envoy. When
the two parties have reached agreement and the treaty is
drawn, the envoys sign it. Although the emissaries write
their own personal signatures, they represent the collective
will of the people in each nation.

The same is true with Buddhism. One who preaches and
propagates the Mystic Law is the envoy of the Buddha; he
acts in the capacity of the Buddha. For this reason, in the
Lotus Sutra, only the original disciples of the Buddha were
entrusted with the task of spreading the Mystic Law. Conversely, those who spread the Mystic Law in the Latter
Day—or those who do *shakubuku* today—are the disciples of
the original Buddha from time without beginning. The
former president Josei Toda proclaimed himself "the teacher
of *shakubuku* in the Latter Day" and defined the Soka Gakkai
as being the group of people devoted to *shakubuku*. This is
why the Head Temple bestowed upon the Soka Gakkai the
Gohonzon on which is inscribed the prayer, "May the
organization attain the supreme goal of *kōsen-rufu* through
the merciful practice of *shakubuku*," to be permanently enshrined in our headquarters. I entreat you to always main-

tain the proud tradition and lofty spirit of the Soka Gakkai and carry on your mission throughout your life as the original disciples of the Buddha.

The phrase, "secretly teaches to one person," does not in any way mean that we should teach in a surreptitious way. It is simply an illustration by way of one extreme case. Needless to say, the greatest and most desirable practice consists in teaching true Buddhism widely among the masses of people. This is evident from the passage in the *Hosshi* chapter which I quoted. There may be times when the age or circumstances do not permit us to openly propagate the Law. No matter what, however, we should always maintain the spirit of *shakubuku* and continue to spread the Law to the limits of our capacities. Only then can we truly be called Bodhisattvas of the Earth—legitimate disciples of the original Buddha, Nichiren Daishonin. I sincerely hope you will understand and make this part of your lives.

The Highest Praise for the Votaries

When one is praised highly by others, he feels there is no hardship he cannot bear. Such is the courage which springs from words of praise. The votary born in the Latter Day of the Law who propagates the Lotus Sutra will encounter the three powerful enemies,* who will cause him to be exiled and even sentence him to death. Yet Shakyamuni Buddha will enfold in his robe of mercy those who nonetheless persevere in propagating. All gods will make them offerings, support them with their shoulders and carry them on their

*Three types of people described in the *Kanji* (13th) chapter of the Lotus Sutra who will persecute those who propagate the sutra in the evil age after the Buddha's death. They are: 1) lay people ignorant of Buddhism who denounce and persecute the votaries of the Lotus Sutra; 2) arrogant and cunning priests who slander them; and 3) influential figures who induce those in power to exile or execute them.

backs. They possess supreme good fortune and qualify as leaders of all mankind. Thus extolled by Shakyamuni Buddha, Tahō Buddha and all of the other Buddhas and bodhisattvas, the seven ranks of heavenly gods and five ranks of earthly gods, Kishimojin and her ten daughters, the Four Heavenly Kings, Bonten, Taishaku, King Emma, the gods of the waters and winds, the gods of the seas and mountains, Dainichi Buddha, Bodhisattvas Fugen and Monju and the gods of the sun and the moon, Nichiren has been able to endure countless harsh trials. When praised, one does not consider his personal risk, and when criticized, he can recklessly cause his own ruin. Such is the way of common mortals.

As a common mortal, Nichiren Daishonin was exiled and even sentenced to death. Still, against all odds, he valiantly continued to spread the Law. Why? Here he explains the reason. It was because, in the Lotus Sutra, Shakyamuni, Tahō, all the other Buddhas, and all bodhisattvas and heavenly gods give only the highest praise to those who propagate the sutra in the Latter Day of the Law. In short, the Daishonin was entirely committed to the Lotus Sutra.

"Shakyamuni Buddha will enfold in his robe of mercy those who . . ." means that he will entitle the votaries of the Lotus Sutra to be his true disciples. He will recognize them as his own children and embrace them with his unbounded mercy. "All gods will make them offerings, support them with their shoulders and carry them on their backs" signifies favorable changes in the votaries' surroundings. To become "the future leaders of mankind" means that they will increase in wisdom and become perceptive, reliable leaders of the people in all areas of society. These suggest the benefits which accrue from doing *shakubuku*.

Then comes the phrase, "Thus extolled by Shakyamuni

Buddha, Tahō Buddha . . ." From the Buddhist standpoint, this means that one who embraces the Mystic Law can set everything in motion—be it the universe, natural surroundings, or people—and that rhythm will work to protect him. To be praised "by Shakyamuni Buddha, Tahō Buddha and all of the other Buddhas" denotes that all the Buddhas in the entire universe will protect the votary of the Lotus Sutra. How reassuring! Wherever he goes, a bright world of human revolution will always unfold before him, where everything is tuned to the rhythm of the Mystic Law.

Specifically, "Shakyamuni Buddha" indicates the enlightened wisdom that wells up in the votary's life. "Tahō Buddha" signifies the actual verification of faith by the blessings the votary receives in the objective world, that is, in his life and environment. "All of the other Buddhas" denotes the Buddhahood within all the people he finds around him. To be praised by bodhisattvas means that everything in nature and society will work in such a way as to protect him. Not only will he himself be able to fully manifest the Bodhisattva power inherent in him—the power to save and give happiness to other people—but the leaders of society, who base their actions on mercy, will also support him and be willing to work for him. The seven ranks of heavenly gods and five ranks of earthly gods (the latter include the Sun Goddess, Tenshō Daijin) are deities of Japan who are said to have existed since before the time of the first emperor. All of these deities in heaven and on earth will function as Buddhist gods, just as an old saying goes, "Heaven knows, earth knows, man knows."

I will touch only briefly on Kishimojin and her ten daughters, since they are quite well known. They were vicious demons before meeting the Buddha, but in the Lotus Sutra they rank among those creatures who protect the votary. They used to feed on the lives of people; now they devour the evil in human lives and promote good. For those who embrace the Mystic Law, they appear as functions to remove causes for unhappiness. The Four Heavenly Kings, Bonten, Taishaku and King Emma symbolize the functions that maintain order in the universe, nature and society. With respect to society, for instance, they denote its leaders, and the power to act for social good.

The gods of the waters, winds, seas and mountains are blessings and functions of nature. Waters and winds have their respective uses and powers. Mountains and seas have lives of their own. All of them are manifestations of the life of the Mystic Law. Therefore, they always work to protect those who practice the Mystic Law. No matter how strong the winds of difficulty or how high the waves of hardship, believers in true Buddhism are invariably protected, as countless experiences testify.

Dainichi is one of the Buddhas present in the ceremony of the Lotus Sutra. He represents one aspect of life force. Fugen refers to learning and Monju, wisdom. The votary of the Lotus Sutra will be enveloped in the light of learning and wisdom. The god of the sun signifies the sun's energy, which nurtures all living things and thereby provides human beings with their glowing life force. The god of the moon symbolizes all that is serene. Casting its soft light, it brings calmness and peace to the people's minds. Thus, all things in the universe, both animate and inanimate, help, protect, embrace and work for those who maintain faith in the Mystic Law.

Now to go on to the phrase, "Nichiren has been able to endure countless harsh trials." We live in the *saha* world, one in which people have to bear all sorts of suffering. It is such a harsh world that whenever we try to do anything at all, we face severe obstacles. Since we must endure anyway, let us do so for the propagation of the Mystic Law. There may be times when we will have to carry out that task even at the cost of our lives. However, when we endure for the sake of the Mystic Law, the Buddhas and Buddhist gods will never fail to come and protect us. This is the Daishonin's conviction that accrued from his enlightenment.

The phrase, "When praised. . . . Such is the way of common mortals," is an insightful thrust into human psychology. They tend to sacrifice themselves when they are praised as well as when they are slandered. In the former, they gladly take on pain. But if they are condemned or criticized or scorned, they often do something foolish and reckless, not knowing that it will thereby bring about their own ruin.

That phrase teaches us a good lesson we must not forget. In our struggle for *kōsen-rufu*, it is important that we praise other members for their efforts and achievements. Encouragement will make them more courageous and build their confidence to continue their march forward.

As Disciples of Nichiren Daishonin

No matter what, maintain your faith as a votary of the Lotus Sutra, and forever exert yourself as Nichiren's disciple.

Beginning with this passage, the Gosho teaches the correct path of faith which the Daishonin's disciples should follow, and describes the practice—exactly how to go about propagating the faith in the Gohonzon. First, the Daishonin tells us to make a firm resolution—which is essential to our faith—to "maintain your faith as a votary of the Lotus Sutra" and "forever exert yourself as Nichiren's disciple." This is as important a teaching as it is famous. It is not too much to say that this phrase, short as it is, contains the key to attaining Buddhahood as well as the fundamental spirit of the Soka Gakkai.

I can feel the Daishonin's outpouring mercy in the words "no matter what." From the infinite past we have lived and died countless times. We have gone through an endless cycle of life and death wrapped in fundamental ignorance, like persons groping their way through the darkness. Fortunately, in this lifetime we have been able to encounter the Mystic Law and meet the original Buddha from the remotest past. This is the rare opportunity to dispel the darkness that envelops the cycle of life and death and discover the true, eternally unchanging entity of life. It is the one chance in a lifetime to enable ourselves to live a happy and secure life, unfettered and undefiled by anything, strolling in a garden of blossoms in the brilliant sun of the Mystic Law and under the crystal-clear sky of eternal enlightenment. That is why the Daishonin emphasizes that "no matter what" situation we may face, in this lifetime we must always maintain our faith. The phrase "no matter what" is crucially important to all of you, and I want you never to forget it.

"Maintain your faith as a votary of the Lotus Sutra" speaks of the practice of faith according to the Law, and "forever exert yourself as Nichiren's disciple" speaks of faith in terms of the Person. Specifically, "a votary of the Lotus Sutra" denotes Nichiren Daishonin himself. Actually, the Lotus Sutra was preached exclusively for the Daishonin. He alone read with his entire being everything written in the Lotus Sutra. He is the only person who declared that Shakyamuni's Buddhism had become powerless in the Latter Day of the Law. He is the one who revealed his identity as the original Buddha, emitting a brilliant light and dispelling the darkness throughout the ten thousand years of the Latter Day and on into eternity. And the Gohonzon is the perfect embodiment of the life of the original Buddha. For us to embrace the Gohonzon throughout our life is to "maintain your faith as a votary of the Lotus Sutra." Even understanding this much, we have still only scratched the surface. Our practice must always be underlined by the fundamental awareness that we are "Nichiren's disciples." Without that consciousness, we can never be "votaries of the Lotus Sutra" in the full sense.

Within our daily practice, to be conscious of being "Nichiren's disciples" is to live in the organization where people work together in *itai dōshin* (perfect unity based on the same faith) to realize *kōsen-rufu*. Indeed, the Nichiren Shoshu Soka Gakkai is the organization directly connected to the life of the original Buddha, Nichiren Daishonin, and the group of people devoted to the attainment of *kōsen-rufu*. The continually increasing opposition given us by the three powerful enemies and the three obstacles and the four devils* is proof that we are practicing exactly according to the Gosho. Therefore, to "forever exert yourself as Nichiren's disciple" means to share the same destiny as the Soka Gakkai. Even if we embrace the Gohonzon, we won't be able to achieve anything without a fundamental awareness of being "Nichiren's disciples." The Daishonin clarifies this in the *Heritage of the Ultimate Law of Life*, one of the most important Gosho, as follows. "Without the lifeblood of faith, it would be useless to embrace the Lotus Sutra." Practice derives from faith, as Nichiu Shonin, the ninth High Priest, says, "For one to practice is itself faith."

To "forever exert yourself as Nichiren's disciple" is of utmost importance, for that alone is the direct way to

---

*The three obstacles are: 1) *bonnō-shō*: obstacles due to the three poisons —greed, anger and stupidity; 2) *gō-shō*: obstacles due to karma created by committing the five cardinal sins. *Gō-shō* also means opposition from one's spouse or children; 3) *hō-shō*: obstacles due to painful retribution caused by actions in the three evil paths—Hell, Hunger and Animality. *Hō-shō* also refers to obstacles caused by one's superiors (sovereign, parents, etc.). The four devils are: 1) *bonnō-ma*: obstructions arising from the three poisons; 2) *on-ma*: the obstacle of the five components—form, perception, conception, volition and consciousness. These five components cause men many kinds of suffering; 3) *shi-ma*: the obstacle of death. The sufferings of death or the untimely death of other believers lead one to doubt Buddhism; and 4) *tenji-ma*: obstruction by the Devil of the Sixth Heaven, which occurs in the form of oppression by men of influence and power and is the most difficult of all to conquer.

attaining Buddhahood. People tend to think that attaining Buddhahood means to become some ideal personality set apart from ordinary people because they envision Buddhas as having the dignified appearance used to describe Shakyamuni. Nichiren Daishonin is a common mortal and at the same time the original Buddha. Herein lies the source of the supremacy of his teaching and the truth of Buddhism. Nichiren Daishonin's Buddhism sheds powerful light on human nature as it is manifested in ordinary people, so even we, common mortals, can relate to it. For us, attaining Buddhahood means to dedicate ourselves to the loftiest mission in the world. This itself is manifesting the Buddhahood inherent in our lives. Going one step further, when you have resolved to "forever exert yourself as Nichiren's disciple" no matter what, you are already living in the state of Buddhahood.

There is a famous passage from the Gosho which states, "Winter never fails to turn into spring." Now we can see that it means that winter *is* spring. The phrase "never fails" has considerable significance. It is synonymous with "definite" or "certain." It also means "equal." The same is true of the passage from *The Opening of the Eyes*: "Let the gods forsake me. Let all persecutions assail me," and another in the same Gosho: "Although I and my disciples may encounter various difficulties, if we do not harbor doubts in our hearts, we will as a matter of course attain Buddhahood."

In connection with the phrase, "forever exert yourself as Nichiren's disciple," let me explain why the faith on which the Soka Gakkai rests produces great benefits. Buddhism expounds the principle of four powers. These are the powers of faith, practice, the Buddha and the Law. In the Daishonin's Buddhism, the powers of the Buddha and the Law indicate those of the Gohonzon, since it embodies both the Person and the Law. Only the powers of faith and practice can bring forth the powers of the Buddha and the Law, the limitless powers of the Gohonzon. Our first president, Mr. Makiguchi, devoted himself to propagating the Law at the cost of his life. The second president, Mr. Toda, exerting magnificent powers of faith and practice, also dedicated his life to spreading true Buddhism. The blessings accumulated through their efforts are so great that now the powers of the Gohonzon brilliantly shine upon those who practice the faith of true Buddhism with the Soka Gakkai. Positive proof lies in the growth of the Soka Gakkai; it has developed into an organization global in scale that walks the Middle Way of Buddhism. It is a truly living religion, and for that, we cannot thank our first two presidents too much.

In the Same Mind

If you are of the same mind as Nichiren, you must be a Bodhisattva of the Earth. And since you are a Bodhisattva of the Earth, there is not the slightest doubt that you have been a disciple of the Buddha from the remotest past. The *Yujutsu* chapter states, "I have taught these people since the remotest past." There should be no discrimination among those who propagate the five characters of Myoho-renge-kyo in the Latter Day of the Law, be they men or women. Were they not Bodhisattvas of the Earth, they could not chant the daimoku.

How are we to become of the same mind as Nichiren Daishonin? It is possible only when you "maintain your faith as a votary of the Lotus Sutra, and forever exert yourself as Nichiren's disciple," that is, when you practice his teaching with your thoughts, words and deeds. This phrase contains the principle of *shitei funi*, oneness of master and disciple. *Funi* is an abbreviation of *nini funi*, meaning "two and yet not two." Superficially, master and disciple are two; there is clearly a difference in standpoint. But, in the ultimate depths of life, they are one and the same.

The oneness of master and disciple constitutes the essence of the relationship between the two, as it is taught in Buddhism. Therefore, true disciples of Nichiren Daishonin are those who "are of the same mind as Nichiren," that is, those who make his mind their own and stake their life on accomplishing the noble mission he left unfinished. Those who give only lip service or pretend to be carrying out their responsibility will sooner or later be severely reprimanded by the Daishonin.

A passage from *Reply to Lord Ueno* reads, "Since Nichiren was born, he has not known a day or even a moment of ease. He has concentrated solely on spreading the daimoku of the Lotus Sutra." Those who concentrate on the mission for *kōsen-rufu* and take responsibility for it just as did the Daishonin—in other words, those who "are of the same mind as Nichiren"—are undoubtedly Bodhisattvas of the Earth. And if we are definitely Bodhisattvas of the Earth, there is not the slightest doubt that we have been "disciples of the Buddha from the remotest past." Let me explain why. When Shakyamuni preached the *Yujutsu* chapter of the Lotus Sutra, innumerable Bodhisattvas of the Earth emerged from the ground. Bodhisattva Miroku, on behalf of the astonished assembly, asked the Buddha what and who they were. Thereupon the Buddha answered, "I have taught these people since the remotest past," meaning that Bodhisattvas of the Earth are disciples of the Buddha from the remotest past.

Superficially, "the Buddha" in the above passage indicates Shakyamuni, who expounded the essential teaching or the latter half of the Lotus Sutra. But actually the term denotes the Tathagata—Nichiren Daishonin, the Buddha in the Latter Day—who embodies the fundamental law by which all Buddhas attain enlightenment. The passage therefore means that Nichiren Daishonin has taught us, Bodhisattvas of the Earth, ever since the remotest past.

We can interpret this to mean that those who are directly connected to the life of Nichiren Daishonin are Bodhisattvas of the Earth and, as such, his true disciples. It was the first president, Mr. Makiguchi, and our mentor, President Toda, who put that into practice in contemporary society. It was especially true for President Toda who, while in prison, attained the realization that he himself was a Bodhisattva of the Earth and a legitimate disciple of the original Buddha, Nichiren Daishonin. From that moment on the Soka Gakkai was destined to become an organization of Bodhisattvas of the Earth, a group of true disciples of Nichiren Daishonin. The Soka Gakkai has advanced and will continue to advance together with Mr. Toda, a leader of unparalleled humanity, as we make his spirit our own. How highly the original Buddha will extol those who belong to this great, vibrant organization! There is nothing that should worry you or cause you fear.

In the life philosophy, "the Buddha from the remotest past" signifies "the Buddha" inherent within our own lives— namely, the Tathagata of Nam-myoho-renge-kyo. That the Bodhisattvas of the Earth are disciples of the Buddha from the remotest past indicates that our life, based on the Buddhahood of Nam-myoho-renge-kyo existing deep within us, manifests the functions of the Four Bodhisattvas—Jōgyō, Muhengyō, Jyōgyō and Anryūgyō. I am convinced that if we hold ourselves completely responsible for the great mission of *kōsen-rufu*, rack our minds and drive our bodies to accomplish this mission, the life of Nam-myoho-renge-kyo will always give us the power to go on, to live our faith. The Daishonin states in the *Tōtaigi Shō* (The Entity of the Mystic Law), "In the final analysis, the entity of the Mystic Law of the Lotus is composed of the bodies, born of father and mother, of the disciples and followers of Nichiren who believe in the Lotus Sutra. . . . The Buddha of the Lotus, the entity of the *Juryō* chapter of the essential teaching, is the disciples and followers of Nichiren." He also explains to embrace the Gohonzon is to attain Buddhahood. Therefore, when we continue our mission exactly as the Daishonin directs, his life will surge forth from within us like a spring. I have always maintained this conviction—even when I had no one to depend on and had to make decisions all by myself. I am also firmly convinced that everything the Daishonin taught is perfectly true, as he stated it.

Now let us go on to the next line, "There should be no discrimination among those who propagate the five characters of Myoho-renge-kyo in the Latter Day of the Law, be they men or women." Those who spread Myoho-renge-kyo, or Nam-myoho-renge-kyo of the Three Great Secret Laws, in this age in the Latter Day are Bodhisattvas of the Earth. Those who spontaneously assume the responsibility of devoting themselves to propagating true Buddhism are all equal as they walk the greatest path of life, no matter what their lot or status. Those who "propagate" Buddhism are the most respectworthy of all, as the *Fugen* chapter of the Lotus Sutra states, "Most certainly you should arise and greet him from afar, and respect him in the same way as you do the Buddha." It is therefore one of the gravest sins to look down upon, censure or slander the Soka Gakkai, the religious organization devoted to spreading true Buddhism.

"There should be no discrimination . . . be they men or women." Men and women are completely equal in that they are Bodhisattvas of the Earth. The social differences between male and female arise because of the different roles they play. Certainly there are occupations that are more suitable for men than for women, and vice versa, although it is not impossible to take on an occupation traditionally held by the other sex. Discrimination on the basis of sex cannot be justified, and salaries should be fixed according to the occupation and not the sex. However, there are inevitable differences between individuals. The real problem arises when such differences stem not from the type of work but simply on the basis of sex, which violates the human equality of both sexes. The attitudes fostered by religion are often influential in social attitudes toward the respective status of each sex.

Many religions, past and present, assume some kind of male dominance. For example, the Christian and Islamic gods are usually envisioned as male. In Buddhism only men were thought to be able to reach salvation by sects whose doctrines derived from the pre-Lotus Sutra teachings. In contrast, Nichiren Daishonin declares that those who propagate the Mystic Law are Bodhisattvas of the Earth, be they men or women. Denying that any difference existed between men and women as far as their religious mission and capability were concerned, Nichiren Daishonin advocated genuine equality between the sexes. I want all of you to know that Nichiren Daishonin's Buddhism endorses the dignity of all human beings with this great democratic principle.

"Were they not Bodhisattvas of the Earth, they could not chant the daimoku." Only Bodhisattvas of the Earth can chant daimoku. In the eternity of life, to be able to live as a human being is a rare and precious thing when we consider all the other innumerable forms of life. Buddhism defines humans as the "correct vessel for the true teaching." Because we are human, we can follow the correct path to the higher states of life, and eventually enlightenment. The correct path is the religious faith which makes people truly human. But when we have no such source of humanity, we lack vitality, become rigid in our ideas and behavior, and become a weak and lifeless fossil. Truly religion is important, but it is very difficult to find a religion with the power to let us attain happiness. How fortunate we are to have faith in the true religion, and proud that we chant the daimoku!

"Were they not Bodhisattvas of the Earth, they could not chant the daimoku," states the importance of continuous, wholehearted chanting, no matter what may happen. Only Nam-myoho-renge-kyo can save us from all trouble. The original mission of bodhisattvas is to fulfill their vows. The Bodhisattvas of the Earth vowed to propagate the Lotus Sutra to the world. Therefore, we Bodhisattvas of the Earth should pray and chant daimoku mindful of our oath to work for *kōsen-rufu*. Without this thought, we cannot chant daimoku as Bodhisattvas of the Earth.

First Man to Stand Alone

Only I, Nichiren, at first chanted Nam-myoho-renge-kyo, but then two, three and a hundred followed, chanting and teaching others. Likewise, propagation will unfold this way in the future. Doesn't this signify "emerging from the earth"? At the time of *kōsen-rufu*, the entire Japanese nation will chant Nam-myoho-renge-kyo, as surely as an arrow aimed at the earth cannot miss the target.

In this well-known passage, Nichiren Daishonin teaches us the eternal formula for attaining *kōsen-rufu* and reveals his conviction that *kōsen-rufu* will be achieved. Nichiren Daishonin alone chanted daimoku first, and then he was followed by two, three and then a hundred. When he says, "Propagation will unfold this way in the future," he means that the process of achieving *kōsen-rufu* will not change a bit in the future, either.

This passage has two important points. First, coupled with the preceding sentence, "Were they not Bodhisattvas of the Earth, they could not chant the daimoku," it tells us that those who chant daimoku are all Bodhisattvas of the Earth. However, as the next sentence says, "Only I, Nichiren, at first chanted Nam-myoho-renge-kyo," there always has to be one who starts chanting and initiates the propagation of the Mystic Law with two, three and then a hundred coming to follow. The propagation of a religion is always started by one person awakened to his mission, followed by a great number of people who come in turn. The initiator is especially important, for his spirit will permeate those who appear later. In our case, the "one" was Nichiren Daishonin, our founder. But as the Daishonin stated, "Propagation will unfold this way in the future," the Soka Gakkai was established by one person, Tsunesaburo Makiguchi, the first president. He stood up alone and began propagation. Following Mr. Makiguchi, two, three and finally three thousand came to chant.

Immediately after World War II, Josei Toda, who succeeded him, came out of prison only to find the organization utterly defunct and lifeless in the ruins of war-torn Tokyo. He embarked upon propagation and was followed by two, three and a hundred people. Today, the Soka Gakkai has more than ten million members. We must never forget these founders, so that we may transmit their spirit correctly. That the propagation of daimoku starts from one person means that his spirit should be shared by all who come later.

The first person who stands alone is important, for he is the source of growth from then on. I want you to be firm in your conviction of this as an unchanging principle of *kōsen-rufu*. Nichiren Daishonin tells us in his *Letter to Niike*: "The relation between cause and effect is like that between flower and fruit. When someone lights a fire in a great plain of dry grass, even a spark as faint as a firefly, the fire will burn one, two, ten, a hundred and thousand blades of grass, and finally reach all the trees and grass of the thousand-mile plain." A single match can cause a great conflagration. Each of us must be a matchstick of faith.

The phrase, "chanting and teaching others," is also very important. "Chanting" is our own practice (*jigyō*), while "teaching others" is practice for others (*keta*). *On the Three Great Secret Laws* has the following statement: "Now in the Latter Day of the Law, the daimoku which Nichiren chants is different from that of previous ages—Nam-myoho-renge-kyo is the practice both for oneself and for others." If we do not practice both for ourselves and for others, we are not truly following Nichiren Daishonin.

The *Ongi Kuden* also mentions the significance of *jigyō* and *keta* concerning "chanting and teaching others." It reads, "The whole *Yujutsu* chapter is devoted to the mission of bodhisattvas sent by the original Buddha. The practice of these bodhisattvas is Nam-myoho-renge-kyo. That is what the sutra means by chanting. Teaching in the sutra means to lead all the people of Japan to the pure land of Eagle Peak." Only those who chant daimoku themselves and teach it to all the people around them are the Bodhisattvas of the Earth. The Daishonin says, "Propagation will unfold this way in the future," meaning that the principle of chanting and teaching is basic to all ages.

Since you believe in the Gohonzon, the entity of Nichiren Daishonin's life, and live up to the spirit of Makiguchi and Toda, I hope you will stand alone courageously, chanting and propagating daimoku wherever you are. To stand alone means to take total responsibility for *kōsen-rufu* in the home, office or community. Buddhism and *kōsen-rufu* lie in the places closest to you and in steady, continuous activities. We all have to be aware that we are here as envoys from the original Buddha, Nichiren Daishonin.

No matter what our circumstances, each of us has his own set of human relationships. He forms his own associations in his home, office and in his community with many types of people. In the light of the Mystic Law, these are the places to carry out his mission, and the people there are all fellow bodhisattvas. In that group of people you are the one and only person who can assume the responsibility and mission for *kōsen-rufu*. To stand up alone to fight for *kōsen-rufu* in your own place and circumstances is to "emerge from the earth."

In addition, the above passage declares that it is the common people who bear the burden of creating the worldwide tide of true Buddhism. Neither power nor authority will ever help to accelerate the movement for *kōsen-rufu*. Never forget the Daishonin's words, "Propagation will unfold this way in the future." *Kōsen-rufu* begins with a single person to reach all strata of people.

"At the time of *kōsen-rufu*, the entire Japanese nation will chant Nam-myoho-renge-kyo, as surely as an arrow aimed at the earth cannot miss the target." Thus we see the Daishonin's conviction—and prediction—that all Japanese would come to chant the daimoku, Nam-myoho-renge-kyo. "The entire Japanese nation" means everyone, housewives, students, educators, statesmen and all others. As all people study and practice Buddhism, create value in their lives and contribute to society, they will bring about a total revolution in society. This is what is meant by "the entire Japanese nation." However, although the Daishonin mentions only Japan, he does not imply that we should neglect propagation of the Mystic Law in other countries. It is clear from the words, "to achieve *kōsen-rufu* throughout the world," which appear in many parts of the Lotus Sutra and the Gosho. It might be noted, however, that Nichiren Daishonin meant Japan as the land where the people's efforts are especially needed in the first stage of *kōsen-rufu*. Japanese members should realize that *kōsen-rufu* in Japan will be a great example to members throughout the world, and act accordingly.

Buddhism for One and All

But now you must build your reputation as a votary of the Lotus Sutra and devote yourself to it. Shakyamuni Buddha and Tahō Buddha, seated in the Treasure Tower in the air, surrounded by all other Buddhas and bodhisattvas, nodded in agreement. What they decided upon was solely for the perpetuation of the True Law throughout the Latter Day. Tahō Buddha had offered Shakyamuni Buddha a place beside him, and when they unfurled the banner of Myoho-renge-kyo, the two leaders of the entire multitude made their decision together. Could there have been anything false in their decision? Their ultimate purpose in meeting was to provide a way for all of us ordinary people to attain Buddhahood.

The most important goal of faith is to "build your reputation as a votary of the Lotus Sutra and devote yourself to it." We feel the infinite mercy of Nichiren Daishonin, who has experienced the truth of life, when he says, "But now you must build your reputation . . ." He was witness to terrible persecution, but with belief in the coming of *kōsen-rufu* he urged his disciples to do what they should. One of the qualities that impresses me most, that is most compelling to me, is his compassion. I can really feel it when he admonishes us not to discard our faith because of shallow, distorted ideas about Buddhism, not to abandon it through ignorance.

I remember something similar that President Toda once said in an essay called "My Problem": "My problem is that too few people stand up strongly in faith. Some, just converted, do not really believe in the Dai-Gohonzon's power and they soon give up, abandoning their faith. How superficial and impatient people can be! They will go to their deathbeds without ever experiencing the clear, fresh outpouring of blessings from the Gohonzon in their lives. How pitiful they are! Just to think of them is like putting a knife through myself."

A spaceship follows a fixed orbit when it goes to the moon. If it should veer from that orbit, it might never return to the earth. We, too, have an "orbit" of life in the universe. If we veer from our own orbit, we might end up wandering in utter darkness for aeons without end. It is a terrible feeling to sense defeat in the ups and downs of life. The Daishonin in effect says, "You may have doubts and questions about the Mystic Law, but now trust what I say and devote yourself entirely to the Lotus Sutra."

To "build your reputation as a votary of the Lotus Sutra" is to live up to *kōsen-rufu* with pride and honor. It is of course very important for each of us to be respected and trusted in whatever work we do. But when seen from the deeper level of eternal life, your efforts for and contribution to the goal of *kōsen-rufu* are vastly more important. That is the only honor whose glory will never fade.

To "devote yourself to the Lotus Sutra" means to make the Gohonzon the sole foundation of your life—the point to which you always return when you need courage and power. It means to keep up your daily practice of gongyo and activities for *kōsen-rufu* to the best of your ability. No other life is stronger or more meaningful than a life devoted to the Lotus Sutra. If we devote ourselves to the Gohonzon, the Lotus Sutra for this day and age, we are rooting our lives in the law and power of the cosmos.

The following part, "Shakyamuni Buddha and Tahō Buddha . . . ," explains why you have to "build your reputation as a votary of the Lotus Sutra and devote yourself to it." The ceremony and teaching of the Lotus Sutra was given for us, people of the Latter Day of the Law. The Buddhist philosophy exists entirely for our sake. If you do not realize that, Buddhism is just another powerless ideology.

In the first nine chapters of the Lotus Sutra, Shakyamuni attempts to awaken his disciples' understanding to his enlightenment and he predicts that they will eventually attain Buddhahood. From the tenth (*Hosshi*) chapter the story is developed on the theme of who is to propagate the Lotus Sutra after Shakyamuni's passing. In the next (*Hōtō*) chapter, the Treasure Tower appears, and the ceremony in the air unfolds. In the *Hōtō* and *Devadatta* (12th) chapters, Shakyamuni asks who is willing to propagate the Lotus Sutra after his passing. In the next two (*Kanji* and *Anrakugyō*) chapters the bodhisattvas taught by the Buddha respond to his call and pledge to propagate the sutra. However, in the *Yujutsu* (15th) chapter, Shakyamuni refuses them and at that moment the Bodhisattvas of the Earth appear. All the other bodhisattvas wondered who they are, and Bodhisattva Miroku, on their behalf, asks Shakyamuni about his relationship to them. In the *Juryō* (16th) chapter the Buddha reveals his aeons of life since *gohyaku-jintengō* to answer the question. In the *Jinriki* (21st) chapter Shakyamuni entrusts the mission of propagation to the Bodhisattvas of the Earth, and in the next (*Zokurui*) chapter, to all the other bodhisattvas present at the ceremony. Therefore, the ceremony in the air was held to pass to the Bodhisattvas of the Earth the mission of propagating the Mystic Law in the Latter Day. This is one interpretation of what is meant by "what they decided upon was solely for the perpetuation of the True Law throughout the Latter Day."

That is still only a literal interpretation of the sutra. For true Buddhism, the ceremony in the air reveals the true object of worship that is to be propagated in the Latter Day of the Law. The ceremony in the air presents a blueprint for the Gohonzon of the Three Great Secret Laws. "The banner of Myoho-renge-kyo" is the essential part of the Gohonzon.

This Gohonzon is the object of worship to be propagated

in the Latter Day, for it can lead all people to enlightenment. That is the meaning of "the perpetuation of the True Law throughout the Latter Day" and "their ultimate purpose in meeting was to provide a way for all of us ordinary people to attain Buddhahood." This is saying that the Gohonzon we worship daily is the ultimate of the "eighty thousand doctrines," the Buddha's teachings. It is the entity that embodies the cosmic law of the Lotus Sutra. This passage reconfirms that we will attain Buddhahood if we carefully follow true Buddhism.

In the Gohonzon, "Nam-myoho-renge-kyo, Nichiren" written in the center is what is meant by "the banner of Myoho-renge-kyo," while Shakyamuni and Tahō on both sides of Nam-myoho-renge-kyo are what represent "Sha-kyamuni Buddha and Tahō Buddha, seated in the Treasure Tower in the air."

Ceremony in the Air

Although I was not at that ceremony, in looking at the sutra, this is crystal-clear. On the other hand, I may have been at the ceremony, but since I am a common mortal, it is beyond my power to know the past. There is no doubt, however, that in the present life I am the votary of the Lotus Sutra, and that in the future I will therefore reach the seat of enlightenment. Judging the past from this point of view, I must have been at the ceremony in the air. There can be no discontinuity between past, present and future.

Here the Daishonin expresses his certain knowledge of attaining Buddhahood in the future because his behavior fulfills exactly the predictions of the Lotus Sutra. Since he is a common mortal, he has no personal memory of his past existences and cannot know from remembered experience whether he was among those who attended the ceremony in the air. But when he reads the sutra, he can clearly see everything that went on during the ceremony. No one can deny the fact that his actions in this lifetime are those of a Bodhisattva of the Earth, the votary of the Lotus Sutra. Therefore, he says, he "must have been at the ceremony in the air."

In the documents the Daishonin transmitted to Nikkō Shonin, and a few other Gosho with equally profound meaning—*On the Three Great Secret Laws*, for instance—he definitely states that he was entrusted with the propagation of the Lotus Sutra during the ceremony in the air on Eagle Peak. Nowhere else is he so articulate; in all his other writings he refuses clearly to commit himself, and maintains a detached objectivity. What we were or what we did in a past existence is beyond our power to know, and any dogmatic assertion of what our past was or what it meant could lead nowhere except to misunderstanding on the part of our listeners. We must try to be objective, as the Daishonin does in this Gosho. First he compares the statements in the sutra with what he is actually doing, and based on that he then deduces what must have occurred in the past, just as historians and scientists do today.

"There can be no discontinuity between past, present and future." Past, present and future are closely interrelated. "If you want to know the cause you formed in the past, observe the effect in the present. If you want to know the effect in the future, observe the cause you are forming now." The Buddhist way is to judge the past as well as the future from what we see and experience around us right now. But to recognize the past and future significance in the facts of the present, we must train our minds to develop a clear grasp of the strict law of causality—the law which determines the effect that a given cause will produce. Because of that ability, a Buddha is said to see through the three existences of life. It requires no mystic or supernatural powers, only the power of true reason. "Buddhism is reason." Remember that always and engrave it in your heart.

Here, let me say a few more words about the ceremony in the air. The ceremony begins in the *Hōtō* (11th) chapter of the Lotus Sutra and ends in the *Zokurui* (22nd) chapter. The Treasure Tower appears in the air above Eagle Peak, and Shakyamuni seats himself beside Tahō Buddha before he begins to preach to the multitude of others also in the air during the ceremony. It is difficult to believe, however, that it actually took place and that it happened in India three thousand years ago. Imagine countless numbers of people airborne without the help of any mechanical device. It is too fantastic to be true. Furthermore, the Treasure Tower is described as having the dimensions $500 \times 250 \times 250$ *yujun*. One *yujun* varies according to interpretation, but using a moderate estimate, 500 *yujun* would equal the radius of the earth!

Is everything in the Lotus Sutra no more than a figment of someone's imagination? No, and it would be a gross misunderstanding to think so. But how does one handle this kind of event as it appears in the sutra? First, we must understand that Shakyamuni could not preach the truth of his enlightenment other than by giving a graphic, almost surrealistic account of the ceremony in the air. Thus, when Mr. Josei Toda said that the solemn ceremony of the Lotus Sutra "took place in Shakyamuni's own life," he meant that Shakyamuni chose that way to portray his enlightenment.

The ceremony in the air conveys the substance of Shakyamuni's enlightenment. The ceremony is itself the entity of the Law to which the Buddha was enlightened. That entity was revealed by Shakyamuni as the ceremony in the air, by T'ien-t'ai as the doctrine of *ichinen sanzen*, and by Nichiren Daishonin as the Gohonzon through which he gave the suffering generations of the Latter Day a means to express their faith and attain enlightenment.

The Daishonin is speaking of Shakyamuni's Lotus Sutra in the above passage, so he says, "Judging the past from this point of view, I must have been at the ceremony in the air." But the real meaning of this paragraph is that by embracing the Gohonzon, doing gongyo and chanting daimoku, we actually participate in the ceremony in the air each day. Our life itself is the ceremony in the air—the manifestation of *kūtai*. Our physical and mental functions are given the power to work by the ultimate entity of life in the state of *kū*. *Kū* is not nothingness, but it is the basis of life filled with infinite creativity and power. Again, eternal life is itself the ceremony in the air. The assembly at Eagle Peak took the form of the ceremony in the air only to reveal the eternity of life—the life itself which continues to exist even after physical death.

Absolute Happiness in Adversity

Because I view things this way, I feel immeasurable delight even though I am now an exile. Joy as well as sorrow brings us to tears. Tears express our feeling for both blessings and misfortune.

Here is an expression of the absolute happiness experienced by Nichiren Daishonin after he had read the Lotus Sutra and absorbed it with his entire being. All of Nichiren Daishonin's writings are beautiful prose. Whenever we read them, our hearts are quickened by the voice of a merciful father, and fill with a stronger determination to move ahead for *kōsenrufu*. The sentences of the Gosho are fundamentally different from the flowery sentences of other writers that are based on mere theory. By reading the Gosho, we can come to see that the Gosho is a living testimony to the Daishonin's state of life—it clearly depicts the inner being of the author.

Confined to Sado Island and forced to endure conditions as bitter as one of the eight cold hells, Nichiren Daishonin reflected in his letters a state of life that encompassed the entire universe. No words are adequate to describe his great courage and mercy.

Countless people were exiled to Sado during the years between the Tempyō era (710–794) and the Edo era (1603–1867). Their despair, indignation, pain and resignation seemed to have soaked into the very soil of the island. Who else but the Daishonin could have remained as serene as the clear autumn sky and as vast and mild as the sea under a warm spring sun, so that he was able to say that he felt "immeasurable delight" in such an oppressive, forbidding place? Philosophers and sages, forced to live in misery, invariably look to the heavens for solace against their frustration or give themselves up to unbearable grief. But Nichiren Daishonin lived through the deepest suffering with unmatched courage, leaving a singularly brilliant example of a personal revolution. Never forget this passage. Make it part of you so that your lives will reverberate with the sound of his voice.

"Because I view things this way" indicates that in the final analysis, the Lotus Sutra was expounded exclusively for Nichiren Daishonin. The magnificent ceremony in the air, Shakyamuni and Tahō Buddhas seated side by side, Buddhas throughout the universe coming to attend the ceremony—all was directed toward "perpetuating the True Law throughout the Latter Day" and "providing a way for all of us ordinary people to attain Buddhahood." The ceremony was held, and the Buddhas assembled, solely to entrust the True Law to Nichiren Daishonin—in a superficial sense the incarnation of Bodhisattva Jōgyō, but in a deeper sense the original Buddha since time without beginning. This, he says, is a thing wonderful beyond words. Tears are the expression of sublime, irrepressible feelings that surge forth against all efforts to contain them. They reveal a tremendous emotion that breaks through to the surface, regardless of circumstances.

"Even though I am now an exile" bespeaks the difficult and painful life of an exile on Sado Island. It is a relative state of unhappiness, which places the Daishonin in a situation with what would appear to be the least security and happiness. However, because of the absolute joy in his heart, his happiness is greater, more effluent and more solid than that of anyone else in the world. Absolute happiness lies on a completely different plane from relative happiness. It is not something that is attained through wealth, good health, and having people close by who care for you.

A person can establish absolute happiness, no matter how dogged he may be by conditions of relative unhappiness. It is also possible to have everything one needs for relative happiness, and still be nowhere near attaining absolute happiness. There are many around us who possess all the conditions for relative happiness and, although they do not believe in Buddhism, they look much happier than we. But they do not have absolute happiness. The happiness of Buddhahood was something completely different from theirs, contingent upon nothing in his objective surroundings and never to be eradicated.

Relative happiness, no matter how great, cannot become absolute. Even a man who is fabulously wealthy or famous throughout the world can tumble into utter poverty and ignominy overnight, and with the disappearance of his fortune, his happiness vanishes also. A man in the prime of life may be badly injured in an accident. Even if he does not meet with any such mishaps, he will suffer from disease and physical frailty as he gets older, as well as many other problems we must all encounter. For most people, happiness mistakenly depends on relative circumstances.

Relative happiness depends totally on the precarious relationship between a person and his environment. Suppose you are hungry, and someone takes you for a sumptuous meal. Your hunger is satisfied by something in your environment—in this case, food—and you feel a momentary sense of relative happiness in your life. In contrast, absolute happiness depends on the relationship between the mission or objective to which you have pledged yourself and the fact of whether or not you are actually carrying it out. This is a sense of fulfillment and satisfaction that you can feel in the depths of your life. It is a state that is unaffected by constant change in your surroundings, a state that you firmly establish by your own will. It can, therefore, become absolute. But first, the mission or objective which you have taken on yourself must be in accord with a law that is as immutable and eternal as the universe itself. That is what makes absolute happiness possible.

A true state of absolute happiness can be established by linking yourself directly to the Mystic Law—the Law that remains immutable since time without beginning—and devoting yourself heart and soul to fulfilling the great wish for *kōsen-rufu*. This is the objective which you have set for yourself. Please be firmly convinced of this, and take the greatest pride in your individual lives, as you follow the noblest course in life that any human being can travel.

"*Thus I Heard*"

The one thousand arhats shed tears in memory of the Buddha, and in tears Bodhisattva Monju chanted Myoho-renge-kyo. From among those one thousand arhats, the venerable Ananda replied in tears, "Thus I heard." Thereupon the tears of all the others fell, wetting their inkstones, and they wrote "Myoho-renge-kyo" followed by "Thus I heard." I, Nichiren, now feel exactly as they did. I am now in exile because

I spread the teaching of Myoho-renge-kyo. I spread this teaching because I, too, "heard thus": Shakyamuni Buddha and Tahō Buddha left Myoho-renge-kyo for the Japanese and all people in the future.

Here we see the meeting held to compile the Buddhist scriptures. Notice in particular the phrase, "Thus I heard." It appears at the beginning of all the sutras, following a title that encapsulates the essence of each sutra. Literally, it means that "I have personally heard Shakyamuni speak these words."

"Monju chanted Myoho-renge-kyo. . . . Ananda replied in tears, 'Thus I heard.' . . . all the others . . . wrote 'Myoho-renge-kyo' followed by 'Thus I heard.' " This means that all the participants had heard Myoho-renge-kyo and agreed it was the ultimate of Shakyamuni's teaching.

"Thus I heard" does not mean simply to listen to something. It is a much stronger declaration. In his *Hokke Mongu*, T'ien-t'ai states that "I heard" indicates a person who upholds [the True Law]. In other words, it implies the believer's affirmation that the sutra he "heard" is the essence of the Buddha's teaching and his resolution to practice Buddhism precisely as the sutra says, devoting himself to showing its validity through his behavior.

Nichiren Daishonin, too, "heard that Shakyamuni Buddha and Tahō Buddha left Myoho-renge-kyo for the Japanese and all people in the future." That is why he fought so valiantly to propagate the Mystic Law, endured persecution to prove the validity of the Lotus Sutra, and at last left the Gohonzon for generations to come in the ten thousand years of the Latter Day and on into eternity.

Our first president, Tsunesaburo Makiguchi, and second president, Josei Toda, were the contemporary masters who "had heard" that the Buddhism Nichiren Daishonin left for us is the fundamental law of human revolution and world peace. Since they "had heard thus," one became a martyr for *kōsen-rufu*, and the other gave his life, also, to the same lofty mission. The conduct of our two presidents exemplifies the Soka Gakkai spirit, and the way of life we, too, should strive for.

After Shakyamuni's passing, Monju, Ananda and the other disciples shed tears in his memory, called his teachings to mind, and in tears compiled them into the Buddhist scriptures. This was the expression of their infinite gratitude for the Buddha's mercy. In short, they could not contain their deep emotion toward Shakyamuni and left his teachings in sutra form, which paved the way for the spread of Buddhism into the future.

Nichiren Daishonin felt "exactly as they did." With gratitude for Shakyamuni and the Lotus Sutra, and with tears of boundless mercy for all mankind, he revealed the supreme law to be propagated throughout the Latter Day and on into eternity. This is what he means when he says in *Requital for the Buddha's Favor*, "If Nichiren's mercy is truly great, Nam-myoho-renge-kyo will spread for ten thousand years and more, for all eternity."

We, too, must thank the original Buddha, Nichiren Daishonin, for the treasury he left for us, despite his hardships. With the great joy we have in our faith in true Buddhism, let us tell everyone we can about it and get them as involved and excited as we are, until it spreads to all mankind in future generations.

Persecution and Enlightenment

I cannot hold back my tears when I think of the great persecution confronting me now, or when I think of the joy of attaining Buddhahood in the future. Birds cry, but never shed tears. I, Nichiren, do not cry, but my tears flow ceaselessly. I shed my tears not for

**worldly affairs but solely for the sake of the Lotus
Sutra. So indeed, they must be tears of *amrita*. The
Nirvana Sutra states that while the tears one sheds
throughout his many existences on the death of his
parents, brothers, sisters, wives, children and followers
may surpass the quantity of water in all the seas, he
weeps not a drop for Buddhism.**

"The great persecution confronting me now," of course,
is his exile to Sado. It was indeed a bitter experience, but
he underwent this persecution as the votary of the Lotus
Sutra. Because he was the votary then, he knew for certain
that he would "attain Buddhahood in the future." Which-
ever way he thought about it, he could not hold back his
tears.

Important here is his teaching that "the great persecution"
at the moment leads directly to "attaining Buddhahood in
the future." To overcome great persecution is to attain
enlightenment. A long succession of hardships lies ahead
on our way to the human revolution. But only by facing
and overcoming them can you attain Buddhahood.

The history of the Soka Gakkai is filled with huge and
painful trials, but that is only further proof that it is an
organization of "envoys of the Buddha, sent to carry out the
Buddha's work." What other person or group in this age
has ever suffered so much for the sake of the Lotus Sutra?
Some religious bodies are hopelessly degraded, concerned
only to deceive their believers and preserve themselves. The
single teaching quoted above makes one realize that the
Soka Gakkai is an organization that echoes the Daishonin's
life, carrying out the Buddha's work exactly as he has
willed.

The Gosho states, "Those who overcome hardships and
embrace the Lotus Sutra from beginning to end are the
envoys of the Buddha." This means that those who endure

persecution and oppression and overcome them are equal to Buddhas. Whenever I read this passage I feel renewed enthusiasm for our mission. Ours is a true revolution, not some game played under the cover of religion. Watched by the Buddhas and bodhisattvas throughout time and space, we are waging a decisive battle with the devil that pervades the universe, showing whether or not we can prove Nichiren Daishonin's Buddhism to be true. We cannot allow ourselves to weaken or retreat even a bit. Continue to advance cheerfully and valiantly together with me, fighting as the original Buddha commands, deceived or swayed by no one. Make this noble campaign a record of your own achievement—one that will be remembered forever.

Tears express the feelings deepest within our hearts. The brief passage above gives a sense of the profound mercy and emotion Nichiren Daishonin felt every moment of his life. "Birds cry, but never shed tears." Birds sing. Some of them are well known for their beautiful calls. But their cries come from instinct, not feeling. "I, Nichiren, do not cry, but my tears flow ceaselessly." This famous phrase seems to show forth the boundless compassion of Nichiren Daishonin.

"I shed my tears not for worldly affairs," he says, "but solely for the sake of the Lotus Sutra." He does not shed tears just because he feels pain, hardship or sadness. His tears are shed as he tries to propagate the Lotus Sutra in order to save people from suffering for all time. "So indeed, they must be tears of *amrita*." *Amrita* (also known as ambrosia), according to ancient legends, is the sweet-tasting drink of immortality. The Chinese believed that the heavens let it rain down on paradise, to relieve human beings of all their sufferings and bring them perpetual youth and immortality. Nichiren Daishonin's tears were crystallized into the Dai-Gohonzon of the Three Great Secret Laws to enrich human life, remove suffering and give people unfading youth and eternal life. We can taste the *amrita* of the Dai-Gohonzon's blessings through our own experience.

The passage of the Nirvana Sutra talks of human life in the past, present and future. It says that we shed more than enough tears for mundane things during the countless lifetimes we live, but not a single tear for Buddhism. It is saying how difficult it is for people to encounter Buddhism and, even when they happen to do so, how rarely they truly have faith in it. Nichiren Daishonin shed tears throughout his life for the sake of Buddhism. In the same spirit let us dedicate our own lives to this noble mission, letting our tears flow for the sake of the True Law.

Mystic Bond

One becomes a votary of the Lotus Sutra by virtue of his practice in past existences. It is karmic relationships that determine which among so many of the same kind of trees are made into images of Buddha. It is also because of karma that some Buddhas are born as provisional ones.

Nichiren Daishonin became a votary of the Lotus Sutra, not because of his relation with the Lotus Sutra in this lifetime, but because of past karma—because he practiced the sutra in his past existences. Trees are insentient, but some of them "are made into images of Buddha"—for example, the Gohonzon. Others become bars in a prison. The Daishonin says that "it is karmic relationships that determine" their fate because plants cannot think or act on their own will. What they are made into depends on their inherent karma, and that decides who will use them.

For every effect, there is always a cause that produced it. The law of causality unites past, present and future. There are Buddhas and Buddhas. Some are the Buddhas of

Hinayana teachings, others of provisional Mahayana teachings. Each has a different task and a different power, and all of this derives from their karma, from their acts in past existences.

We are engaged in the propagation of Nam-myoho-renge-kyo as true disciples of Nichiren Daishonin, but what about those who have no firm basis for their lives? What they consider to be happiness is as ephemeral as a thin blanket of snow in the noonday sun, as fleeting as a mirage, and as rootless as duckweed floating at the mercy of waves. How fragile, illusionary and empty their way of living is, engulfed in the constant changes of life! Think of the misery a man feels when stripped of a reputation that once intoxicated him. Or of the petty, short-lived "haughtiness of ashura"—those who were in some position of authority yesterday, but are removed from power today.

Such people are to be pitied for the weakness and shallowness of their foundation in life. For I know that in the depths of all that flux and phenomenal impermanence, unaffected by anything, lies the ultimate foundation—the Mystic Law. You must be convinced that people who make that foundation their own have the most meaningful lives of all. My mentor, Josei Toda, was awakened to the fact that his true entity was that of a Bodhisattva of the Earth. When we are awakened to our mission and our true entity, we, too, will feel infinite power welling forth from within. Toda's words, filled with a thousand emotions, still ring in my heart, as in his poem written for me:

> Now in bud is the mystic bond
> Which we formed of old.
> Let it come into full bloom
> Stout-hearted and magnificent.

Our predecessors, who developed the Soka Gakkai into what it is today, were always aware of "the mystic bond which we formed of old" as they continued their struggle. You are now fighting as members of the Soka Gakkai, the group of Bodhisattvas of the Earth. Believe that it is because of your past karma, and fight courageously on to accomplish your mission. Attain your ultimate purpose in this life, for only by so doing can you lead a life of complete fulfillment.

Faith, Practice and Study

In this letter, I have written my most important teachings. Grasp their meaning and make them part of your life. Believe in the Gohonzon, the supreme object of worship in the world. Forge strong faith and receive the protection of Shakyamuni, Tahō and all the other Buddhas. Exert yourself in the two ways of practice and study. Without practice and study, there can be no Buddhism. You must not only persevere yourself; you must also teach others. Both practice and study arise from faith. Teach others to the best of your ability, even if only a single sentence or phrase. Nam-myoho-renge-kyo, Nam-myoho-renge-kyo.

With my deep respect,
Nichiren
The seventeenth day of the fifth month

I touched on the meaning of "my most important teachings" earlier. This Gosho contains the essence of all of Nichiren Daishonin's teachings: the supreme law and core of Buddhism that must be spread in the Latter Day; the revelation of the Buddha of the Latter Day; the way the Daishonin's disciples should practice their faith. Here he tells us again to understand them deeply and make them part of our lives.

"Make them part of your life" means for us to engrave

his teachings in our hearts and practice exactly as this Gosho directs. Our Gohonzon is "the supreme object of worship in the world." I believe that the Daishonin's Buddhism is the very religion that can bring peace to humankind and that the Dai-Gohonzon is the crystallization of its essence. The rest depends entirely on our faith. He therefore urges us to "forge strong faith and receive the protection of Shakyamuni, Tahō and all the other Buddhas."

Faith is not something that will someday deepen of itself. We must progress positively, with confidence, and no matter what obstacle may hinder us, we must resolve to tuin it around and use it to advance another step, with the Gohonzon as our pillar. This requires courage, but if we continue in courageous faith, Shakyamuni, Tahō and all the other Buddhas will always protect us.

Shakyamuni's protection is the welling up of Buddha nature—the most fundamental change that can occur in our lives. Tahō's protection appears as a life filled with benefits. The protection of all the other Buddhas means that all those around us will be awakened to the True Law and will, together with us, build an ideal, harmonious human society where peace, equality and justice are at last attained.

"Exert yourself in the two ways of practice and study. Without practice and study, there can be no Buddhism." I hope you have memorized this and all the sentences that follow. I have talked about "practice and study" as stressed in this Gosho on many occasions, so here I will go into the teaching, "Without practice and study, there can be no Buddhism." Buddhism exists in practice and study, in the efforts of living people who practice and study it. Buddhism is not contained in sutras, books, or the characters with which they are written. Nor is it found in the temples or other buildings. Buddhism exists and manifests itself only in the life of each person who studies the Gosho and practices his faith strictly according to the Daishonin's teachings. The

Soka Gakkai is carrying out a global movement to propagate Buddhism. Its members remain in close contact with each other and concentrate upon developing the faith of others as well as their own. Remember that the true stream of Buddhism only lives and breathes in the association and mutual encouragement of us believers.

"You must not only persevere yourself; you must also teach others." This is the principle of *jigyō* and *keta*: to practice Buddhism for ourselves and also teach it to other people. We must become happy ourselves, and at the same time make others happy.

"Both practice and study arise from faith." Faith is the basis of both practice and study, and faith is always manifested as practice and study. These three—faith, practice and study—become the most important objective of the Soka Gakkai.

"Teach others to the best of your ability, even if only a single sentence or phrase." This tells us to do *shakubuku* to the full extent of our capabilities and to the degree that our circumstances allow, even if we can only teach others a single sentence or phrase of Buddhism.

Eternally Master and Disciple

Postscript:
I have already passed on to you many of my important teachings. Those I have revealed to you in this letter are especially important. Is there not a mystic bond between us? Are you not the embodiment of one of the Four Bodhisattvas of the Earth headed by Jōgyō who led bodhisattvas equal in number to the sands of the sixty thousand Ganges Rivers? There must be some profound reason for our relationship. I have given you some of the most important teachings relating to my own life and practice. Nichiren may

be one of the countless Bodhisattvas of the Earth, for I have been chanting Nam-myoho-renge-kyo out of my desire to guide all the men and women in Japan. Hence the phrase of the sutra: "Among the bodhisattvas are four who led the entire multitude: The first is called Jōgyō; [the second, Muhengyō; the third, Jyōgyō; and the fourth, Anryūgyō.] They are the four highest leaders." Our deep relationship in the past has made you one of my disciples. By all means keep these matters to yourself. Nichiren has herein committed to writing the teachings of his own enlightenment. I will end here.

"Those I have revealed to you in this letter are especially important." I discussed this sentence at the beginning of this lecture. Nichiren Daishonin gave several very important Gosho to Sairenbō, including *Heritage of the Ultimate Law of Life*, *Enlightenment of Plants*, and *On Prayer*. Here he says that this Gosho, *The True Entity of Life*, contains the most important of all the teachings he has ever conveyed to Sairenbō. He asks if there is not a mystic bond between the two of them, master and disciple. This Gosho carries "the main teachings" concerning Nichiren Daishonin himself— those on the enlightenment and practice of the Buddha of the Latter Day. Sairenbō, the Daishonin declares, must be one of the Bodhisattvas of the Earth, born with a vital mission for *kōsen-rufu* in the Latter Day.

The Daishonin is using strong understatement when he says, "Nichiren may be one of the countless Bodhisattvas of the Earth," but it implies that in a transient sense he is Jōgyō, the foremost of the four greatest leaders of those bodhisattvas, and that his true entity is the original Buddha from time without beginning. In a word, it expresses his conviction that he is the Buddha of the Latter Day of the Law.

"For I have been chanting Nam-myoho-renge-kyo out of my desire to guide all the men and women in Japan." He says "all the men and women in Japan," but what he really means is "all the people in the world for all eternity." No one other than Nichiren Daishonin ever strove to save all mankind with the Law of Nam-myoho-renge-kyo in the Latter Day. He is therefore the supreme leader of the Bodhisattvas of the Earth and the Buddha of the Latter Day.

"Our deep relationship in the past has made you one of my disciples." Here again he stresses the mystic bond and reminds Sairenbō of his mission. A passage from *Reply to Sairenbō* reads, "In your letter you say, 'From now on I will forsake all the heretical teachers I have hitherto followed, and regard you, and you alone, as the teacher of the True Law.' But I do not understand this." Why does he say he doesn't understand it? He gives the reason in a fairly long paragraph that follows, but the heart of it is this: "We have been master and disciple ever since the infinite past. This is not a relationship which we just happened to form for the first time in this life. It is not an accidental encounter."

From the Buddhist viewpoint, "I do not understand this" has profound meaning. Sairenbō's words are fitting from a superficial standard. But the Daishonin delved much deeper into the Buddhist master-disciple relationship because he knew of the three existences of life.

This applies to us as well. We did not "just happen" to encounter the Daishonin's Buddhism in this lifetime. Nichiren Daishonin and we have been master and disciples since the infinite past. The members of the Soka Gakkai have always been brothers, sisters and friends. And now we have again come together in this world, assuming new personalities and positions, and are marching onward to accomplish our mission for *kōsen-rufu*.

The infinite past is here and now. Let us always remember

that we, united by bonds we established in the infinite past, must advance hand in hand as brothers and sisters of Buddhism. As we learned earlier, "There can be no discontinuity between past, present and future." Our togetherness at this moment is a mirror of life reflecting both the remote past and the distant future. Believing this, let us continue to enlarge our circle of *itai dōshin* (many in body, one in mind), studying together, respecting and encouraging one another.

To borrow the Daishonin's words, "our deep relationship in the past has made" us members of the Soka Gakkai. You have great capabilities accruing from that relationship, and your responsibilities are equally great. As a line in the "Song of Human Revolution" goes, "You have a mission to accomplish in this world."

"By all means keep these matters to yourself. Nichiren has herein committed to writing the teachings of his own enlightenment." The people in the Daishonin's day could not grasp the ultimate essence of his Buddhism. Out of consideration for the unthinking doubts they might harbor, he told Sairenbō to keep the letter to himself. But it also means that we must imprint his teachings indelibly on our lives. He concludes by saying that this, *The True Entity of Life*, is an important writing which consists of "the teachings of his own enlightenment."

TWO

Heritage of the Ultimate Law of Life

Gosho Text

I have just carefully read your letter. To reply, the ultimate law of life and death as transmitted from the Buddha to all living beings is Myoho-renge-kyo. The five characters of Myoho-renge-kyo were transferred from the two Buddhas inside the Treasure Tower, Shakyamuni and Tahō, to Bodhisattva Jōgyō, carrying on a heritage unbroken since the infinite past. *Myō* represents death, and *hō* represents life. Life and death are the two phases passed through by the entities of the Ten Worlds, the entities of all sentient beings which embody the law of cause and effect (*renge*).

T'ien-t'ai said, "You must realize that the interrelated actions and reactions of sentient beings and their environments all manifest the law of the simultaneity of cause and effect." "Sentient beings and their environments" here means the reality of life and death. The law of simultaneity of cause and effect is clearly at work in everything that lives and dies.

The Great Teacher Dengyō said, "Birth and death are the mysterious workings of the life essence. The ultimate reality of life lies in existence and nonexistence." No phenomena—heaven or earth, Yin or Yang, the sun or the moon, the five planets, or any life-condition from Hell to Buddhahood—are free from birth and death. Thus the life and death of all phenomena are simply the two phases of Myoho-renge-kyo. In his *Maka Shikan*, T'ien-t'ai says, "The emergence of all things is the manifestation of their intrinsic nature, and their extinction, the withdrawal of that nature into the state of latency." Shakyamuni and Tahō Buddhas, too, are the two phases of life and death.

Shakyamuni who attained enlightenment countless aeons ago, the Lotus Sutra which leads all people to Buddhahood, and we ordinary human beings are in no way different or separate from each other. Therefore, to chant Myoho-renge-kyo with this realization is to inherit the ultimate law of life and death. To carry on this heritage is the most important task for Nichiren's disciples, and that is precisely what it means to embrace the Lotus Sutra.

For one who summons up his faith and chants Nam-myoho-renge-kyo with the profound insight that now is the last moment of his life, the sutra proclaims: "After his death, a thousand Buddhas will extend their hands to free him from all fear and keep him from falling into the evil paths." How can we possibly hold back our tears at the inexpressible joy of knowing that not just one or two, nor only one or two hundred, but as many as a thousand Buddhas will come to greet us with open arms!

One who does not have faith in the Lotus Sutra will instead find his hands firmly gripped by the guards of hell, just as the sutra warns, ". . . After he dies, he will fall into the hell of incessant suffering." How pitiful! The ten kings of hell will then pass judgment on him, and the heavenly messengers who have been with him since his birth will berate him for his evil deeds.

Just imagine that those thousand Buddhas extending their hands to all Nichiren's disciples who chant Nam-myoho-renge-kyo are like so many melons or moonflowers extending their slender vines. My disciples have been able to receive and embrace the Lotus Sutra by virtue of the strong ties they formed with this teaching in their past existences. They are certain to attain Buddhahood in the future. The heritage of the Lotus Sutra flows within the lives of those who never forsake it in any lifetime whatsoever—whether in the past, the present or the future. But those who disbelieve and slander the Lotus Sutra will "destroy the seeds for becoming a Buddha in this world." Because they cut themselves off from the potential to attain enlightenment, they do not share the ultimate heritage of faith.

All disciples and believers of Nichiren should chant Nam-myoho-renge-kyo with one mind (*itai dōshin*), transcending all differences among themselves to become as inseparable as fish and the water in which they swim. This spiritual bond is the basis for the universal transmission of the ultimate law of life and death. Herein lies the true goal of Nichiren's propa-

gation. When you are so united, even the great hope
for *kōsen-rufu* can be fulfilled without fail. But if
any of Nichiren's disciples should disrupt the unity of
itai dōshin, he will destroy his own castle from within.

Nichiren has been trying to awaken all the people
of Japan to faith in the Lotus Sutra so that they too
can share the heritage and attain Buddhahood. But
instead they attacked me time and again, and finally
had me banished to this island. You have followed
Nichiren, however, and met with sufferings as a
result. It pains me deeply to think of your anguish.
Gold can neither be burned by fire nor corroded or
swept away by water, but iron is vulnerable to both.
A wise person is like gold and a fool like iron. You
are like pure gold because you embrace the "gold"
of the Lotus Sutra. The Lotus Sutra reads in part,
"Sumeru is the loftiest of all mountains. The Lotus
Sutra is likewise the loftiest of all the sutras." It also
states, "The good fortune of the believer cannot be
burned by fire or washed away by water."

It must be ties of karma from the distant past that
have destined you to become my disciple at a time
like this. Shakyamuni and Tahō Buddhas certainly
realize this truth. The sutra's statement, "In lifetime
after lifetime they were always born together with
their masters in the Buddha lands throughout the
universe," cannot be false in any way.

How admirable that you have asked about the
transmission of the ultimate law of life and death!
No one has ever asked me such a question before.

I have answered in complete detail in this letter, so I want you to take it deeply to heart. The important point is to carry out your practice, confident that Nam-myoho-renge-kyo is the very lifeblood which was transferred from Shakyamuni and Tahō to Bodhisattva Jōgyō.

The function of fire is to burn and give light. The function of water is to wash away filth. The winds blow away dust and breathe life into plants, animals and human beings. The earth nourishes the grasses and trees, and heaven provides nourishing moisture. Myoho-renge-kyo too works in all these ways. It is the cluster of blessings brought by the Bodhisattvas of the Earth. The Lotus Sutra says that Bodhisattva Jōgyō should now appear to propagate this teaching in the Latter Day of the Law, but has this actually happened? Whether or not Bodhisattva Jōgyō has already appeared in this world, Nichiren has at least made a start in propagating this teaching.

Be resolved to summon forth the great power of your faith, and chant Nam-myoho-renge-kyo with the prayer that your faith will be steadfast and correct at the moment of your death. Never seek any other way to inherit the ultimate law and manifest it in your life. Only then will you realize that earthly desires are enlightenment and the sufferings of life and death are nirvana. Without the lifeblood of faith, it would be useless to embrace the Lotus Sutra.

I am always ready to clear up any further questions you may have.

With my deep respect,
Nichiren, the *Shramana* of Japan

The eleventh day of the second month in the ninth
year of Bun'ei (1272)

Lecture

Mirror for Believers

The *Shōji Ichidaiji Kechimyaku Shō* (Heritage of the Ultimate Law of Life) brings back fond memories of my master, Josei Toda, for he lectured on it many times. "*Shōji Ichidaiji Kechimyaku Shō* is one of the most difficult letters of all the Gosho," he used to say over and over again. "Whenever I read it, it seems so clear at first, but then I find myself wondering again what it means. The higher my state of life becomes, the more fully I understand this Gosho." Mr. Toda also said it contains the essence of faith for disciples of Nichiren Daishonin. In fact, he said, without the spirit of this Gosho we cannot accomplish *kōsen-rufu* nor can we achieve the essence of faith and the ultimate in Buddhism. "*Shōji Ichidaiji Kechimyaku Shō*," he added, "is a spotless mirror of the practice of the Bodhisattvas of the Earth."

I am convinced that what he said is true, for it can be proven—there is documentary, theoretical and actual proof. I myself have often lectured on this Gosho and have pondered deeply on it. Each time I am astonished and again impressed by all that is condensed into each sentence, each phrase. I can only call it a mystic work. Without my even being aware of it, this Gosho has come to bear a decisive influence on my life. Here I want to share with you the thoughts I have developed after many years of study and reflection on the *Shōji Ichidaiji Kechimyaku Shō*. I would like to think of this as a commemoration of the seventeenth anniversary of my inauguration as president, and also of this year, 1977, the Year of Study. I have only one goal: knowing that the movement toward *kōsen-rufu* will continue far into the future, I want us to delve deeply into the basic point of faith of the Soka Gakkai through this Gosho. I want to confirm the fundamental spirit of our faith, the lifeblood of faith.

This is a very short Gosho, but the doctrine it contains is profound, for it probes directly into life and death, the ultimate question of Buddhist philosophy. It is that question to which Shakyamuni Buddha and all the others who lived for Buddhism devoted their wisdom and passion in the search for a solution. All of the so-called eighty-four thousand teachings and all the innumerable theses and commentaries on them, without exception, focus on one theme: life and death. Sairenbō was a scholar of the Tendai sect which was regarded as the highest school of Buddhist philosophy in those days. Eager to break through the mystery of life and death, he asked Nichiren Daishonin for illumination. The Daishonin's reply is the *Shōji Ichidaiji Kechimyaku Shō*. There he presents the conclusions he has reached, based on his enlightenment as the Buddha of the Latter Day, and at the same time he explains how all mankind can actually attain Buddhahood.

In *Shohō Jissō Shō* (The True Entity of Life), the Daishonin discusses general themes, such as universal phenomena and the true entity, the Ten Worlds and the Mystic Law, the common mortal and the Buddha. Then he reminds us of our mission to propagate the Mystic Law as Bodhisattvas of the Earth, people "of the same mind as Nichiren." In contrast, the *Heritage of the Ultimate Law of Life* deals specifically with the ultimate purpose of Buddhist practice—attaining Buddhahood—and tells us clearly the type of practice which leads directly to that objective.

The True Entity of Life, it will be recalled, contains the main points of two of the Daishonin's major theses: *The Opening of the Eyes*, which explains the object of worship from the viewpoint of the Person, and *The True Object of Worship*, which discusses it from the viewpoint of the Law. The *Heritage of the Ultimate Law of Life* is no less important, for it contains the teaching based on Nichiren Daishonin's own enlightenment as the original Buddha. It is the place where the Daishonin reveals the state of his Buddhahood. Since this Gosho is so important to Buddhist teaching, it should be read and reread, until it becomes a part of your life.

This Gosho was written on February 11, 1272, at Tsukahara on Sado Island. As in the case of *The True Entity of Life*, it was written to Sairenbō Nichijō, whose background I have described elsewhere.* Of course the original was a personal letter, and the title it now has was affixed later. However, because it begins with a discussion of *shōji ichidaiji kechimyaku*, I will begin by examining this phrase.

Shōji is life destined to repeat the endless cycle of birth and death. *Ichidaiji* may be rendered as "the most fundamental essence." *Ichi*, literally "one," here means not "one of many," but "the one and only." *Ichidaiji*, then, is "the one and only fundamental essence." *Shōji ichidaiji*, as a result, denotes the most important thing in our lives—the ultimate law of life. *Kechimyaku* is the "pulse" of the flow of life, which continues on, unchanged, beneath the superficial passages of life and death. The master-disciple relationship is vital in Buddhism, for through this relationship the Buddha, as teacher, transmits the law of life—which he has fully realized—to the lives of his disciples. The transmission of the law is also called *kechimyaku*.

Shōji ichidaiji kechimyaku conveys, in effect, the way the Buddha endows people undergoing the endless cycle of

*See page 19.

birth and death with the ultimate law so they can manifest it in their lives. That is the crux of Buddhism, the quality that makes Buddhism a practical philosophy involving living relationships, carrying it far beyond the reach of mere ideas.

The Ultimate Law of Life

Having roughly explained *shōji ichidaiji kechimyaku*, I would like to elaborate now on the meaning of *shōji* and *ichidaiji*. I will speak about *kechimyaku* in detail later. *Shōji* has basically two meanings. One is its significance as an abbreviation of *shō-rō-byō-shi* (*ji* of *shōji* is a phonetic change of *shi*)—birth, old age, sickness and death—including all human suffering. The other meaning is derived from belief in eternal life and signifies the entity that repeats the endless cycle of birth and death. *Shōji*, as used in this Gosho, denotes the latter.

Life and death are the two phases that all living beings must pass through. Conversely, a living being can exist only in the state of life or death. The ordinary person can see his life only as it begins with birth and ends with death. The Buddhist perspective goes beyond this limited view, however, extending its horizon to life as a changeless entity that exists eternally, sometimes in the manifest phase called life, and at other times in the latent phase called death. What is the Buddhist view of the two phases of life and death? The *Juryō* chapter of the Lotus Sutra says, "There is no ebb and flow of birth and death, . . ." Since "ebb and flow" indicate death and birth, the *Juryō* chapter, based on belief in eternal life, denies the ebb and flow of life, that beings are born and die. In the *Ongi Kuden* (his oral teachings of the Lotus Sutra), however, Nichiren Daishonin says that this denial of birth and death is not the truth of life. We should instead regard birth and death—the ebb and flow—as essential phases in the ultimate entity of life. This, he says, is the only valid view of life. Life is the state in which its ultimate entity is manifest, and death the state in which it lies dormant. The ultimate entity remains unchanged, repeating the endless cycle of birth and death.

Buddhism also teaches us that life and death are one and the same. What allows life to continue is the mystic energy accumulated in its latent state. When the latent form is aroused by some external influence, it becomes manifest once again, giving full expression to its individuality. Eventually, it quietly recedes into the state of death. However, during this latent state, that being stores up fresh energy in preparation for its coming rebirth.

Life is like the explosion and combustion of a force stored up during its rest period. When it has completed its lifetime, it passes away, merging into the universe. During this latent state it refuels itself with cosmic force, awaiting the time when it can spring to life once again. Thus birth and death are intrinsic to the ultimate entity of life. The source of its rhythm that accords perfectly with the rhythm of the universe is Nam-myoho-renge-kyo. A deformed life, out of step with the intrinsic rhythm, must go through a cycle of birth and death burdened by a limiting destiny, and it is usually in the state of Hell, Hunger or Animality. This is what we call evil karma. One possessing such a karma is born, lives and dies constrained by bonds as heavy as any iron chains. There is only one way to transform such a misdirected cycle of birth and death and bring it into step with the cosmic rhythm, and that is to return to, and start anew from, the Law of Nam-myoho-renge-kyo.

That is a macroscopic view of life, seen in terms of one lifetime within the eternity of past, present and future. We must also look at life microscopically, seeing the births and deaths that occur within each of us at every passing moment. A lifetime is made up of the repetition of this process, for births and deaths of smaller lives combine to ensure the continuation of a greater life.

First, consider birth and death in terms of space. Galaxies wax and wane in size as stars within them are born and perish. In the existence of each star are the births and deaths of myriad living beings, as well as the appearance and disappearance of mountains, rivers and valleys. What about our own lifetime? We do not maintain the same matter we were born with from beginning to end. Most of our body cells continually die, to be replaced by new ones. Their births and deaths—metabolism—keep the body constantly provided with fresh life force and enable it to live on.

Life and death coexist in our bodies. Fingernails and hair are "lifeless," insentient things, but they originate from living material. They move from a living to a dead state in a smooth, unruffled change, followed by new fingernails and hair. The births and deaths of these and other parts of the body all combine to form a greater life. Thus life is neither a single-unit entity nor a mere assembly of parts that work independently of each other. It is something that consists of multiple components functioning in perfect unity, smaller lives combining to form a greater life. Tiny streams of births and deaths flow into broader rivers of births and deaths, which in turn pour into the vast ocean of cosmic life. The mystic nature of life is truly incredible in its working.

Now let us look at life in terms of time. We experience life and death at every moment. If our life at the present moment is in Hell, the state of Hell is "alive," and the other nine worlds are "dead." Suppose you are finally cured of a long, drawn-out disease. You dance with joy in the state of Rapture. The agony of Hell you felt a moment ago is gone; it has died. Hell and the other worlds have passed away, replaced by the vigorous life of Rapture. You want to tell other people of the joy of your recovery and attribute it to your Buddhist practice so they can possibly benefit from your experience. Then Rapture vanishes and your life changes to the state of Bodhisattva. Each moment one of the Ten Worlds is alive and the others dead, and the next moment another state takes over. Our lifetime is an accumulation of momentary lives and deaths. Even if Rapture is alive now, the other nine worlds have not in the least ceased to exist; they have merely become dormant. Since they are latent, any one of them can come to life in the next moment.

Since our lifetime is an accumulation of moments, the most important thing is the state of life we assume at each moment. Eternity consists of moments, and each moment has a lifetime condensed in it. Hence our state of life from moment to moment determines the overall course of our life. This, more broadly, is the key to changing one's karma. When we value each moment and live actively, enthusiastically, ready to greet the next moment, we go through a state of life and death free from suffering and directed toward enlightenment. If not, we will have to go through lifetime after lifetime in the six paths (from Hell to Rapture), passing from one dark state to another. That is why we must embrace Nam-myoho-renge-kyo, the Law which penetrates the ultimate in life and death. Only this Law will enable us to attain the state of life in which it is possible to live eternity in a single moment.

Next, consider *ichidaiji*. It signifies "ultimate." *Shōji ichidaiji*, therefore, means that the ultimate in Buddhism lies only in the question of life. What then is the ultimate law of life? Nichiren Daishonin gives a clear answer in the *Ongi Kuden*, in the section on the purpose of the Buddha's advent. Here let me enlarge on this question, relying on his explanation. *Ichi* of *ichidaiji*, as we have seen, indicates "the most fundamental essence." *Ichi*, literally "one," is not just a number like three, five or seven; it means "the absolute one and only," something that has no equivalent. All human affairs originate from, and return to, the one and only fundamental question—life and death. This is what *ichi* signifies. No matter what grand system of thought a scholar may develop, should he overlook or evade the question of life and death, his achievement will be nothing but a castle built on sand.

Dai, literally "great," here is used to mean that the ultimate law of life is the fundamental force which penetrates and pervades not only humanity but all things in the universe. It denotes the universality of the law of life. All phenomena, from the tiniest particle of dust to the galaxies, move in rhythm to the law of life. There is nothing in the entire universe which is not touched by it.

Ji literally means "fact." That the ultimate law of life is constantly present and working in man and in the universe is not a mere idea; real phenomena are themselves the law. We live from day to day, the seasons come and go—all of this is part of the law of life and death, and *ji* expresses this incontrovertible fact.

Ichidaiji also symbolizes *en'yū-santai* or the perfect union of the three truths: *kūtai* (potential), *ketai* (form) and *chūtai* (entity or source). In the *Ongi Kuden* we read, "*Ichi* refers to *chūtai*, *dai* to *kūtai*, and *ji* to *ketai*. What is meant by the 'perfect union of the three truths'? It is that which is called Nam-myoho-renge-kyo." *Ichi* here is the ultimate entity that embraces everything; it therefore corresponds to *chūtai*, or the Middle Road. *Dai* tells us that the ultimate law of life and the universe is as extensive and all-inclusive as space; it therefore corresponds to *kūtai*. *Ji* implies that this law manifests itself in the kaleidoscopic changes of all actual phenomena; it therefore corresponds to *ketai*. In the final analysis, *ichidaiji* is Nam-myoho-renge-kyo, the Law which perfectly incorporates the three truths. Nam-myoho-renge-kyo is the ultimate law of life and the universe. At the same time it contains all things in the entire cosmos. It is not just an idea or something abstract and vague; it manifests itself in actual phenomena. The true entity of life completely free and unobstructed—this is *ichidaiji*.

In the *Ongi Kuden*, Nichiren Daishonin also says: "*Ichi* represents the life-moment (*ichinen*), and *dai* indicates conditions of life (*sanzen*). What creates the conditions of life are the internal and external causes of reality (*ji*)." "Reality" is the fundamental power that makes each life-moment actually work within all phenomena in the universe. *Ichidaiji* therefore means the same thing as the manifestation of *ichinen sanzen*. In the final analysis, Nichiren Daishonin is saying that *ichidaiji* is the Gohonzon, the power house of the Mystic Law.

The Eternal Heritage

I have just carefully read your letter.

Nichiren Daishonin wrote this Gosho during his exile on Sado Island. In an environment filled with almost indescribable hardships, he carefully read every letter from his disciples and devoted himself heart and soul to giving them guidance. For him, even that desolate island was a field for his battle, a field of his Buddhist practice. His simple statement, "I have just carefully read your letter," makes me realize that nothing could destroy or obstruct the sublime state of life of the original Buddha, Nichiren Daishonin.

To reply, the ultimate law of life and death as transmitted from the Buddha to all living beings is Myoho-renge-kyo.

He gives his conclusion first: *shōji ichidaiji kechimyaku*—the ultimate law of life and death as transmitted from the Buddha to the people—is Myoho-renge-kyo, which is Nam-myoho-renge-kyo itself. The doctrine of *shōji ichidai-*

ji kechimyaku was originally developed by the Tendai school. Sairenbō, formerly of that school, apparently asked in his letter what this doctrine was all about. The Daishonin's words, "I have just carefully read your letter," suggest that Sairenbō's letter described in detail what he, as a priest of the Tendai sect, had learned about that teaching and how in the end he had become confused as to its true meaning. In his reply to the lengthy and complicated inquiry, Nichiren Daishonin revealed the ultimate law in a single sentence, and dispelled the priest's delusion completely. The conclusion seems to be simple enough, but a profound philosophical process took place before it would be reached, as we will see by studying the sentences which follow.

The five characters of Myoho-renge-kyo were transferred from the two Buddhas inside the Treasure Tower, Shakyamuni and Tahō, to Bodhisattva Jōgyō, carrying on a heritage unbroken since the infinite past.

Why does the Daishonin regard Myoho-renge-kyo as the entity of *shōji ichidaiji kechimyaku*, the heritage of the ultimate law of life? His first reason is as follows. Myoho-renge-kyo was expounded during the ceremony of the Lotus Sutra as the law to be propagated in the Latter Day. Bodhisattva Jōgyō was entrusted with that task because, the Daishonin states, the true entity of his life, which has continued on since the infinite past, is Myoho-renge-kyo. It follows, therefore, that the above sentence is written from a double viewpoint. The statement, "The five characters . . . to Bodhisattva Jōgyō," is made from the standpoint of Shakyamuni Buddha's Lotus Sutra, while the phrase, "carrying on a heritage unbroken since the infinite past," is stated from Nichiren Daishonin's position.

According to Shakyamuni's teaching, Bodhisattva Jōgyō inherited Myoho-renge-kyo from Shakyamuni and Tahō during the ceremony of the Lotus Sutra in the air. From the standpoint of the Daishonin's Buddhism, however, his true identity is *jijuyūshin nyorai* of *kuon ganjo*—the original Buddha who simultaneously embodies the Person and the Law, and who has dwelt in the world of the Mystic Law since the infinite past. Therefore he "carries on a heritage unbroken since the infinite past." The powerful life in the original Buddha since the infinite past is Nam-myoho-renge-kyo itself.

Life Itself Is the Mystic Law

Myō represents death, and hō represents life. Life and death are the two phases passed through by the entities of the Ten Worlds, the entities of all sentient beings which embody the law of cause and effect (renge).

Nichiren Daishonin next reveals that the ultimate entity of life in all sentient beings—in all people—is also *shōji ichidaiji kechimyaku*, or Myoho-renge-kyo. "*Myō* represents death, and *hō* represents life" is another way to say that the law of life and death is in itself *myōhō*, the Mystic Law. The two phases of life and death, which are manifested in the ultimate entity of life, are together the Mystic Law. The law does not exist outside the realities of living and dying; our life itself is the Mystic Law. Then again, our lives in their repetition of the cycle of birth and death are also the entities of the Ten Worlds. Earlier I explained how birth and death occur in a moment of life by referring to the Ten Worlds. They do not mean types of environments or surrounding situations; the Ten Worlds are to be found in the life of everyone—in its rise and fall, ebb and flow.

Some people are harassed by bill collectors. Some students go through agony as they cram for examinations. There are many more examples of life in the state of Hell, but basically the tortures of Hell always come back to the question of life and death. The intense desire to live on and the desperate attempt to escape death give rise to the anguish and agonies of Hell, which are, then, nothing but the results of such desires. The state of Hunger revolves around greed, and so that, too, is related to life and death. In this way everyday life, in its depths, always involves life and death. Patients groan with and fear the pain of illness because they do not want to die. Some seek fame and status; others set their minds on learning. All derive from their attitudes toward life.

As long as we take the occurrences of every day lightly, we will not understand life's true meaning. Joy, anger, sorrow and pleasure may seem trivial, but they are ultimately related to the question of life and death. Because we are human, we may consciously or unconsciously evade relating our feelings and activities to life and death, but in the depths of the changing phenomena of the Ten Worlds, this problem of life and death is the most serious question of all. Only when we squarely confront it, recognize it, and reflect our recognition in the way we live, can we improve the state of our life. The human revolution is the process of transition from the six paths to the four noble worlds, from the two vehicles (Learning and Realization) to Bodhisattva to Buddhahood. It is a revolution that can only take place when we seek the ultimate law and root our attitude toward life and death firmly within it.

Let us next consider why the Daishonin says, "*Myō* represents death, and *hō* represents life." It is impossible to imagine anything about the state of death. Where does it exist, and how? Even if told that it continues to exist as part of universal life, we remain unconvinced. Death, therefore, is *myō*, a mystic phenomenon. In contrast to death, manifest life appears in many ways, shapes and forms. Like a law, it manifests one or another of the Ten Worlds in

accordance with the workings of the Ten Factors of Life.*
When you do not eat for a long time, you crave food—the
state of Hunger. When ridiculed, you are upset or angry—
the world of Anger. This is the natural law of life. Life,
therefore, is *hō*, or law.

The Chinese character for *hō* consists of the ideographs
for "water" and "passing away" combined. Together they
mean "flow of water." Water represents the even, eternal
and impartial, that which pervades the universe. "Passing
away" symbolizes the flow of time from the infinite past to
the infinite future. In some ancient literature we read that
the radical "passing away" also indicates "an existence that
banishes evils." All streams, be they rapids rushing down
mountainsides or large rivers meandering through plains,
flow on and on, never stopping, until they finally empty
their waters into the ocean. The Buddhist sees the rise and
fall of all phenomena, sometimes manifest and at other times
latent, in terms of causality. He observes law within the
movements of everything, not in a still, abstract form. It is
probably for this reason that Buddhism regards the flow of
water as symbolic of law. Buddhist law exists in the realities
of everyday life, in the actual feelings of being alive. Hence
shohō (literally, all laws) of *shohō jissō* is translated as "all
phenomena."

The usual concept of a law or laws is much closer to death
than it is to life. The law of gravitation, the theory of
relativity and the principles of political economy are but
rules of relationships among real phenomena; laws, theories
or principles themselves do not appear in any concrete form.
In contrast, one of the special qualities of Buddhism is that
it makes it possible to see the law within each phenomenon
that occurs. It is not an abstract concept one step removed
from the realities of life, but the living relationships that
real people experience and express from moment to mo-

*See pp. 24–26.

ment. Thus it becomes clear why Nichiren Daishonin states, "*Hō* represents life."

If Buddhism were limited only to the observation of phenomena, it would be no different from scientific research. The study of the flow of a river belongs to the realm of science. To understand the fundamental force that creates the flow—this is the true object of religion. That fundamental force is never divorced from real phenomena, but neither can it be grasped as a form or a shape. Hence it is described as *myō*, mystic.

Earlier I explained the sentence, "*Myō* represents death, and *hō* represents life," in terms of the life and death of people, but it also applies to all other phenomena as well. Suppose we see an angry man. He may be furious over an argument he had, or he may be angry with himself for something he did. No matter what the cause, his countenance and attitude are *hō*, and since they are visible, they represent "life." On the other hand, his psychological state—the causes and circumstances which have brought about his anger—is impossible to see or fathom. This is exactly what the phrase, "*Myō* represents death," is talking about.

The movement of the universe is *hō* and therefore "life." The fundamental force that causes this movement is *myō* and therefore "death." But what *is* this fundamental force? The three meanings of *myō* given in *On the Daimoku of the Lotus Sutra* should be helpful. They are: "to open," "to be endowed and perfect" and "to revive." Concerning the first, Miao-lo stated that "to reveal is to open." "To open" indicates the quality or force which activates a life, like opening a secret repository, and causes it to pervade the entire universe. "To be endowed and perfect" means, for instance, that each drop in the ocean contains the same elements and properties as the ocean itself. "To revive" is, in other words, to create value. Insentient or inorganic matter such as wood and stone is transformed into a building, a place of bustling activity—that is revival. So, too, is the human act of reforming oneself so that a person can change his or her karma and be able to contribute to society.

The fundamental force is invisible. Suppose a star is born. Physicists see it as the result of a recombination of matter. But something definitely activated that process, some force on which universal life depends for its growth. This is the meaning of "to open." All things in the universe contain each other—they do not exist separately—and together they form the greater life of the macrocosm. This is what "to be endowed and perfect" means. The meeting and parting of various forms of life creates new values and new lives. This is "to revive."

All these workings can be traced back to the fundamental force of the universe. Without this force the universe would only be a lifeless chunk of matter. I suspect that the late Dr. Toynbee had such a force in mind when he said that he believed in the existence of "the ultimate spiritual reality behind the universe." Since the fundamental force is beyond the imagination, it is *myō* (mystic), and since we cannot see it, it is "death." But the force does exist, unseen but definitely permeating all phenomena (*hō*).

The entities of the Ten Worlds which pass through the phases of life and death can be called *renge*, because they embody the law of cause and effect. The Mystic Law or *myōhō* means life and death, and *renge* means the entities that manifest this law. Therefore, all forms of life in the Ten Worlds are in themselves *myōhō-renge*.

T'ien-t'ai said, "You must realize that the interrelated actions and reactions of sentient beings and their environments all manifest the law of the simultaneity of cause and effect." "Sentient beings and their environments" here means the reality of life and death.

The law of simultaneity of cause and effect is clearly at work in everything that lives and dies.

Here Nichiren Daishonin backs up his previous statement by quoting from T'ien-t'ai's *Hokke Gengi* (Profound Meaning of the Lotus Sutra). "The interrelated actions and reactions of sentient beings and their environments" refers to the law of causality manifested in life. It signifies life as it actually exists—in other words, people in the Ten Worlds. In terms of time, we see that all life is invariably destined to be born and to die—the reality of life and death. In terms of space, we discover the relationships between sentient beings and their environments. Nichiren Daishonin shows how the spatial relationship that T'ien-t'ai grasped as the law of cause and effect between sentient beings and their environments is in perfect agreement with the law of life and death. From this derived his statement that " 'sentient beings and their environments' here means the reality of life and death."

Life as it actually exists—the interrelation of sentient beings and their environments within the reality of life and death—manifests the law of cause and effect. In this law of life, the cause and its effect always take place simultaneously; it is therefore called "the Law of the Lotus." Let me say a few words about the Law of the Lotus and simultaneous cause and effect. As we know, the lotus plant puts forth flower and seed at the same time, which is why it is such an eminent symbol of the principle of simultaneous cause and effect. However, it is important to understand what this principle means in relation to our actual lives.

In the physical and chemical sciences as well as in the affairs of society, the cause and effect are invariably observed at different times. Simultaneous cause and effect is only found in vital phenomena—more specifically, in the law of life which Buddhism was the first to elucidate. *The True*

Object of Worship contains a passage which explains the Ten Worlds. It reads, "Rage is the world of Hell, greed is that of Hunger, foolishness is that of Animality, perversity is that of Anger, joy is that of Rapture, and calmness is that of Humanity." Rage, part of the workings of life, is the cause, and Hell is its effect. You don't become angry now and reach the state of Hell some time later. You are angry (cause) and experience the state of Hell (effect) at the same time. This is simultaneous cause and effect. Rage is one way the sentient being expresses himself. In this case his environment will reflect the state of Hell. The sentient being is the cause and his environment the result. Hence T'ien-t'ai's expression, "the interrelated actions and reactions of sentient beings and their environments." Likewise, precisely when we believe in the Mystic Law (cause), we are in the state of Buddhahood (effect), which means that the law of simultaneous cause and effect is the principle which enables us to attain enlightenment.

Life's Mysterious Workings

The Great Teacher Dengyō said, "Birth and death are the mysterious workings of the life essence. The ultimate reality of life lies in existence and nonexistence." No phenomena—heaven or earth, Yin or Yang, the sun or the moon, the five planets, or any life-condition from Hell to Buddhahood—are free from birth and death. Thus the life and death of all phenomena are simply the two phases of Myoho-renge-kyo. In his *Maka Shikan*, T'ien-t'ai says, "The emergence of all things is the manifestation of their intrinsic nature, and their extinction, the withdrawal of that nature into the state of latency." Shakyamuni and Tahō Buddhas, too, are the two phases of life and death.

"The life essence" in Dengyō's statement is Myoho-renge-kyo, and "the ultimate reality of life" describes the state of life of the Buddha who has realized this Mystic Law. "Birth and death" signifies life's workings, the transition from death to life and from life to death. In contrast, "existence and nonexistence" concerns whether or not that life appears in this world. We might say that life comes into existence with birth and recedes into nonexistence with death. Nonetheless, nonexistence here does not mean absolute nothingness, but the potential state which in Buddhism is called *kū*. In any event, both "birth and death" and "existence and nonexistence" are the workings of Myoho-renge-kyo, the two phases of Myoho-renge-kyo. Conversely, while all things are born and die, come into existence and recede into nonexistence, their entities are the eternally unchanging law of Myoho-renge-kyo.

With this basic understanding of the above passage, I will now discuss Dengyō's statement from the standpoint of faith and daily life. "The life essence" refers to our state of mind toward faith, our determination to chant Nam-myoho-renge-kyo in perfect harmony with the Gohonzon. To be resolved to believe in and chant to the Gohonzon is to be endowed with the power to fully utilize the law of life and death. Our lives are adrift in the sea of suffering of life and death, but when we base both our life and death on the Mystic Law, we will be able to cross that sea without fear. The same is true with the phenomenal world of existence and nonexistence. By fixing our minds on the Mystic Law, we are able to move throughout that world in any way we please. In the final analysis, neither happiness nor good fortune comes to us of itself; we are the ones who must build it.

We can make the law of life and death work for us by harnessing the mystic functions of the life essence. This is still not the same as saying that birth and death will cease, or that we will become immortal, a legendary sage. We will live on as ordinary people, but we will no longer have to repeat a continually more painful cycle of suffering as we go through birth and death. Making the law of life and death work for us means that we can instead find joy, by discovering the essential reality of life and death themselves. Then we can live freely and as happily as a butterfly floating from flower to flower.

The *Ongi Kuden* states, "We repeat the cycle of birth and death secure upon the earth of our intrinsic enlightened nature." Our life from past to present to future is like going for a drive. From birth to death, in lifetime after lifetime, we travel upon the great earth of life. But even though birth and death are repeated by everyone, there is a great difference between struggling across a dangerous swamp in an old rattletrap and speeding along a freeway in one of the latest models. The former is the result of living your life with the idea that everything ends with death, and the latter the result of a life lived with a knowledge of the essential reality of birth and death. By harnessing the mysterious functions of the life essence, we are able to enjoy the enlightened cycle, but we can only do so by continual practice of gongyo.

Ponder the practical implications for a moment. Which law will we manifest in life and death, and which path will we travel through existence and nonexistence? The deciding factor will be the attitude and feelings we have toward the Mystic Law innate within us, the strength of our faith in the Gohonzon. The phenomenal world has its own, natural law of causality. We live our life in the world of phenomena—the phenomena of birth and death, and existence and nonexistence. Can we transform our entire being into an entity filled with good fortune, or will we have to plunge into an abyss of misery? Steering and directing us is our state of mind which, though invisible, is always at work.

Nichiren Daishonin states, "It is because one's entire being is contained in each life-moment that the Buddha preaches of the great benefits in experiencing even a moment of joy when hearing the teachings of Buddhism." The happiness to have encountered the Mystic Law and the joyful, courageous faith and practice as a Soka Gakkai member carrying out an unprecedented Buddhist movement—from these feelings immeasurable benefits come forth, and they lead to a life of true success and victory as a human being. The difference between an active and a passive attitude may at first seem negligible, but in the long run it grows into a tremendous difference, which no one can help but see.

"No phenomena—heaven or earth, Yin or Yang, the sun or the moon, the five planets, or any life-condition from Hell to Buddhahood—are free from birth and death." Nothing in the ceaselessly changing universe can avoid the law of life and death. The earth on which we live and the limitless expanse of space—they too repeat the cycles of birth and death. The sun and the moon were formed in the distant past; eventually they, too, will become extinct. The "five planets" indicate five of the earth's fellow planets which, like it, revolve around the sun. Going outward from the sun, they are: Mercury, Venus, Mars, Jupiter and Saturn. Thanks to the telescope, today we know that there are three more planets in the solar system—Uranus, Neptune and Pluto—which were still unknown in the Daishonin's day.

In any event, the entities of all things and all phenomena are Myoho-renge-kyo. Therefore, their inevitable birth and death are, in the final analysis, that of Myoho-renge-kyo. That is precisely what T'ien-t'ai means when he says, "The emergence of all things is the manifestation of their intrinsic nature, and their extinction, the withdrawal of that nature into the state of latency." The "intrinsic nature" is the Mystic Law, and the manifestation and extinction of all phenomena in the universe is, therefore, that of Myoho-renge-kyo.

"Shakyamuni and Tahō Buddhas, too, are the two phases of life and death." Shakyamuni represents life and Tahō death. The two Buddhas, seated side by side in the Treasure Tower during the Lotus Sutra's ceremony in the air, symbolize the two phases of life and death. We can also say that Shakyamuni represents subjective wisdom and Tahō, objective truth. Subjective wisdom refers to one who acts, which in turn implies life. Objective truth is that which is proven to exist through wisdom, and implies death. Thus, Shakyamuni symbolizes life, and Tahō, death.

Beyond Discrimination

Shakyamuni who attained enlightenment countless aeons ago, the Lotus Sutra which leads all people to Buddhahood, and we ordinary human beings are in no way different or separate from each other. Therefore, to chant Myoho-renge-kyo with this realization is to inherit the ultimate law of life and death. To carry on this heritage is the most important task for Nichiren's disciples, and that is precisely what it means to embrace the Lotus Sutra.

So far, Nichiren Daishonin has revealed the ultimate law of life and death, the ultimate law to which the Buddha was enlightened, and which constitutes our own entities. From this passage onward, he teaches us how, practically, we can manifest the law, limitlessly, within ourselves. The above passage is especially important in that it speaks about the basic posture we should assume toward faith.

The entity of life of "Shakyamuni who attained enlightenment countless aeons ago" is Myoho-renge-kyo. "The

Lotus Sutra which leads all people to Buddhahood"—this is the law through which Shakyamuni, as the Buddha who attained enlightenment countless aeons ago, expounded the teaching of his own enlightenment. By believing in and embracing this law, all people in the Ten Worlds can perceive the existence of the Mystic Law inherent within themselves and attain Buddhahood. The entity of the Lotus Sutra as well is Myoho-renge-kyo.

The phrase, "we ordinary human beings," corresponds to that part of the previous passage which reads, "No phenomena... are free from birth and death." We are only ordinary people, but we possess the seed of Buddhahood. Here the Daishonin makes it unmistakably clear that we, too, are entities of Myoho-renge-kyo. Taken literally, "Shakyamuni" here is the Buddha who attained enlightenment in the distant past called *gohyaku-jintengō*, as revealed in the essential teaching of the Lotus Sutra; "the Lotus Sutra" denotes the sutra's entire twenty-eight chapters. On a deeper level, however, "Shakyamuni" is intended to mean the original Buddha from the infinite past who appeared in this world as Nichiren Daishonin, and "the Lotus Sutra" signifies the Dai-Gohonzon of true Buddhism. So the above passage tells us we should realize that Nichiren Daishonin, the Dai-Gohonzon and all common people like ourselves are alike entities of Nam-myoho-renge-kyo, and are in no way different or separate from each other.

True Buddhism does not differentiate or separate these three from each other. It is a serious misconception to take the Buddha as a unique, superior existence, and to assume that the ordinary people of this world are, in contrast, lowly and ugly, utterly incapable of attaining Buddhahood. It would also run against the spirit of the above passage to decide that both the ceremony and the teaching of the Lotus Sutra are just the products of someone's imagination, divorced from the people and their daily life in this or any age. That kind of misconception is all the more insupportable when it comes to belief in true Buddhism. To think that there is an unbridgeable gap between Nichiren Daishonin and us, or that the Gohonzon exists somewhere outside of ourselves, would break the heritage of the ultimate law of life and death. Of course it is difficult for us to "realize" subjectively the oneness of the Daishonin, the Gohonzon and ourselves. We should consider "realize" to mean "have profound faith in," for Buddhism teaches that "one enters Buddhahood through faith," and also that one should "rely on faith instead of one's limited understanding."

In any event, the life of the original Buddha, Nichiren Daishonin, is Nam-myoho-renge-kyo. And the Gohonzon is of course Nam-myoho-renge-kyo, as the Daishonin himself states: "I, Nichiren, have inscribed my life in *sumi*." Unworthy as we are, the life of each one of us is also Nam-myoho-renge-kyo. When we maintain firm faith in this as we chant daimoku, the heritage of the ultimate law of life and death, the great life of Nam-myoho-renge-kyo, will well forth endlessly in our lives. This is "the most important task for Nichiren's disciples," those who practice his Buddhism. As the Daishonin says, this is "precisely what it means to embrace the Lotus Sutra."

"Now Is the Last Moment"

For one who summons up his faith and chants Nam-myoho-renge-kyo with the profound insight that now is the last moment of his life, the sutra proclaims: "After his death, a thousand Buddhas will extend their hands to free him from all fear and keep him from falling into the evil paths."

"The profound insight that now is the last moment of one's life" does not just mean to make up one's mind to accept the end. It means to fill one's life and being to its depths with the knowledge of inevitable death as part of life itself. Nearly everyone assumes there are many more years to live. No one knows exactly when he will die, but the fact is that death may come at any moment. That is the reality of life. Another way to look at the words, "now is the last moment of one's life," is to consider that even if we live twenty, thirty or fifty more years, they are but a moment in comparison with eternity. Such knowledge surely ought to make any thoughtful person keenly aware of the great significance of being able to live and embrace true Buddhism. Glory, fame and fortune in this life are nothing. We must devote ourselves wholeheartedly to the practice of our faith, always focusing on the true purpose of our lives. We must do so in order to accumulate the kind of good fortune which will not vanish after death, but will remain for all eternity.

This is the most important aspect of our attitude toward faith. It does not follow, however, that we, as Buddhists who are also ordinary members of society, must discard everything but Buddhism. As we continue to practice our faith, upholding the goal of _kōsen-rufu_, everything we do and everything we possess will be given new meaning because it is based on the Mystic Law. That is how we can live "with the profound insight that now is the last moment of life." When we live from moment to moment, always maintaining that resolution, "a thousand Buddhas will extend their hands to free us from all fear and keep us from falling into the evil paths." This means that we will live in a state of perfect peace and security, as if carried in the arms of a thousand Buddhas, and that we will never fall into the evil paths of Hell, Hunger, Animality and Anger. In a literal sense, the phrase means that we will enter a state of perfect peace and security at the last moment of our life, but in a deeper sense, it refers to each moment in this lifetime.

In the final analysis, to have "the profound insight that now is the last moment of our life" is to put our entire being into the present moment. It means to live with all our vigor from day to day, fighting to the last ounce of our energy to achieve *kōsen-rufu* and attain Buddhahood in this lifetime. When you engage in religious talks with someone, you must decide that this is the last opportunity to talk to him about Buddhism and that if you miss this chance, he will never be able to change his karma. If you act on that resolution, you are already living with the spirit of knowing that now may be "the last moment" possible for this. It is important to do everything with utmost sincerity, whether you are chanting to the Gohonzon, studying the Gosho, or writing a letter of encouragement.

In this connection, I would like to think about life and death in terms of the last moment and what happens after death. Many scholars have studied this subject, among them, Mrs. Elisabeth Kübler-Ross. She was formerly professor on the psychiatric faculty of the University of Chicago. Although a Protestant, she did not really believe in life after death. But after eleven years of working with some one thousand dying patients, she confides that she was forced to change her mind and came to realize that life goes on continuously, even after death. In her study of death, she interviewed patients who had been declared dead but later revived, and asked them if they were able to share any of their impressions or experiences. She reports the results of those interviews as follows, giving us an idea of a sort of out-of-the-body experience.

> With many of these patients we found out that their experience is that, at the moment of physical death, they float out of their physical body and they float a few feet above the hospital bed or the accident scene. They can see themselves lying in the bed and they can distinguish many things. They can describe in minute, very fine detail who came into the

room and they can describe a resuscitation attempt. They can say which doctor or which nurse, which family member, which priest was in the room. They describe the color of their dress, at the time they have no vital signs.

"At the first instant of death," Mrs. Ross's report continues, "the moment of physical separation is a good experience. Like getting out of a prison." But the question is what happens the next moment. "What Christians call 'hell,' heaven or hell, the difference between good people and bad people, people who have led very enlightened lives and those who have not, comes afterwards, after separation. What Christians call 'hell' is not as Christians describe it. (Some of these patients were Christians.)

"After they leave, they go through the walls—they don't need an open door or window—and then they go toward a light, through a tunnel, over a bridge or river. After they have passed over, then comes what a Christian would call 'hell.' There is no god who condemns you, but you are forced to review your own life.

"It's like watching a television screen and your whole life is passed in front of you, not only deeds but also thoughts. This is going through hell, because you see everything you have ever done and thought." We may safely say, then, that some of the dead go through heaven and some others through hell. "So it is not a god who condemns you, but you condemn yourself."

Based on many years' experience with dying patients, Mrs. Ross emphatically agrees with the Buddhist concept of karma, that all of our acts are ingrained in our lives and will never disappear. She says, "It's a beautiful thing. I really believe that what you plant as seeds is what you will reap. . . . It's an absolute law. I know that." She believes in karmic debts only because she has verified that it is true. "It's not really a question of just believing," she says. "All these things can be scientifically verified."

Mrs. Ross is very pleased to know that her thought accords with Buddhism. "People will live a very different quality of life," she says, "if they knew this [concept of karma], if they could understand that they alone are responsible for all the good things and bad things that happen to them."

Ernest Hemingway also experienced such out-of-the-body travel. After he had been badly wounded, he wrote to a friend in his unique style: "I died then. I felt my soul or something coming right out of my body, like you'd pull a silk handkerchief out of a pocket by one corner. It flew around and then came back and went in again and I wasn't dead any more." He used this episode in *A Farewell to Arms*.

There is a collection of essays on death compiled by Dr. Michio Matsuda, a critic. It contains the essay "Shi no Gen'ei" (Death's Illusion) by Masaru Kobayashi. It is quite a lengthy account of his own experience, so I will give you a summary of it. Kobayashi underwent a critical surgical operation, and his account begins when he was lying on the operating table and the anaesthesia began to wear off.

> At midnight on the tenth, consciousness returned and with it the pain. It was like raging waves. When they engulfed me, everything before my eyes and inside my head became pure crimson, the color of blood.... When the pain became absolutely unbearable, I felt myself coming apart and beginning to fly away. I clearly saw myself, broken to bits, a black burnt-out chunk of matter, flying at tremendous speed through the vast reaches of space.
>
> I left the warm earth, and felt the cooling atmosphere rush by me. Everything, myself included, was cold. As I went deeper into the universe, the space around me gradually changed from light to deep blue and on to a deeper and deeper black. I felt that death lay at the pitch-black extremity of the universe.
>
> As I felt myself getting colder, I had no emotions at all.

I had lost all sense of joy or sorrow for my family, even for myself. There was nothing of loneliness, pain or grief, even though I had parted with many relatives and friends. This was something I had never imagined.

But I did sense one thing that seemed inextinguishable— an indescribable feeling of frustration. It was not mere frustration at having to part with my life. I had once been a human being and had lived a life which I could never live again. My sense of loss was at having to go away without leaving the slightest mark on history—history which would continue after my death.

This came as quite a shock to me. I thought I had lived as full a life as I could. I had never imagined that such a feeling would come at the last moment....

Perhaps there is no despair more concentrated than that at the last moment when you realize for the first time that your life has been meaningless, and you plunge toward death with indescribable remorse in your heart.

The one feeling which remained when joy, anger, sorrow, pleasure and all other emotions had gone was the feeling of frustration. It must have been what he felt at the core of his being. The meaninglessness he felt at not having contributed a thing to mankind threw him into a trough of despair on the borderline between life and death, a point of no return. Mr. Kobayashi's account is very precious for its description of a feeling which came from the very source of his being.

Eternity in the Moment

Henri Bergson, the eminent philosopher, also believed in an afterlife. After years of contemplation on the human body and mind, Bergson came to agree that life continues after death. Dr. Arnold Toynbee once said that he believed death to be a return to "the ultimate spiritual reality" underlying the universe, the sea of immortality. As a scholar, he sought his answer to the question of life and death in higher religions, especially in the Buddhist concept of *kū*. He said:

> I conclude that the phenomenon of death, followed by the disorganization of the physical aspect of a personality that we encounter as a psychosomatic unity, is, in terms of reality-in-itself, an illusion arising from the limitations of the human mind's conceptual capacity. . . . I believe that reality itself is timeless and spaceless but that it does not exist in isolation from our time-and-space-bound world. . . .
>
> Does life persist *after* death? And where does the soul go when the body goes back into the inorganic section of physical matter? To sum up, I believe that these questions can be answered in terms of *kū* or of eternity, but not in terms of space-time.*

Jun Takami, a professional writer who died of cancer, wrote a poem "Kako no Kūkan" (Space of the Past) in his work, *Shi no Fuchi yori* (From the Abyss of Death). In this poem he described how he felt as he lived facing imminent death.

> *As sand scooped in hands*
> *Falls through the emaciated fingers,*
> *So does time with a gritty sound run out of me,*
> *My time—so short and precious.*
> . . . . .
> *I can only hear the ceaseless sound of time slipping away.*

This poem suggests how much the author valued the short time left to him and how he wished he could live for eternity. To value each second more highly than a drop of blood—this is the true way of life for people born in this world. Most people, however, waste all too much of their time before they are confronted with death. I once heard

*Arnold Toynbee and Daisaku Ikeda, *Choose Life* (London: Oxford University Press, 1976), pp. 259-60.

the story of a gifted free-lance reporter who succumbed to cancer. After being told he had cancer and would soon die, he began to use a daily pad calendar. To him, each day that remained was precious. He could not bear the sight of a calendar which showed all the days of the month or even of the whole year on one sheet of paper, as if every day was just another day. When each day came to a close, he would tear off one sheet from the calendar and tell himself, "Congratulations! You have lived one more day," relishing the feeling of being still alive.

We do not need Martin Heidegger, or anyone, to tell us that "human existence is itself a being-unto-death" in order to know that death underlies life. Indeed, at each moment we meet death and at each moment are revived. It is the consciousness of death which really gives our life a sense of fulfillment. Without the consciousness of death one can neither live humanely nor spend time meaningfully. The question of death is in itself the question of life. As long as the question of death remains unsolved, life cannot be truly substantial.

Four years ago in spring, I went to London at the invitation of Dr. Toynbee for my second meeting with the British historian. After spending five days talking with him, I went to Paris, and from there rode a train for two hours to the Loire. Clear streams washing grassy banks, flocks of sheep, steeples of ancient castles, paths where birds chirped, quiet woods, flowers in full bloom, ageless farmhouses built of stone—in such surroundings stood the ivy-covered house where Leonardo da Vinci spent his later years. In the bedroom where he ended his life there was a copper plate on which were engraved his words:

> *A substantial life is long.*
> *Meaningful days give one a good sleep.*
> *A fulfilled life gives one a quiet death.*

C. G. Jung said, "From the middle of life onward, only he remains vitally alive who is ready to *die with life*."* Jung's remark probably originated from his belief that the latter half of one's life is especially important. In a way, however, to be ready to "die with life" may be necessary throughout one's lifetime. Perhaps we can say that only those with such a determination will prove to have lived a truly vital life.

In his study, "The Relation between Life and Death, Living and Dying," Dr. Toynbee wrote: " 'In the midst of life we are in death.' From the moment of birth there is the constant possibility that a human being may die at any moment; and inevitably this possibility is going to become an accomplished fact sooner or later. Ideally, every human being ought to live each passing moment of his life as if the next moment were going to be his last." Although conceding that perhaps it may be too difficult for any human being to live permanently on this ideal level, he went on to say, "What can be said with assurance is that, the closer a human being can come to attaining this ideal state of heart and mind, the better and happier he or she will be."†

It is also instructive to learn how a natural scientist regards life and death. Dr. Kinjirō Okabe, physicist and professor emeritus of Osaka University, wrote a book entitled *Ningen wa Shindara Dōnaruka* (What Happens to Man after Death?). In this book he takes a unique approach, starting with the concepts of modern science, and calling his speculation "scientific inference" about the problem of death. Dr. Okabe's view may be summarized as follows:

> In the world of physics, there is a law called the energy conservation principle. Never does energy or matter come

*C. G. Jung, *The Meaning of Death* (New York: McGraw-Hill Book Company, Inc., 1959), p. 6.

†*Man's Concern with Death* ed. Arnold Toynbee (London: Hodder and Stoughton Ltd., 1968), p. 259.

from nothing. Nor is energy or matter actually lost.

Man's soul is supra-matter and supra-energy; it cannot be felt by the five senses. I, too, must concede the existence of the soul. Matter which composes the human body is completely replaced, through metabolism, by new matter in several years. Materially, one becomes a totally different person from what he was in his childhood, though he may retain some of the physical characteristics he used to have as a child. Therefore, if there is to be identity between what we are today and what we were as children, then we are forced to admit that there must be something which may be called the human soul.

If the soul really exists, the energy conservation principle must also be applicable. In other words, it seems very possible that a human life does not become extinct upon death but continues to exist in some state or other.

I postulate the existence of a "core of the soul." Life is a state during which the core of the soul is inseparably merged with the body and manifests itself in the workings of life. In other words, it is in an active state. Death is a state in which the core of the soul is inactive. It cannot manifest itself in life-functions as it did during the active state. But it still contains the ability to sustain manifest life. When the dormant state passes into the active state, the core of the soul again begins to perform its functions.

Thus, man's life or death depends on whether the core of the soul is in the active or the inactive state. The core itself continues to exist throughout life and death.

I suspect that Dr. Okabe's "soul" or "core of the soul" is different from the meaning usually given the word. The Nirvana Sutra speaks for Buddhism when it categorically denies the concept of the soul as applied in the ordinary sense. I think that what Dr. Okabe calls the core of the soul has something in common with what is called "the self" of life in Buddhism—that which sustains our identity.

Life is the accumulation of all the moments we live. One who cannot live meaningfully today cannot hope to lead a brilliant life tomorrow. No matter what grand plans one makes, if he does not value each moment, they will be just so many castles in the air. All the causes in the past and all the effects in the future are condensed within the present moment of life. Whether or not we improve our state of life at this moment will determine whether we can expiate the evils we have caused since the infinite past and be able to build up good fortune to remain for all eternity. The key is whether or not we have faith strong enough to decide that this may be the last moment of our life. The above passage, therefore, gives us the principle for changing our karma.

"After his death, a thousand Buddhas will extend their hands to free him from all fear and keep him from falling into the evil paths." This is a sentence in the *Kambotsu-hon*, the twenty-eighth chapter of the Lotus Sutra. Why do we need the assistance of those Buddhas? Because a life, once inactivated and merged with the universe, can no longer do anything of its own will. It has to suffer the effects of its lifetime, or the state it was in at the time of death, and those effects are strict and absolute. At that time a thousand Buddhas extend their protecting hands. What could be more reassuring!

The passage does not simply mean that Buddhas, literally, "extend their hands." It also means that we will be able to stand on an eternal footing, that we will attain happiness that can never wane with time. Of course, all this becomes possible only when you keep your faith strong enough to determine that now is the last moment of your life. As the Gosho tells us, "The firmer one's faith, the stronger the gods' protection." It is a serious mistake to expect that those Buddhas will come to protect you if you don't strive for your human revolution. Literally, the passage means that the Buddhas "extend their hands" because an inactivated life is in a latent state of existence. Its true meaning is that we have to strive through our own human revolution to bring forth the protection of a thousand Buddhas who reside within our hearts.

The Buddha's Protection

How can we possibly hold back our tears at the inexpressible joy of knowing that not just one or two, nor only one or two hundred, but as many as a thousand Buddhas will come to greet us with open arms?

This is a denunciation of Nembutsu. The Nembutsu sect preaches that if one dies invoking the name of Amida (Skt., Amitabha or Amitayus) Buddha, he will be able to go to the land where this Buddha is said to dwell. Two bodhisattvas, Kannon (Avalokiteshvara) and Seishi (Mahasthamaprapta), come as messengers riding on a cloud to take him to that land. Most people in Nichiren Daishonin's day believed in Amida. The passage quoted above reveals his indignation at the Nembutsu sect for deluding the people with such a doctrine. Not just one or two Buddhas, much less two bodhisattvas, but as many as a thousand Buddhas will extend their arms to protect us, giving us so much more solace than what Nembutsu preaches. Even if one is destined to fall into the three evil paths, he will escape that fate. The *Ongi Kuden* says, "One thousand Buddhas signify the teaching of One Thousand Factors of Life.*" In other words, all the protective functions of the universe will work to guard the votary of the Lotus Sutra.

If there were only one or two Buddhas to save us, all beings in this world would be necessarily subordinate to them—something akin to absolute monotheism. Such a

*At each moment, life experiences one of ten conditions or the Ten Worlds. Each of these worlds possesses the potential for all the ten within itself, thus making one hundred possible worlds. Each of these hundred worlds possesses the Ten Factors, thus becoming one thousand factors. In short, one thousand factors are the forces and phenomena manifest by one's life essence.

dogma in effect says that the people are powerless beings who can seek salvation only by beseeching those Buddhas. The Buddhas, on their part, would have to be magnificent-looking so that people would seek them out with awe and respect. That kind of teaching centering on the "person" lacks universality. It becomes something like a "cult of personality" and only acts to separate Buddhas from the people.

The Lotus Sutra is very different. It assures that a thousand Buddhas will protect us, which ultimately indicates the Hundred Worlds and Thousand Factors of Life. As a teaching, it centers on the "law." If we abide by that law, the functions of the universe work to protect our lives. Furthermore, what sets those functions in motion is the individual's life force. Thus the Lotus Sutra teaches true independence, and it is a universal teaching. Buddhas need not be august or magnificent in appearance, and we, common people, are able to make all the Buddhas and heavenly gods throughout the universe work for us and protect us, just as we are.

How does this principle apply to our daily life? Suppose a member of the Soka Gakkai dies. Many friends and acquaintances come to his or her funeral and chant daimoku for the deceased. Those who struggled together with that person to accomplish their lofty mission and shared the hardships, joys, winter storms and mild springs, are themselves Buddhas, and they will all be there praying for their loved companion.

The Strict Law of Causality

One who does not have faith in the Lotus Sutra will instead find his hands firmly gripped by the guards of hell, just as the sutra warns, ". . . After he dies, he will fall into the hell of incessant suffering." How pitiful!

The ten kings of hell will then pass judgment on him, and the heavenly messengers who have been with him since his birth will berate him for his evil deeds.

This relates a situation, the opposite of the preceding passage. The quoted portion appears in the *Hiyu* (third) chapter of the Lotus Sutra. It says quite clearly that people who oppose the faith in this sutra will end up in the hell of incessant suffering—the most terrible of hells—after they die. And instead of a thousand Buddhas, demons will be there to drag them away. No one would be happy to meet demons. Such is the great difference after death between those with faith in the Mystic Law in their lifetimes and those who opposed it. In life, people may wield unmatched power, accumulate great wealth, or enjoy a good reputation, but all that is nothing after death. Only their worth as humans remains. It is said that a female demon divests them of all their possessions and a male demon hangs them on a tree to determine the weight of their sins. Everything they have done—that is, their karma—is revealed just as it is, and they have to face its reward or retribution.

The "heavenly messengers" will censure them for their evil acts, and the "ten kings" will pass judgment on them. The heavenly messengers are the gods who stay with an individual from the moment of his or her birth. Their duty is to report all acts, both good and bad, to King Emma, the lord of hell. In this age they might be something like prosecutors. The ten kings of hell are said to try the dead beginning on the seventh day after death and continuing until the second anniversary of their passing away. King Emma is one of them—something like the judges in today's courts of law.

It is possible to commit some evil act and get away with it, as far as the morals of society or the laws of the land are concerned. But never with the Buddhist law. The heavenly messengers, also called Dōshō and Dōmyō, are always with their charge and constantly watch him. He can never elude them. This is what Buddhism teaches us, that the law of causality is always at work in the depths of our lives. No lies can go undetected in the world of Buddhism.

It is generally believed that hell is just a fable, contrived to make people rectify their conduct while they are alive. This may be the case with some of the more primitive representations we have from past ages of hell. But whatever the general belief, it is true that hell-like conditions exist in actual life. It is said undeniably that the world is filled with all kinds of suffering—people anguished by the hardships and losses they must endure, people condemned to frustration because of their surroundings, people suffering terrible afflictions. Life continues through past, present and future, so the situation will not change a bit, even after one dies. Whether dead or alive, one will always have to experience both hardship and joy in the depths of his being.

I mentioned the male and female demons who divest the dead of their possessions. They symbolize the fact that, according to the strict and constant law of causality, vanity is worth nothing after one dies. The only thing of value is the essential reality in the innermost core of one's life. The ten kings and the heavenly messengers are but a figurative way of teaching us that our physical and mental acts at each and every moment invariably become engraved in the karma of our lives. Though they are all fables, they are very enlightening ones indeed.

We can see, then, that a person who refuses to believe in or slanders true Buddhism causes his own life force to weaken with each moment. Eventually he will be completely drained of life force and find himself restrained from accomplishing anything, as if inextricably mired in a swamp. There are many dreadful things in the world, but nothing is more horrible than the hell of incessant suffering. It is said that if one were even to hear a description of that hell, he would cough up blood and die. True, this suggests the horrors of hell, but it also indicates that, in contrast to outward appearances, the misery in the depths of life is terrible beyond description.

Nothing is sadder and more miserable than to find one's very life a prison of agony, without the slightest energy or hope for the future. Such a person will fail in everything he does. The Gosho teaches that those who revile the votary of the Lotus Sutra may seem at first to receive no retribution, but they ultimately end in disaster. When a building is wrecked by a natural calamity of some sort, we can see the damaged parts and repair them. But we see nothing at all when it is rotting from within. If the rot spreads to the point that the house starts to crumble, it is almost impossible to repair. To slander the Lotus Sutra is to cause the palace of one's life to rot from within. This is most dreadful—perhaps no less horrible than finding one's hands seized by the guards of hell. No matter what hardship or sorrow befalls you, never part with the Gohonzon. If you do, you will only be throwing away all your good fortune and utterly destroying the seed of Buddhahood within you.

Buddhism places strong emphasis on the last moment of life, for in the Buddhist view it contains the sum total of one's lifetime, and it is also the first step toward the future. All phenomena manifest the true entity; all the acts done during one's lifetime, both good and bad, decide the way one dies. It is almost frightening, for nothing can be hidden. The way one dies, whether peacefully or horribly, is a perfect reflection of the life he has led and a spotless mirror of his future. In his *Reply to Myōhō-ama*, Nichiren Daishonin wrote:

> Ever since my childhood I, Nichiren, have studied Buddhism with one thought in mind. Life as a human is truly a fleeting thing. A man exhales his last breath with no hope to

draw in another. Not even dew borne away by the wind suffices to describe life's transience. No one, wise or foolish, young or old, can escape death. My sole wish has therefore been to solve this eternal mystery. All else has been secondary.

This passage guides us in the attitude we need in order to live our irreplaceable life without any regret, and with total joy.

What are the most important matters? They are one's lifelong objective and the question of life and death. If we let our minds stray from those most basic things, and become enwrapped in trivial affairs, nothing important can be gained. We need not become morose, but we should never forget the necessity to look soberly and sincerely straight at death and strive to live each moment to the fullest. How often today's writers and critics lament that modern humanity and civilization are drowning in "the luxuries of life." A frivolous way of life that ignores the gravity of death cannot bring true fulfillment. The Daishonin's words, "with the profound insight that now is the last moment of life," become all the more significant, now that our society is becoming so hopelessly confused.

Nichiren Daishonin talks about the hell of incessant suffering throughout the Gosho. But his almost too frequent reference to it, I believe, comes from his boundless mercy to do everything possible to keep people from falling into that hell. But what is the hell of incessant suffering really like? *On Slanderous Acts* states:

The eighth hell is *avichi*, the hell of incessant suffering. . . . Ringing it are seven great iron fortifications. . . . To the prisoners in this hell, those in the hell of scorching heat are like people enjoying themselves in the sixth heaven. The stench of this hell is so noxious that the heavenly beings and people on the entire earth and in the six heavens of the world of desire would all die should they ever chance to smell it. . . .

If the Buddha should but describe all of the sufferings in this hell, those listening to him would cough up blood and die. That is why the Buddha refrains from giving a detailed description.

Those passages, showing how deep life goes and how strict the retribution for slander is, really make us sit up and take notice. There is also the parable of the one-eyed turtle and a floating piece of sandalwood, a parable which is as profound as it is well known. The *Reply to Widow Matsuno* reads:

The turtle symbolizes ordinary people like us. Its lack of limbs signifies our lack of endowment with causes for good fortune. Its burning stomach denotes the eight hot hells of anger, and its freezing back the eight cold hells of greed. That the turtle has to stay at the bottom of the ocean for one thousand years represents the difficulty of extricating ourselves from the three evil paths. Every thousand years it comes to the surface, which signifies how rare it is to escape from the three evil paths and be born as human beings—perhaps once in countless aeons—and how rare it is to be born in Shakyamuni Buddha's lifetime.

We are told here how difficult it is to escape the three evil paths of Hell, Hunger and Animality and be born in the human world. Having been fortunate enough to live as human beings now, we have all the more motive to take seriously what this passage says.

In the Face of Death

The other day I read an article by Jun'ichi Watanabe, a physician-turned writer, describing the behavior of an eminent surgeon when faced with his own death. An expert in abdominal surgery, the doctor had treated thousands of cancer cases. Then, ironically, he was found to have cancer himself. The discovery came too late, and he could do nothing but await his own death. He remained calm and composed at first, but as his condition declined he began to change.

At midnight a low growl would come from his room; then suddenly a scream would shatter the dead silence of the ward.

"No! No, I don't want to die!"

"Help me! Help me!"

The nurses would rush into his room and find the doctor in tears, kicking his legs and beating his fists against the bed like a child. Sometimes he would take things off the bedstand and throw them across the room. At other times, his eyes filled with hatred, he would just lie and glare at his elderly wife, who stayed with him to look after him, and at the nurses who treated him.

"You hypocrites!" he would shout angrily at them. "You're thinking what fun you can have by yourselves after I go. You're all just waiting around like vultures, glad that I'm going to die." Once on the rampage, no one could control him. It took the combined power of all the nurses and his wife just to pin him down and give him an injection to put him to sleep.

The next day the doctor would wake up and look around with eyes hollow and gaunt as if he had just escaped from hell. When an occasional visitor came, he would hardly say anything at all. At such times he seemed like a man who was looking death calmly in the face. When night came, however, he would again lose all control and become as violent as another Mr. Hyde. It seemed as if he was being alternately tormented by his daytime exhaustion and nightly hell. The physicians were completely taken aback—they had never seen anyone struggle with such desperate fear of death as this doctor. Unable to remain indifferent, someone suggested that religion might give him some consolation. But he was in no state to accept any kind of religious faith. He simply continued to writhe in agony.

Was the doctor more frightened or cowardly than other

people? No; there was no one who believed that. But there was no hope of his being cured. Death would definitely take him in a few more weeks and *he knew it better than anyone else.* The problem was that he was all too clearly aware of the fact.

He was like a criminal in death row; in a way, even worse. Even a condemned criminal still has that one chance in a thousand for reprieve, some slight hope that somehow his sentence might not be carried out. For the doctor, however, there wasn't the tiniest glimmer of hope that he would live. He knew too much about medicine to expect any such thing.

He had devoted himself to medicine and for several decades had studied and accumulated professional knowledge. But all his knowledge was now completely worthless. All it did was make him more acutely aware of his own death. He had diagnosed and operated on thousands of cancer cases. All this experience only told him that he would soon breathe his last. There was not the slightest possibility for survival in which he could believe. His precious learning had turned into a demon that did nothing but torture him.

In despair even more intense than that of a condemned criminal, the doctor continued to writhe and cry in anguish until he finally breathed his last, as if exhausted of all his abusive language. There was no longer the slightest vestige of the lofty-minded scholar. Here was but an ordinary old man, egotistic and suspicious of everything, thrashing about in the horror of death.*

This fairly lengthy quotation brings into bold relief human frailty when faced with the final hurdle of death, a frailty which is part of our pitiful karma. Reading the article, I realized afresh how wonderful it is to be able to live aware of the philosophy of eternal life expounded by Nichiren Daishonin. Learning, genius, power, wealth, reputation, science, technology—all become nothing when one is confronted by death. Faced with his end, man finds himself

Mainichi Shimbun (Tokyo: The Mainichi Newspapers, February 13, 1977)

hopelessly overpowered, and there is nothing able to salve his conscience. That article and numerous other similar stories make us realize all the more clearly the significance of the phrase, "My sole wish has therefore been to solve this eternal mystery. All else has been secondary." Buddhism holds the answers to the questions man has struggled with since his beginning, the questions of death and the last moment of life. Buddhism is the philosophy of how to live, and every one of us, being human and existing as "beings-unto-death," should study it with equal zeal.

In his *Exegesis on The True Object of Worship*, Nichikan Shonin quotes the Great Teacher Dengyō as saying, "The unified perception of the three truths of life* at the moment of death is entirely different from that during ordinary practice at ceremonies. For, at the last moment, death's agony comes quickly and grips the body with ever-increasing strength, and the mind becomes so confused that one can no longer distinguish between right and wrong." Here is something we must think of in our own lives. Nichikan Shonin continues, "Unless you master the essential practice that will free yourself from illusion and suffering at the moment of death, all ordinary learning is completely useless. ... At the last moment of your life you should chant Nam-myoho-renge-kyo." This phrase indicates that "the essential practice" is the practice of Nam-myoho-renge-kyo. Only a life devoted to the Mystic Law will lead to the state of true peace and security that is described as "happiness in this life and good circumstances in the next."

Just imagine that those thousand Buddhas extending their hands to all Nichiren's disciples who chant Nam-

---

*To perceive the three truths as an indivisible entity—*kū* (the spiritual or qualitative aspects of life), *ke* (all phenomena of life) and *chū* (essential, unchangeable entity of life)—in a momentary state of life. T'ien-t'ai defined this unified perception of life as stemming from the correct practice of concentration and meditation.

myoho-renge-kyo are like so many melons or moon-flowers extending their slender vines.

Earlier we discussed the sentence in the *Kambotsu* (28th) chapter of the Lotus Sutra which states, "After his death, a thousand Buddhas will extend their hands. . . ." Here the Daishonin says that this sentence was written for those who would believe and practice the Great Pure Law in the future, which meant all his disciples and believers. Just as melons or moonflowers extend their "slender vines," the thousand Buddhas will extend their hands to support us, who embrace the Gohonzon, with all their might. We are, as it were, traveling aboard a ship as huge as the macrocosm, the ship of the Gohonzon. No other ship is as secure and powerful, for the blessings of the Gohonzon are as vast as the universe.

The quoted passage also says a great deal about the attitude leaders should have. The Buddhas extend their hands to prevent people from falling into hell or suffering from unbearable fear. This is the spirit we need when dealing with friends both inside and outside of our Buddhist organization. We should be constantly thinking of ways to let them enjoy their lives and to keep them from misery. To do that is to carry out the spirit of the Buddha, "to free him from all fear and keep him from falling into the evil paths." As we extend our hands to help others and encourage them, we are the "thousand Buddhas extending their hands." Just as melons or moonflowers extend their vines, so must we extend our helping hands to our friends, always watching them with special care, and thinking of their problems as our own. This is the spirit of the leader, filled with love for other members and for our neighbors and for all mankind.

Life always has its ups and downs. Everyone meets with times of failure and defeat. But it is at exactly such times that the people around should go to help and encourage. In doing so, they perform the work of the thousand Buddhas, the work which I believe causes a change in individual karma and, in the long run, growth in our respective communities. I always think of this whenever I meet with members or non-members.

This Moment Decides the Future

My disciples have been able to receive and embrace the Lotus Sutra by virtue of the strong ties they formed with this teaching in their past existences. They are certain to attain Buddhahood in the future.

The *Shinjikan* Sutra states, "If you want to know the cause you formed in the past, observe the effect in the present. If you want to know the effect in the future, observe the cause you are forming now." Thus, we have been able to take faith in true Buddhism because of the strong ties we formed with the Gohonzon in our past existences—the cause in the past. The fact that we have been able to receive and embrace the Gohonzon is the effect in the present, and at the same time it is the cause we are forming now. This cause makes it certain that we will attain Buddhahood—the effect in the future.

It is truly mysterious that we have been able to receive and embrace the Gohonzon and are now practicing true Buddhism for *kōsen-rufu* and to attain Buddhahood in this lifetime. It is possible only because we accumulated good causes in our past existences. The seventh chapter of the Lotus Sutra reads, "In lifetime after lifetime they were always born together with their masters in the Buddha's lands throughout the universe." It is saying that we must have formed the cause by unbroken dedication to propagating the Mystic Law. That has enabled us to encounter the Gohonzon in this life—the effect in the present.

Although you have been able to take faith in the Gohonzon, if you regard this only as the effect and nothing more, you are severing all the ties you once formed and cutting yourself off from the good fortune you have accumulated. It is important to understand that you must instead make that effect a cause for the future, a springboard for further growth. Only then can you cause your life to blossom in the future.

"My disciples have been able to receive and embrace the Lotus Sutra . . ." In this phrase, "receive" can be considered the effect received from the past. On the other hand, "embrace" is the cause aimed toward the future. To "embrace" means ceaseless effort and devotion, the continuous, unwavering practice of faith. Nichiren Daishonin means precisely that when he says, "To accept is easy; to continue is difficult. But Buddhahood lies in continuing faith."

The passage, "My disciples . . . ," teaches us that the ties we formed in the past have led us to receive and embrace the Gohonzon, and that our acts to do so now guarantee that we will attain Buddhahood in the future. Here we see the processes of planting, nurturing and reaping the seeds of Buddhahood—processes which span all eternity. Some of you may wonder, "Some people cannot bring themselves to take faith in true Buddhism. Is it because they did not form ties in the past? Must we abandon all hope of saving them?" No, we should not. If one is able to hear Buddhism in this life, that is equal to having formed ties in the past. Man is not an entity inescapably bound and controlled by past karma. He is an independent being whose present state of mind can change his future in any way he pleases. Actually it is beyond anyone's capacity to know whether or not he formed strong ties with Buddhism in the past. The essential thing is the fact that we embrace the Gohonzon now. This is what *The True Entity of Life* means by: "Were they not Bodhisattvas of the Earth, they could not chant the daimoku." We do not chant daimoku because we are Bodhisattvas of the Earth. But we are Bodhisattvas of the Earth *because we chant daimoku.*

Be convinced, therefore, that you formed strong ties with Nichiren Daishonin as his true disciples in the past, and that you were born in this age with the pledge to spread the Mystic Law throughout the world. Live earnestly each and every moment with this conviction, so that you will be able to forge a path through life—a life which is an accumulation of moments of good fortune. This is fundamental to the spirit of Buddhism. Be firmly resolved that when you strive to attain *kōsen-rufu,* you will prove yourselves as noble Bodhisattvas of the Earth. Keep this resolution as you devote yourselves wholeheartedly to your daily activities.

Upholding the Eternal Heritage

The heritage of the Lotus Sutra flows within the lives of those who never forsake it in any lifetime whatsoever—whether in the past, the present or the future.

Earlier in this Gosho, Nichiren Daishonin explained that the ultimate law in life is Myoho-renge-kyo and that to chant Nam-myoho-renge-kyo is to bring forth the law. In the passage above he is saying that this heritage is only transmitted through the continuous practice of faith. Just as parents' blood is by nature transmitted to their children, it is equally certain that the heritage of the ultimate law flowing within the life of the original Buddha from the infinite past is transmitted to the lives of us, his true disciples. Thus the passage assures us that the heritage of the ultimate law also flows within our lives eternally. Because we embrace the Gohonzon and chant daimoku, our lives are entities of the ultimate law. The heritage of the ultimate law is never interrupted in the lives of those who continue to embrace the Gohonzon throughout the past, present and future.

Sairenbō had only recently become Nichiren Daishonin's disciple, and the Daishonin sensed a tendency in him to place greater emphasis on theory than on practice. It was probably for these reasons that the Daishonin wrote in this particular way, to remind Sairenbō that the continuous practice of faith is most important of all. The heritage of the ultimate law is passed on to lives elevated through faith to a level where perception and communication with the Buddha's life is not only possible, but assured. But to fully receive that heritage requires practice continuing not just throughout a single lifetime but throughout the three existences of life. It is difficult, of course, to maintain one's belief even for a single lifetime. Since past, present and future are contained in a single moment—the present moment—we must sustain our faith without interruption through a succession of moments, now and into the future. Although it may seem easy, there is actually nothing more difficult, or more important.

For us, the transmission of the ultimate law should be the solemn ceremony taking place in the depths of our lives—a ceremony in which we perceive our own Buddhahood and bring it to the surface. Is there anything concrete about the way we inherit the ultimate law flowing within Nichiren Daishonin's life? The Daishonin passed away long ago. But he left behind the Gohonzon, the object of worship that combines the Person and the Law. We inherit the ultimate law from the Gohonzon, but we require no special ceremony. We only need to have a firm faith and chant daimoku to transfer the Gohonzon's life into our own. Or, putting it another way, we need only to bring forth the Daishonin's life—Buddhahood—from within ourselves.

Let me repeat this: Inheriting the Daishonin's life means bringing forth Buddhahood from within our own lives. The Gohonzon may be compared to a bird in the sky, while the Buddhahood in our own lives is like a bird in a cage.

Bringing forth our own Buddhahood is like the caged bird responding to the song of the bird in the sky. The heritage of faith flows entirely within our own lives. Only through our own faith can we realize this.

There is no reality other than the life we have, which continues throughout past, present and future. Reality is not something someone else gives you. The only thing there is, is our wonderful life which, though changing from moment to moment, continues to exist eternally. The heritage of the ultimate law flows here and nowhere else.

But those who disbelieve and slander the Lotus Sutra will "destroy the seeds for becoming a Buddha in this world." Because they cut themselves off from the potential to attain enlightenment, they do not share the ultimate heritage of faith.

All in all, then, there is no way for those who disbelieve or condemn true Buddhism to possess the heritage of the ultimate law. No matter how severe our situation may be, as long as we maintain strong life force through faith in the Gohonzon, we will someday be able to make the seed of enlightenment grow, ripen and bear fruit. You probably remember a news report not so long ago that a lotus seed that was found to be more than three thousand years old still retained enough life force to bloom and bear fruit. However, if one prevents the seed of his own Buddhahood from sprouting, he cannot expect it to bear fruit. Hence the Daishonin's statement that disbelievers and slanderers cut themselves off from enlightenment. "Destroy the seeds . . . in this world" means that no matter where they go they can never be saved. For them there is no place to escape. The only course open to them is hell.

The line, "destroy the seeds for becoming a Buddha in this world," appears in the third chapter of the Lotus Sutra. Look again at the phrase, "in this world." It tells us that we can attain Buddhahood only in the world we are living in. Proof of enlightenment becomes manifest as we try to live sincerely and humanely. You will never, never attain enlightenment if you run away from society to some quiet place to meditate. Buddhahood exists within us as we live from day to day. The seed for Buddhahood inherent in all people is Nam-myoho-renge-kyo. Those who derogate or refuse to believe in the Mystic Law will destroy the seeds for becoming a Buddha in this world.

Perfect Unity

All disciples and believers of Nichiren should chant Nam-myoho-renge-kyo with one mind (*itai dōshin*), transcending all differences among themselves to become as inseparable as fish and the water in which they swim. This spiritual bond is the basis for the universal transmission of the ultimate law of life and death. Herein lies the true goal of Nichiren's propagation. When you are so united, even the great hope for *kōsen-rufu* can be fulfilled without fail.

Here we learn that the heritage of the ultimate law flows within the group of believers who maintain perfect unity (*itai dōshin*) among themselves. The passage is a concrete lesson in the way of practice to follow and thereby inherit the lifeblood which enables any and all people to attain enlightenment.

Then where in particular does the heritage of the ultimate law flow? The answer is given at the beginning of this Gosho, in which the Daishonin states, "The five characters of Myoho-renge-kyo were transferred from the two Buddhas inside the Treasure Tower, Shakyamuni and Tahō, to Bodhisattva Jōgyō, carrying on a heritage unbroken since the infinite past." In a literal sense, the heritage exists in the life of Jōgyō, leader of Bodhisattvas of the Earth, whom Shakyamuni and Tahō Buddhas entrusted with the propagation of the Lotus Sutra. From the standpoint of true Buddhism, the entity of the ultimate law is the life of Nichiren Daishonin himself, the reincarnation of the original Buddha from the infinite past who appeared as Bodhisattva Jōgyō when Shakyamuni taught the Lotus Sutra. Therefore, the above passage concludes that the heritage, which in particular dwells within the Daishonin's life, flows in general within the group of his disciples who maintain perfect unity among themselves.

The quoted passage also makes it clear that the Buddha's lifeblood flows in the actions of people—not those who act divisively or egotistically, but within the lives of those who chant daimoku and advance together toward the common goal of *kōsen-rufu*. It is an important passage, for it shows a practical way for common people of little understanding to attain Buddhahood in the Latter Day.

"Herein lies the true goal of Nichiren's propagation." What is the objective that Nichiren Daishonin strove for as he propagated the Mystic Law? He did not intend to keep the heritage of true Buddhism to himself or just to transmit it to a limited number of people. He wanted to open the way to Buddhahood and pass the heritage on to all people—those in his own country and throughout the world. He wanted to pass it on to mankind, and for all eternity. This was the spirit that underlay everything he did, and it shows us the fundamental difference between *shōju* and *shakubuku*. *Shōju* was the method used during the Former and Middle Days to transmit the True Law for all generations, but *shakubuku* in the Latter Day aims at enabling all people to attain Buddhahood.

With infinite mercy for all, Nichiren Daishonin established the Dai-Gohonzon as the ultimate entity of enlightenment. He taught us *itai dōshin* (literally, many in body, one in mind) as the spirit in which to carry on the practice and the movement. In the light of this teaching, the noblest aspect of Nichiren Daishonin's Buddhism lies in faith based on the spirit of *itai dōshin*. Today in the Soka Gakkai we are firmly joined to the Gohonzon and dedicate ourselves to propagating the Mystic Law. The training and study we do is always undertaken within a fine, harmonious web of human relationships. The Soka Gakkai's very existence becomes extremely important in the light of this teaching of the Daishonin. Our organization carries out the lofty mission to achieve "the true goal of Nichiren's propagation."

Josei Toda used to say, "The organization of the Soka Gakkai is more important than my own life." Soka Gakkai members maintain perfect human harmony and transcend all differences between them. Ours is an organization which has unmistakably inherited the ultimate law of life—the key to enabling all people to attain Buddhahood. I am certain Mr. Toda made his remark because he knew this all too well.

Any group, no matter what kind, has capabilities greater than the sum total of the individual abilities of its members. If each member is given the suitable position according to the principle of *itai dōshin*, the group as a whole will be much more versatile than one would imagine. Think of a family, the smallest unit in society. Human culture and traditions are always created by groups or organizations and passed on down to posterity.

The Soka Gakkai is an organization established with the objective of enabling the individual to revolutionize his own life, attain enlightenment in this lifetime and carry out the great mission for *kōsen-rufu*. That is why the organization is endowed with the powers and abilities of the Buddha, the ultimate law of life flowing through it in ceaseless torrents. You can see this immediately when you study the Soka Gakkai's development and the myriad examples of human revolution attained by the people who have woven its history. We are Mr. Toda's disciples. It is our foremost duty to respect, nurture and protect the organization of life-to-life unity he left us. The Soka Gakkai, the world of *itai dōshin*, is the living organization of Buddhist practice and the training ground for human revolution in our day.

The Daishonin teaches us that the heritage of the ultimate law flows only in a group of people with the same faith, who work together in perfect unity. I think it is important to say a few words about the genuine nature and significance of *itai dōshin*.

We frequently meet in order to encourage the movement for *kōsen-rufu*, study the Gosho or make plans for events. We support and give guidance to each other. All this is *itai dōshin* in miniature, and the *Letter from Teradomari* states: "Those who have a seeking mind should all gather and read this letter together." People's minds change from moment to moment, so our members meet to keep themselves oriented on the right path of faith. Then they split up and go their various ways, some to create an unshakable foundation in their homes, others to contribute to the prosperity of their respective communities. Then they gather again at a discussion meeting to seek the true way of Buddhism. Repeated meetings and partings are a practical way for the members to manifest the essence of Buddhism in their own lives. This, I believe, is what is meant by the phrase, "If *itai dōshin* prevails among the people, they will achieve all their goals." The Soka Gakkai owes what it is today to the countless meetings and partings by members who were many in body but one in mind, firmly united with President Toda at their center.

The objective of our faith lies in the continuous revolution of our own lives. *Kōsen-rufu* is just that revolution, aimed at contributing to the peace and culture of mankind. An organization, no matter what kind, which ceases to strive for continuous revolution—which is really the accumulation of daily reform—is but a living corpse with no future. Another thing makes our organization special: *Kōsen-rufu* lies in an entirely different dimension from revolutions carried out solely for a certain class or group of people. Ours is the crystallization of man's noblest endeavor, a universal, eternal revolution carried on to benefit all people on earth. By now you probably know that it is only the unity of *itai dōshin* that makes such a revolution possible.

Itai dōshin contains two important principles. The first, of course, is *itai*, or many different individuals. Nichiren Daishonin's Buddhism deeply respects each person's individuality, situation and character and shows the way to display one's particular abilities to the fullest. The *Ongi Kuden* says, "Cherry, plum, peach and damson blossoms all have their own qualities, and they manifest the three properties of the life of the original Buddha without changing their own character." People, in other words, should give full play to their unique capabilities as they struggle toward *kōsen-rufu*. Their struggle brings about their own human revolution, and the circle of unity they form is the Soka Gakkai.

Because organizations must maintain internal order, they tend to reject individual differences and make their members conform as much as possible. Perhaps the best examples of such are the military and "in-family" groups. An "in-family" group may appear firmly united, but because in reality it forms an inner core closed to outsiders, it eventually grows unable to respond to the changes of the times. Although it seems to be one body, it usually becomes divided into countless opposing factions. It becomes corrupt and depraved eventually, giving rise to evil among the members. This explains why many religious bodies find themselves at a standstill. They have turned into "in-family" groups so poisoned with the evils of nepotism that they are unable to move.

The members of the Soka Gakkai have always maintained mutual respect for each other and each other's special talents. I want you to carry on this noble tradition eternally. Each member has his own mission to accomplish in the land of the Buddha. We aim at a total revolution. In its ideal form, this revolution has people from all walks of life gathering together in the garden of the Soka Gakkai, each blossoming forth in a unique way. An association of fishmongers may be able to effect reform in the fish market, but they cannot achieve a total revolution. The total revolution will be achieved only when people with all sorts of characters and talents fully live up to their abilities as they scale the peak of *kōsen-rufu* on into the coming century.

Gohonzon and Kōsen-rufu—Our Foundation

The second principle of *itai dōshin* requires that people different in body (*itai*) act in one spirit (*dōshin*). This is the more important of the two principles. The phrase "transcending all differences among themselves" does not mean to reject differences. Rather, it repudiates failure of heart-to-heart communication between people. It rejects egotism and actions based only on personal feelings. Such attitudes lead people to emphasize their differences and finally cause them to sever their bonds. No spiritual bond can long exist in such disunited groups of people.

In contrast, fish and water are two totally different things, but fish cannot live for a moment without water. "To become as inseparable as fish and the water in which they swim" is to realize that our existence flourishes within, and even depends on, the beautiful tapestry of human relationships woven together with the people around us. We must treasure those relationships. "Water" then represents the human relations surrounding us—the organization—and "fish" indicates ourselves. Just as fish feel perfectly comfortable in the water they swim in, so must we merge with the group of *itai dōshin*, respecting each and every member. Then we can "become as inseparable as fish and the water in which they swim."

Buddhist teaching puts heavy emphasis on a strong sense of gratitude: gratitude to parents, teachers, society and mankind. The Buddhist regards our existence as being inseparably connected to all other forms of life. We learn from Buddhism that we must be as grateful for other people's existence as we are for our own. Realize that the principle of *itai dōshin* is based on this teaching. But look at the society in which we live. It is filled with people who assert only their differences, and it is beset with conflict and selfishness, hostility and hate, discord and destruction. Like so many foxes and wolves, people cunningly, almost hungrily, watch for the chance to pounce on each other. We must see this for exactly what it is. We must not allow ourselves to give in to or be ridiculed by wicked people. This harsh reality totally surrounds us, but there is one remaining force capable of overcoming all viciousness and establishing a society in which true humanism prevails. It is ourselves, members of the Soka Gakkai. Indivisible and united in the spirit of *itai dōshin*, we must advance toward the lofty goal willed to us all, together, by the original Buddha, Nichiren Daishonin.

Dōshin (one mind) means to believe in the Gohonzon and to take the supreme goal of *kōsen-rufu* as our own, personal mission. The Gosho tells us to be "of the same mind as Nichiren" and says that his disciples should "form your ranks and follow him."

If people follow only their own subjective opinions and personal whims, they will become divided, both in body and mind, and find themselves in a whirlpool of complaints, discontent, hatred and jealousy. But when all stand together in the spirit of *itai dōshin*, each one will be able to see how intensely the others are fighting, each in his own capacity. They will clearly see that members are taking the lead in their own spheres of action and work on their own, and helping the whole movement one step at a time. Everyone is living the best way he can, constantly feeling purified and filled with new vigor. If we are aware of their individual efforts and feelings, we sense a new respect for them all, and at the same time try all the harder in our own positions to accomplish our own mission. Ours is a living organization because it is composed of just such people. It is only natural, therefore, that the heritage of the ultimate law flows within it in a broad, clear river of abundant joyful benefits. Until now the Soka Gakkai has continued to support its faith by the purest form of *itai dōshin*—a purity that is very difficult to appreciate if one is not a part of our organization. Part of my will for all who are members is that you preserve this tradition eternally and never destroy it.

On Itai Dōshin, one of the best-known Gosho, states, "King Chou of Yin led 700,000 soldiers into battle against King Wu of Chou and his 800 men. Yet King Chou's army lost because of disunity while King Wu's men defeated him because of perfect unity." This episode took place in China about the eleventh century B.C., an incident which marked the passage of one dynasty into the next. Although the age and historical background are far removed from us today, the story contains an eternal truth for human behavior. According to the *Shih Chi* (Records of the Historian) by Ssu-ma Ch'ien, King Chou of the Yin dynasty was a bloody tyrant. He was infatuated with a woman named Ta Chi and indulged in sensual pleasures day and night. He killed anyone who dared oppose him and sometimes made salted or dried meat of his victims' flesh. When his loyal retainer, Pi Kan, remonstrated with him, the king gouged out his heart. Naturally he cared nothing for the happiness of his people.

Yin had many countries under its control. One of them was Chou. Its king, Wen, was a wise ruler who enjoyed the confidence of the kings of other countries. When he died, his son, Wu, succeeded him. Following his father's last will, Wu took up arms against the tyrannical King Chou. His action was well-timed, as eight hundred lords with the same intent as he came to participate. King Chou commanded 700,000 soldiers in the battle against Wu. Wu's army was a motley group of lords from many different countries, but they were firmly united in the common desire to punish the abominable king for going against Heaven's will. Their morale was very high. In contrast, King Chou's troops way outnumbered King Wu's, but they had no will to fight. Actually, they were secretly glad that Wu was coming. When the expeditionary force arrived, they all rose together in revolt against their king and let Wu into their country without resisting at all. The Yin dynasty fell, and the Chou dynasty was born. Wu had won the hearts of the people and enjoyed their trust. From the very beginning his army had been united in *itai dōshin*, which is why he succeeded so magnificently.

We, too, must advance in the spirit of *itai dōshin* with strong faith in the Gohonzon, holding high the banner of human revolution. All other people will soon find that their only hope lies in our progress, and they will come and join in, one after another. Now is the time. If we are united in *itai dōshin*, "even the great hope for *kōsen-rufu* can be fulfilled without fail."

Kōsen-rufu will not come our way if we merely sit and wait or repeat empty phrases like parrots. It can only be realized when we continuously practice our faith in the spirit of *itai dōshin*. In this sense, can any religious body in this age other than Nichiren Shoshu Soka Gakkai be called "the envoy of the Buddha, sent to carry out the Buddha's work"? Which other group is carrying out "Nichiren's propagation" in our world? I declare that there is absolutely no other. Therefore, Soka Gakkai members will certainly obtain immeasurable benefits, as the Gosho states, "Not even the wisdom of the Buddha can fathom the blessings you will obtain." Our path in life is illuminated by both an important mission and great good fortune. March straight along this road until you finally enter the highest state of happiness and satisfaction.

The Pitfall of Arrogance

But if any of Nichiren's disciples should disrupt the unity of *itai dōshin*, he will destroy his own castle from within.

Here Nichiren Daishonin points out that those disciples whose spirit is not one with his are like parasites in a lion's body and are enemies of true Buddhism. Since they break the unity of *itai dōshin*, and thereby cut themselves off from the heritage of the ultimate law, their sin is extremely grave. In Buddhism the most serious of the five cardinal sins* is "causing disunity in the Buddhist community." It also corresponds to a still more deadly act—"slandering the True Law." They are violating Myoho-renge-kyo—the heritage of the ultimate law and the core of Buddhism.

In the final analysis, to be of a "different mind" is to go against Nichiren Daishonin's spirit. But those who sometimes seem to turn against the Daishonin do not do so intentionally. Then what makes some people develop strong, intractable opposition? The cause, I believe, is selfishness, personal feelings and conceit. In Shakyamuni's day some people turned traitor and disrupted the flow of Buddhism because of those reasons. Devadatta was one of them. He

*The five most serious offenses in Buddhism. They are: 1) killing one's father; 2) killing one's mother; 3) killing an arhat; 4) injuring a Buddha, and 5) causing disunity among believers.

is said to have been a villain who committed three of the five cardinal sins. He was initially one of Shakyamuni's disciples, but later left the group of Buddhists, taking five hundred monks with him, and began to attack Shakyamuni and his disciples. What made him backslide and eventually caused him to fall into hell? The following passage from *The Opening of the Eyes* vividly describes the situation:

> The World-Honored One scolded Devadatta to his face, saying, "You are a fool! You drink the spittle of other people." Devadatta felt as if he had been shot in the heart with a poisoned arrow. In fierce resentment he said, "Gautama cannot be a Buddha. I am the heir to King Dronodana, an elder brother of the revered Ananda and a cousin of Gautama. No matter what evil I might have done, he should have admonished me in private. Instead he scolded me severely in the presence of a large assembly of people and heavenly beings. How can such a man rank among the Buddhas and bodhisattvas? Earlier he took my sweetheart away from me. This time he has humiliated me in the presence of a large assembly. From today on I am his arch enemy, for each and every lifetime I am born."

It is clear that Devadatta disrupted the unity of *itai dōshin* out of rancor, which originated in a personal grudge. The immediate cause of his treachery was Shakyamuni's reproof at a place of Buddhist practice where many other disciples were gathered. There he was called a fool and reproached, and he resented it. How haughty he was, and how keenly he wished the admiration of others! Shakyamuni could see that, given such a nature, Devadatta would not attain enlightenment unless he did away with his arrogance. That is why the Buddha purposely scolded his cousin in front of everyone.

Shakyamuni knew Devadatta's heart inside and out. As the teacher, he sincerely wanted his pupil to grow. He wanted to correct Devadatta's wicked mind and purge the benighted nature in his life, which would otherwise cause him to fall into misery. There was nothing personal involved, he simply had to be severe in his guidance. The Buddha's harsh words were the expression of mercy for a single person. But Devadatta could not see that far. His arrogant mind was already so bent on fame and fortune that he rejected the guidance and help Shakyamuni offered him.

I know of many instances in which people have deviated from the path of human revolution out of pride. There may be times when someone harshly admonishes you or gives you severe, straightforward guidance. At such times tell yourself that you are standing at a crucial point which can decide the success or failure of your human revolution. President Toda often gave me extremely strict guidance. He would even scold me for mistakes other leaders had made. Whenever I look back on those days, I am filled with memories and deep gratitude to my late master. How I wish I could have had his severe guidance for at least ten more years!

We saw that the immediate cause of Devadatta's revolt was Shakyamuni's humiliating treatment in the presence of the large assembly. However, the original cause went back many years earlier, which comes out in Devadatta's remark, "Earlier he (Shakyamuni) took my sweetheart away from me." Devadatta came from a royal family. When he was young, he vied with Prince Siddhartha (Shakyamuni's name as a youth) for the hand of Princess Yashodhara, who was reputed to be the most beautiful woman in India, but he lost. We are told that it was because Siddhartha far excelled his rival. With all that, it might have been hard for Devadatta to accept the Buddha's words with an open heart. But his response was so utterly personal that revolt was completely unjustified. At any rate, we can see that his heart was full of rancor—jealousy and hatred for his superior cousin, lingering over a lost love.

Now let us turn to Sanmibō, a disciple who turned against Nichiren Daishonin. Sanmibō was one of the leading disciples, but, like Devadatta, he disrupted the unity of the Daishonin's followers and finally died a violent death. About him the Daishonin states:

> There was something extremely strange about Sanmibō. However, I felt that whatever I said about it would be taken by the foolish as mere jealousy of his wisdom, and therefore I refrained from speaking out. It was because he had a wicked mind that he met his doom during the great persecution. If I had scolded him more strictly, he might have been saved, but since it was much too mysterious I have not mentioned it before.

In this passage the Daishonin indicates an important point. He wanted to give guidance to Sanmibō and point out his errors, but his surroundings prevented him from doing so. Before he was aware of it, his disciples had created an atmosphere in which it would have caused more harm than good to scold Sanmibō. Sanmibō Nichigyō was an educated priest who had studied at Enryaku-ji temple in Kyoto, then the highest seat of learning in Buddhism. Learned and eloquent, he breezed to a brilliant victory in his debate with Ryūzōbō, a famed scholar of the Tendai sect. He had the tendency, however, toward false pride in his talents and, at the same time, obsequiousness to social power. He lacked the true pride and determination to uphold the supreme teaching of Buddhism, no matter what. In his reply to this priest, the Daishonin writes, "In your letter you mentioned the great honor you had to give a lecture at the family temple of a court noble. But it seems very strange for you to say that kind of thing. . . . by speaking of your 'great honor,' are you not in essence expressing your low opinion of me, Nichiren?" It seems that Sanmibō placed the Daishonin's Buddhism below the aristocratic authority of the country's religious center in Kyoto.

During the Atsuhara Persecution, Sanmibō was dispatched to the Fuji area to assist Nikkō Shonin, who ranked below him. Then, becoming victim to the scheming of Gyōchi, acting chief priest of Ryūsen-ji temple of the Tendai sect, he turned against Nikkō Shonin. The consequence you know well: "He met his doom," dying a violent death. I suspect he was not pleased about having to go and assist one of his juniors who was leading the struggle against the persecution. On that struggle hinged the rise or fall of the Daishonin's Buddhist order. Even in such a decisive battle, he was preoccupied with his own resentment that he had not been assigned the leading position. He was completely dominated by egoism, and a desire for fame and fortune.

The Daishonin, of course, had long before discerned this dark tendency in Sanmibō's life. Once, when Sanmibō was in Kyoto propagating true Buddhism, the Daishonin wrote him a letter admonishing his inclination toward selfish pride. The Daishonin highly regarded Sanmibō's learning, but did not want it to go to his head and eventually cause him to backslide. He must have felt it necessary to scold Sanmibō on a number of occasions but, as I said, there was some turn of events which prevented him from doing so. In the final analysis, this brought him to his death. Remember that the principle, "There can be no discontinuity between past, present and future," stands, no matter what the age.

After the Daishonin's demise there were traitorous moves on the part of the five elder priests who had been the closest disciples of the Daishonin. After he had passed away, they tried to identify his teaching with the Tendai school and, shamelessly calling themselves followers of that school, they abandoned true Buddhism. It was not so much because they failed to comprehend the Daishonin's Buddhism, as because they wanted to preserve their authority in the already well-established Tendai sect. But they went about it by altering the Daishonin's teaching. You may know that the Daishonin wrote many of his Gosho in the simple Japanese syllabary. The five elder priests considered any Gosho not written in classical Chinese characters harmful to their sect's prestige. So, on the excuse that such writings were a disgrace to their late master, they either tore them up and made new paper of them or burned them. They were doing nothing less than trampling on the very spirit of Nichiren Daishonin, the original Buddha who consecrated his own life for the sake of all people.

Nichirō, one of the five, had taken part in the propagation campaign, spiritually exalted by his perfect master-disciple relationship with the Daishonin. For his effort he was even imprisoned. In his *Letter to the Imprisoned Disciple*, the Daishonin extolls his strong faith. Then, after Nikkō Shonin succeeded the Daishonin, even Nichirō turned against the second high priest and rejected true Buddhism. It is a sad story, but for us, becomes a very important lesson, which generations of believers must remember as they advance toward *kōsen-rufu*. Nichirō was very active during the lifetime of Nichiren Daishonin. But when Nikkō Shonin became high priest, Nichirō turned on him. By so doing he violated the teaching, "There can be no discontinuity between past, present and future." This principle should be a mirror for all who propagate Buddhism, both now and in the future.

President Makiguchi, the founder of the Soka Gakkai, was a pioneer who built the foundation for *kōsen-rufu*, propagating the True Law at the cost of his own life. In the face of oppression from the government he resolutely continued on, pitting himself against the persecution in order to spread true Buddhism until he was finally imprisoned. By then he had a large group of followers, but no sooner had he been imprisoned than many of them abandoned their faith. Then, when Mr. Toda became the second president, a number of Mr. Makiguchi's disciples turned away from true

Buddhism. The leaders in the early days of the Soka Gakkai, nonetheless, were not swayed a bit by the turncoats. They had unshakable conviction in their faith, and it is through their unity that the Soka Gakkai has been able to move ahead in its unprecedented development. Today their names and their meritorious achievements stand out in the history of *kōsen-rufu*.

These and other episodes, both ancient and recent, make it absolutely certain that those who try to take advantage of the Soka Gakkai in the present age are no better than subversives attempting to break up the spirit of *itai dōshin*. There always have been, are, and will be, people who seek to satisfy their own selfish desires by using our organization. Some may try to use us for financial purposes. Others, completely underestimating the strength or purity of our organization, may try to use us as a means in their pursuit of fame and power. Such people exist both inside and outside the Soka Gakkai. Some also undoubtedly join simply out of curiosity, which can also be damaging.

In a time of trial, those who disrupt the unity of *itai dōshin* "will destroy their own castle from within." As long as everything goes as they wish, they will go along with the organization and praise it to the skies. But if the Gakkai is attacked, or when things do not go as they hoped, it is this kind of person who will betray the Gakkai. I have seen such people become more and more miserable, their lives growing constantly darker. It is a very sad thing, but it is inevitable, a result determined by the law of causality.

Mercy for All Mankind

Nichiren has been trying to awaken all the people of Japan to faith in the Lotus Sutra so that they too can share the heritage and attain Buddhahood. But instead they attacked me time and again, and finally had

**me banished to this island. You have followed Nichi-
ren, however, and met with sufferings as a result. It
pains me deeply to think of your anguish.**

From this passage on, Nichiren Daishonin demonstrates
concern for Sairenbō, giving him deep encouragement and
enfolding him with compassion. The heart of the Daishonin was filled with one thing, and one thing alone—the
infinitely merciful wish to let all people "share the heritage
and attain Buddhahood." The only reason he so categorically denounced misleading teachings was to bring the
heritage within reach of the people. He was especially
severe with Ryōkan of Gokuraku-ji temple, to whom many
in those days looked up as a great spiritual and philosophical
leader. The Daishonin carried through everything he did
in righteousness to the end. He fought for the people,
courageously, in utter disregard of his own life.

We of the Soka Gakkai carry on the struggle in the same
spirit. The Daishonin fought to bring happiness to all the
people in the world, and we follow in his footsteps to let
them "share the heritage and attain Buddhahood." Being
ourselves entities of the Mystic Law, whatever we do to
encourage others to join us is a noble endeavor, whether we
are aware of it or not. By encouraging them to join, we
bring them the chance to inherit the ultimate law and let it
take root firmly in their lives.

"But instead they attacked me time and again, and finally
had me banished to this island." The country's leaders
during the Daishonin's time were easily cajoled by the
cunning, villainous priests into persecuting and finally
banishing him to Sado Island. Exile on Sado was almost a
living death, as the Gosho confirms, "Exiles to this island are
seldom able to survive. Even if they do, they can never
return home." He was forced to dwell in a small temple
called Sanmaidō at Tsukahara. It was in a state of utter ruin.

The howling wind swept through the wide gaps in the roof and walls. Any other person would have felt as if he were living in hell itself, but the Daishonin's heart was filled with joy. He felt the kind of joy that could only be felt by the original Buddha. In spite of being in such terrible surroundings, or rather, because he found himself there, he could perceive people's misery all the more acutely. That sense made him want to bring them happiness and bring the merciful light of his Buddhism to shine over the whole earth, a Buddhism as bright and powerful as the sun.

The Daishonin's mercy takes on added significance and depth from the fact that he wrote this important Gosho, the *Heritage of the Ultimate Law of Life*, while on Sado Island. In spite of being made to live in the worst environment imaginable, he recharged and polished his life all the further to leave unfading landmarks of true Buddhism that would guide mankind for eternity. Perhaps only the original Buddha could achieve this, but we nonetheless must try to follow suit. The more trying and harsh our circumstances become, the more faith and courage we must call forth.

"You have followed Nichiren, however, and met with sufferings as a result." Nichiren Daishonin was going through persecution that came at him from all over the land. Flames of hatred roared up against him from all quarters. Under these circumstances Sairenbō dared to follow the Daishonin and, as a result, he too met with suffering. We do not know for certain what agonies he underwent, but it is certain that he was a man of great courage. The kind of attacks that caused him such pain were aimed less at him as an individual than they were part of a greater persecution to which the Daishonin's entire Buddhist order was subjected. Sairenbō stood his ground, and continued to follow his master. Such perseverance must have required extraordinary conviction. On the other hand, his faith was undoubtedly put to a real test.

The *Ongi Kuden*, interpreting the phrase "to follow this master and study," which appears in the tenth chapter of the Lotus Sutra, says, "To follow means to believe and accept." In another part it explains that to follow means to devote both mind and body to the Lotus Sutra. Thus, in saying, "You have followed Nichiren . . . ," the Daishonin was offering deep encouragement to Sairenbō, the man who shared the greatest hardship his master ever had to suffer. To me, one of the reasons that the Daishonin was not only a peerless master but a source of warm, human inspiration was his capacity for unbending sternness—which in itself indicates concern—combined with a limitless, personal interest in all his followers.

What Nichiren Daishonin went through was no ordinary abuse. It was a fierce attack by *senshō zōjōman*, the third and worst of the three powerful enemies.* The authorities of some of the religious groups had schemed and prevailed upon the government to publicly punish the Daishonin. The entire nation was like a hive of angry bees swarming in hatred around him. Sairenbō made his commitment to follow the Daishonin right at that point, at a peak of his distress and unpopularity. And Sairenbō never faltered, despite the trials he had to face. At the same time, Sairenbō's courage and perseverance made it possible for the Daishonin to place unqualified confidence in him. Josei Toda used to say, "I trust only those people who have stuck to their faith through thick and thin for at least twenty years—especially those who have overcome hardship after unbearable hardship. I trust them with my very life." I also remember Dr. Toynbee saying during one of our talks, "I can correctly appraise a person's value only when I have reviewed the past twenty years of his life."

"It pains me deeply to think of your anguish." This sentence expresses the Daishonin's very personal consider-

*See page 54.

ation for his disciple. He knows the terror that must have gripped Sairenbō's heart, and understands the mental conflict and indignation that must have been raging within him. He thinks of this disciple's distress even more than his own suffering, which is possible only from the heart of the original Buddha.

People of "Pure Gold"

Gold can neither be burned by fire nor corroded or swept away by water, but iron is vulnerable to both. A wise person is like gold and a fool like iron. You are like pure gold because you embrace the "gold" of the Lotus Sutra. The Lotus Sutra reads in part, "Sumeru is the loftiest of all mountains. The Lotus Sutra is likewise the loftiest of all the sutras." It also states, "The good fortune of the believer cannot be burned by fire or washed away by water."

Gold is one metal that will not oxidize even in fire, nor can it be corroded by water. And, because of its density, it is not even budged by a flood. In contrast, iron rusts and eventually disintegrates in either fire or water. A wise person, therefore, is one who, like gold, does not waver the slightest in his faith, no matter what suffering he meets or how difficult his life becomes. A fool, on the other hand, is as vulnerable and corruptible as iron.

Fire and water are like the trials we meet in daily life. The Gosho, *The Eight Winds*, reads, "A truly wise man will not be carried away by any of the eight winds: prosperity, decline, disgrace, honor, praise, censure, suffering and pleasure. He is neither elated by prosperity nor grieved by decline." Most people lose their integrity when they receive prosperity, honor, praise or pleasure, and they become morose in the face of decline, disgrace, censure or suffering. Fire and water are symbols of the temptations and troubles of this constantly changing world. Unswayed by praise or blame, we must not let them move us, but instead, we must advance straight along our path of faith, making the life we live shine like polished gold.

Because of his faith in true Buddhism, Sairenbō went through suffering as withering as a fire and as relentless as a flood. But he never gave in. He upheld his faith to the end. That is why Nichiren Daishonin praises him, saying, "You are like pure gold." A passage in the "Precepts for Youth" written by President Toda states, "For a wise person it is a shame to be praised by a fool. But for him to be praised by the Buddha is a lifelong honor." I hope each of you will steadily lead your life in your own way and be worthy of praise from the Daishonin.

"Pure gold" is talking about those of unquestionable integrity of faith and practice. The test is whether a person has the insight to get to the core of things, whether he can carry through his faith while living a truly humane life, and whether he can keep on the path of righteousness to the end. I hope all of you will become people with insight and conviction based on Buddhism, who can discern the truth of things and who never falter or doubt, no matter what may happen. When the Daishonin was banished to Sado, quite a few of his disciples began to doubt, wondering whether his Buddhism was really true or not. However, it was precisely because he was exiled to Sado that he could prove in the way he responded to exile that he was the original Buddha and was able to complete so many important works. None who only saw into superficial aspects of what was happening could have anticipated this.

Much, much later, when Mr. Makiguchi and Mr. Toda were imprisoned, once more many followers began to doubt and eventually abandoned their faith. More than thirty years have passed since the Soka Gakkai was fiercely oppressed by the Japanese military authorities, and during this period our organization has achieved phenomenal growth. Looking back, we can see profound significance in Mr. Makiguchi's death in prison. He left us with the spirit of determination to propagate the Law even at the cost of our lives. It was also in prison that Mr. Toda discovered that Buddha is life itself, awakening to his mission as a Bodhisattva of the Earth. Thus, even the cruel, wartime oppression had considerable meaning. It was through that persecution that the spiritual core of the Soka Gakkai solidified. It produced the seed which has since blossomed into our organization today. Continue to live as people of "pure gold," no matter what situation you may face. People of pure gold will eventually reveal their inner light and their true ability, no matter where they may be.

"Because you embrace the 'gold' of the Lotus Sutra" means that we are able to walk a golden path only because we embrace the Lotus Sutra, the highest philosophy of life. As the Gosho states, "If the Law is supreme, so is the person who embraces it." Buddhism teaches that the content of one's life is determined by the quality of the belief he upholds, whether it is noble or base, deep or shallow. We have already received the Gohonzon and based our lives on it. This is the supreme teaching of which the Buddha of the Latter Day, Nichiren Daishonin, declared, "So long as men of wisdom do not prove my teachings to be false, then I will never accept the practices of the other sects!" There is no alternative; we must make the Gohonzon part of us throughout our lives, and it will take us on a golden journey in life.

Both quotations from the Lotus Sutra appear in the twenty-third chapter, *Yakuō-hon*. "Sumeru is the loftiest of all mountains. The Lotus Sutra is likewise the loftiest of all the sutras," extolls the Lotus Sutra. The sentence, "The good fortune of the believer cannot be burned by fire or washed away by water," concerns the good fortune of those who receive and embrace that sutra. President Toda explained that "fire" in this sentence indicates the fire of desire and that "water" denotes the water of suffering. The *Ongi Kuden*, interpreting the same phrase, states that "fire" represents the flames of the hell of incessant suffering and that "water" signifies the ice of the hell of unspeakable cold. In any case, the second quotation clearly tells us that the life of each person who embraces the Gohonzon will be illuminated by good fortune and he will find absolute happiness. Neither his fortune nor happiness can be disturbed by any of the fires or floods in life.

Bonds in the Depths of Life

It must be ties of karma from the distant past that have destined you to become my disciple at a time like this. Shakyamuni and Tahō Buddhas certainly realize this truth. The sutra's statement, "In lifetime after lifetime they were always born together with their masters in the Buddha lands throughout the universe," cannot be false in any way.

The fact that Sairenbō became Nichiren Daishonin's disciple during the most severe persecution in the Daishonin's lifetime cannot be understood in terms of worldly relationships. That is why the Daishonin states, "It must be ties of karma from the distant past that have destined you to become my disciple at a time like this."

"Shakyamuni and Tahō Buddhas certainly realize this truth." Literally, this means that since the Daishonin is an ordinary person, he does not himself realize the fact but that Shakyamuni and Tahō, being Buddhas, do. More than that, however, it means that the eternal law of Buddhism reveals that Sairenbō shared the Daishonin's difficulties because of the deep bonds they had formed in the past.

"In lifetime after lifetime they were always born together with their masters in the Buddha lands throughout the universe." This is a well-known passage from the seventh chapter, *Kejōyu-hon*, of the Lotus Sutra. According to this chapter, in a distant past called *sanzen-jintengō* a Buddha by the name of Daitsū expounded the Lotus Sutra. He had sixteen sons, and taught each of them the Law. They in turn preached the Law to as many people as there are grains of sand in six hundred billion Ganges Rivers, forming a master-disciple relationship with all. Since then, in lifetime after lifetime these people were continually born together with their masters in the Buddha's lands throughout the universe. They heard the teaching, and practiced Buddhism together with their masters. Three thousand years ago, the sixteenth of those sons came into the world as Shakyamuni and attained enlightenment. At that time the people he had taught in the past existences were also born into this world, heard him expound the Law, and attained Buddhahood.

In a word, the quotation from the *Kejōyu* chapter confirms that the master and his disciples are always born in the same world to practice Buddhism together. In Japan, Nichiren Daishonin made his advent in the Kamakura era. So Nikkō Shonin and many other disciples and followers appeared during the same period and devoted themselves to spreading the Mystic Law. Therefore, Nichiren Daishonin is the "master" in the Latter Day of the Law.

How, then, should we read the passage from the *Kejōyu* chapter after the Daishonin's death? By inscribing the Dai-Gohonzon, Nichiren Daishonin provided the answer for us and our future generations. Also, he transmitted the entirety of his teachings to Nikkō Shonin, his immediate successor. We live together with Nichiren Daishonin when we worship the Gohonzon enshrined at our own homes with the same attitude we have toward the Dai-Gohonzon. Hence the statement of the *Kejōyu* chapter. We are now fighting for *kōsen-rufu* because we are brothers and sisters joined by the deep bond of the Mystic Law we have formed in the past. What strengthens our relationship is the prayer that we offer to the Gohonzon, with the same mind, as well as the mental and physical struggle we undergo together to save mankind and attain *kōsen-rufu*.

At times the Soka Gakkai may enjoy smooth sailing; at other times it may face a fierce wind. No matter what, stay firm within the Soka Gakkai and grow together with it. The karmic relationship we have shared since the distant past has destined us to become Soka Gakkai members. Therefore, live your whole life together with me and together with the Soka Gakkai so that, with the Gohonzon's mercy, we may be born again together and enjoy the happiest of possible lives.

The quotation from the *Kejōyu* chapter is very significant from the viewpoint of faith. Whether we are true disciples of Nichiren Daishonin or not depends on how we display the spirit of that sentence in our practice. There are many kinds of relationships: flesh-and-blood relationships between parents and children or brothers and sisters, work relationships between superior and subordinates, social relationships between friends or teachers and students. These are very important relationships, and the happiness and prosperity of families and society rest on whether those ties remain strong and whether individuals can associate with each other on a constructive basis or not. But of all human relations, that between master and disciple is the deepest and most important. Only through the master-disciple relationship can we learn and teach each other how to develop ourselves as human beings and how best to deal with life. This is the only life-to-life bond which continues for all eternity and which remains firm no matter where we may be.

Ties based on common interests collapse when interests diverge. Relationships forced upon us by external circumstances all change according to the time and place. However, the symphony played by master and disciples in one mind, creating harmony in the depths of their lives, will send forth its echoes throughout the universe and on into eternity. We are all legitimate disciples of Nichiren Daishonin. And now growing numbers with pure faith assemble in perfect harmony in countries around the world. You should have the pride and conviction to know that this is the purest crystallization of human relationships ever achieved in the history of man.

Whenever I read the quotation from the *Kejōyu* chapter, my heart is rent by the memory of Mr. Toda's words to his late master at the second memorial service on November 17, 1946:

> Your mercy was so boundlessly great that you even took me to prison with you. Because you did so, with my very life I was able to read the phrase in the Lotus Sutra which states, "In lifetime after lifetime they were always born together with their masters in the Buddha's lands throughout the universe." The wonderful result was that I awoke to the mission of Bodhisattvas of the Earth and could understand even a little of the meaning of the Lotus Sutra. Nothing could have made me happier.

Even in prison, Mr. Toda visualized the Gohonzon and chanted daimoku to it sincerely. As a result, he discovered himself in perfect fusion with the Gohonzon as the passage from the *Kejōyu* chapter reads. Also, he realized his deep sense of mission, with which he would devote his remaining years to spreading faith in the Gohonzon. "Your mercy was so boundlessly great" and "Nothing could have made me happier" are the expressions of his pure, genuine faith in the Gohonzon. Mr. Toda's struggle reminds me that every individual can feel the statement of the *Kejōyu* chapter with his faith in true Buddhism.

"The Buddha's lands throughout the universe" indicate worlds inhabited by human beings. In theory all forms of life are entities of *ichinen sanzen*, but only the human being can reform and direct himself toward attaining Buddha-hood. Therefore, we can be born as humans in world after world and devote ourselves to the construction of a Buddha land in each lifetime. This is the greatest good fortune. According to the third chapter, *Hiyu-hon*, of the Lotus Sutra, those who slander the sutra will sometimes be born as stray dogs, emaciated and lean, hated and scorned by others. At other times they will be born as asses, destined to forever carry burdens on their backs, beaten with sticks. At still other times they will receive a serpent's body and wriggle about on their bellies, shunned. In contrast, we will always be born to live a joyful life, strolling, as it were, in the beautiful garden of our hearts, enjoying music that rings from within our lives. We are able to lead the noblest life possible. It is a remarkable achievement that deserves our most grateful thanks. It gives all the more reason to earnestly ponder what we must do in this life.

A Buddha land is not some particular part of the universe where the Buddha resides. The principle of the oneness of life and its environment teaches that the condition of a land depends on the entities who dwell there. Thus, where we pursue the truths of Buddhism with firm faith in the Gohonzon is transformed into a land of eternal enlightenment. The Buddha land is a place where master and disciple strive together in perfect unity.

"The Buddha lands throughout the universe" indicates that such lands exist everywhere in the universe. Mr. Toda used to tell us his grand view of the cosmos in a straightforward manner: "I'll continue to do *shakubuku* until we attain *kōsen-rufu* on this Earth. Then I'll go to another planet and do the same thing." According to Buddhism, the Buddha land is not limited to the Earth; it exists across the universe and throughout time.

Modern astronomy seems to endorse the Buddhist view. Scientists have asserted the possibility of cosmic dust floating between nebulae to form the building blocks of life. We may assume, therefore, that among the myriad stars many are inhabited by beings as advanced as man. This, I believe, is what "the Buddha lands throughout the universe" indicates. Be convinced that we will always be born in one or another of the Buddha lands spread throughout the universe and that there we will be able to devote ourselves to building an ideal human society.

No Enlightenment without Practice

How admirable that you have asked about the transmission of the ultimate law of life and death! No one has ever asked me such a question before. I have answered in complete detail in this letter, so I want you to take it deeply to heart. The important point is to carry out your practice, confident that Nammyoho-renge-kyo is the very lifeblood which was transferred from Shakyamuni and Tahō to Bodhisattva Jōgyō.

Nichiren Daishonin praises Sairenbō for having asked this vital question, which no one had ever asked before. Then he stresses that "the important point is to carry out your practice, confident that Nam-myoho-renge-kyo is the very lifeblood which was transferred from Shakyamuni and Tahō to Bodhisattva Jōgyō." The Daishonin thus emphasizes the importance of the seeking spirit, and at the same time gives his disciple profound guidance so that he could elevate his state of life and live the life of that spirit.

Perhaps one of the best-known stories about a seeking spirit is that of Sessen Dōji and the particular process by which he attained enlightenment. Sessen Dōji was practicing austerities in search of the Law when he heard a voice say, "All is changeable; nothing is constant. This is the law of birth and death." Certain that the verse contained the law for enlightenment he had so seriously been seeking, he beseeched the demon which appeared in front of him to tell him the rest of the verse. The demon—actually Taishaku in disguise—looked horrible and lowly. Why did Shakyamuni, in telling this story, have such an abominable creature enter the scene? It may have symbolized the many crimes and evils widespread in Shakyamuni's day. Shakyamuni may also have wanted to teach that we must seek the law on the basis of its philosophy, not on the appearance or station of the person who preaches it.

We can look still deeper into the significance of the story. The demon demanded warm human flesh as the price for its teaching. Sessen Dōji, by offering his own body to the demon, was finally able to hear the rest of the verse. This lesson could not be clearer: seekers of Buddhism should be prepared to offer even their own lives for the sake of the law. But why was it that the price was human flesh? Why did Taishaku, disguised as the demon, demand it? To find the answer, recall the latter half of the verse the demon told Sessen Dōji. It reads, "Extinguishing the cycle of birth and death, one enters the joy of nirvana." This represents extinguishing the suffering of birth and death in the phenomenal world and entering the unshakably happy state of nirvana in which there is neither birth nor death. This is a Hinayana doctrine, and it does not come anywhere near the highest teaching, the Lotus Sutra, much less Nam-myoho-renge-kyo. However, the verse contains an eternal truth in teaching us not to be blinded by births and deaths in the world, but instead to seek nirvana in the depths of those phenomena.

In order to truly understand the teaching, therefore, Sessen Dōji first had to rid himself of the tendency to cling to his physical self. This was where the demon came in. The demon appeared and demanded that Sessen Dōji give him human flesh. That demand was itself the answer to his quest. When he resolved to offer himself to meet the demon's request, he became qualified to hear the latter half of the verse or, right then and there, he attained enlightenment.

Some who heard the Buddha explain this were incapable of comprehending it. For them Sessen Dōji's act of offering his body was the substance of that teaching. The abundance of parables in the sutras reflects an attempt to make the philosophy comprehensible to all people. To go a step further, the fact that the demon would not preach the law until Sessen Dōji vowed to offer his body is saying that enlightenment lies only in practice. Aside from the degree of Sessen Dōji's enlightenment, his act tells us that Buddhism exists only within human behavior. Had he not offered his body for the sake of the law, he would not have been able to attain enlightenment, no matter how profound a teaching he came across. Without practice, no one can acquire the law of Buddhism. For Buddhism is a philosophy that was systematized only to reveal the enlightenment the Buddha attained after many long years of practice.

While it is true that Buddhism embodies a profound philosophy of life, and we must not depreciate the intellectual side, in its essence Buddhist doctrines enlarge on the Buddha's own enlightenment—enlightenment which can be acquired only through practice. Buddhism is not just a compilation of abstract, theoretical teachings. It is a dynamic guide to a better life, the way to live most humanely, and how to reform ourselves. Since Buddhism is the true way of life, we can naturally find a profound philosophy behind it. Therefore, the heritage of the ultimate law of life exists *only* within our own lives. The spirit of this Gosho lives only within a life that continues to grow from day to day and month to month.

"Nam-myoho-renge-kyo ... was transferred from Shakyamuni and Tahō" tells us that the entity of the Lotus Sutra manifested by the two Buddhas in the Treasure Tower is Nam-myoho-renge-kyo. Nichiren Daishonin was aware that Sairenbō, a former scholar of the Tendai school, tended to see only the literal interpretation of the Lotus Sutra. He reiterates here, therefore, that the ultimate of the Lotus Sutra is Nam-myoho-renge-kyo.

"The very lifeblood which was transferred . . . to Bodhisattva Jōgyō." Here again the Daishonin emphasizes the same point. Bodhisattva Jōgyō, who was entrusted with the mission of spreading the Law during the ceremony of the Lotus Sutra, is the supreme leader of propagation in the Latter Day. It follows therefore that the teaching he spreads is the one and only True Law for that age.

The Functions of the Mystic Law

The function of fire is to burn and give light. The function of water is to wash away filth. The winds blow away dust and breathe life into plants, animals and human beings. The earth nourishes the grasses and trees, and heaven provides nourishing moisture. Myoho-renge-kyo too works in all these ways. It is the cluster of blessings brought by the Bodhisattvas of the Earth.

In this passage the Daishonin explains that the functions of earth, water, fire, wind and *kū* are themselves the workings of Myoho-renge-kyo—the blessings brought by the Bodhisattvas of the Earth. Earth, water, fire, wind and *kū* are the basic constituents of all things in the universe. They are called the five elements, which by inference are represented by the five characters of Myoho-renge-kyo. *On the Ultimate Teaching Affirmed by All Buddhas* states, "When Shakyamuni Buddha was still a common mortal, at a time more distant than *gohyaku-jintengō*, he perceived that his body consisted of earth, water, fire, wind and *kū*, and he immediately attained enlightenment." "His body consisted of earth, water, fire, wind and *kū*" is another way of saying that "his body consisted of Myoho-renge-kyo."

Buddhism is in part the declaration to mankind that Myoho-renge-kyo—the ultimate law of all things—does not exist outside the phenomenal world, and the five elements that make up the physical world are themselves Myoho-renge-kyo. The Lotus Sutra teaches that this world is itself the land of eternal enlightenment, that a common mortal can attain Buddhahood just as he is, that the nine worlds and Buddhahood are mutually inclusive, and that suffering leads to nirvana. All of these are revolutionary philosophical concepts, and they all originate in this single insight that is so basic to Buddhism.

Buddhism does not exist apart from this world; any system of religious thought that evades the realities of life and concentrates on fleeting pleasures or escapism, or ends up with dreams of heavenly pastures, is powerless to help the plight of man. How should we deal with our constant, and often agonizing, reality? How should we live in the tumult of society? What can we do to open the path from chaos to a bright future? It is by seeking out answers to these questions that we can discover the revitalizing power of Buddhism. Religions that teach escapism or resignation, or religions that exist only in ceremony, are not religions in the true sense of the word.

Our movement has, from the beginning, advanced together with the masses, and today, it continues to be borne forward by a broad section of the populace. It lives among them and supports them in their sorrows and joys, sharing their sufferings and pleasures. Maintain this constant path for the Soka Gakkai, and always be proud in following it. It is the road Presidents Makiguchi and Toda built for us and led us to. No matter what others may say, let us proceed without fear along the Soka Gakkai's noble path and live the most precious life of all.

To go back to the text, the above passage enumerates the functions of the five elements. Their physical workings are exactly as the passage describes, but I feel that we must also study them in the light of the phrase, "Myoho-renge-kyo too works in all these ways. It is the cluster of blessings brought by the Bodhisattvas of the Earth."

First, consider fire. The text says, "The function of fire is to burn and give light." What does this mean for the life philosophy? A careful answer is given in the section of the *Ongi Kuden* concerning the first chapter, *Jo-hon*, of the Lotus Sutra. It states that "fire" means the fire of enlightened wisdom. "Giving light" is what wisdom does as it adapts to each new circumstance, and "burning" relates to the unchanging law of the universe. Nam-myoho-renge-kyo itself possesses both the virtue of burning and of giving light. The *Ongi Kuden* goes on to say that we who chant Nam-myoho-renge-kyo "can illuminate the darkness of suffering in life and death and can eventually see clearly the fire of nirvana's wisdom." It also says that we "can burn the firewood of desires and reveal the fire of enlightened wisdom." Since flames burn upward, fire represents Bodhisattva Jōgyō, as *jō* means "upward."

"The function of water is to wash away filth." This is the function of washing away evil karma and eliminating the five impurities of life.* It symbolizes life's innate power—coming from the Mystic Law—to purify itself. Water represents Bodhisattva Jyōgyō, *jyō* meaning to purify. The many evil deeds we committed in past existences destine us

*They are: 1) impurity of the age caused by war, natural disasters, etc.; 2) impurity of thought, or illusion, caused by confusion in philosophy and religion; 3) impurity of desires, or ugly tendencies such as greed, anger and stupidity; 4) impurity of the people, weak both physically and spiritually; and 5) impurity of life itself.

to suffer for countless lifetimes in succession. When we take faith in the Gohonzon, however, all that cumulative suffering comes to us all at once here in the present, but with far less intensity. This is the principle of lessening karmic retribution. When you flush water through an old hose, all the dirt in it is washed out the end. You may have to undergo hardship after hardship during this lifetime, but after the last dregs are purged, you will be able to live in comfort for the rest of your life and accumulate great good fortune.

Third, "The winds blow away dust" means to sweep away the difficulties that occur during our lifetime and the obstacles that try to block our path of faith. Just as the winds blow away dust and dirt, so can we clear away obstacles and difficulties by chanting powerful and resounding daimoku. The winds represent Bodhisattva Muhengyō, *muhen* meaning "without bounds." The Daishonin says that the winds also "breathe life into plants, animals and human beings." From old, wind has symbolized the vitality of nature and the universe, blowing the breath of life into all things.

Fourth, "The earth nourishes the grasses and trees" indicates the stabilizing factor of life. Just think of how life works. Nothing is more complicated or delicate. Our body, for instance, maintains a temperature that averages about 36.5°C. A fever, even if only two or three degrees above normal, feels uncomfortable. It is a wondrous system that maintains our temperature at the same level, except in times of illness, when it changes to tell us that something is wrong. The thoughts and feelings in our mind change from moment to moment, but always with well-coordinated balance. The stability-maintaining function of our mind and body represents Bodhisattva Anryūgyō, *anryū* meaning "harmonious support."

Finally, "heaven provides nourishing moisture." "Heaven" here corresponds to *kū*, the fifth element. Rather than any of the Four Bodhisattvas, it symbolizes Myoho-renge-kyo itself. Just as heaven lets life-giving rain fall upon all things, so Myoho-renge-kyo bestows its benefits on all phenomena and is the fundamental force by which they work.

A passage similar to the one above appears in the *Ongi Kuden*:

> Now Nichiren and his disciples who chant Nam-myoho-renge-kyo are all Bodhisattvas of the Earth. The benefits of the Four Bodhisattvas are as follows: The natural function of fire is to burn things [Jōgyō], that of water to purify [Jyōgyō], that of wind to blow away dust and dirt [Muhen-gyō], and that of earth to nourish plants and trees [Anryū-gyō]. The roles of the Four Bodhisattvas are not the same, but all of them are derived from Myoho-renge-kyo. The Four Bodhisattvas dwell underneath, and T'ien-t'ai's interpretation in the *Hokke Mongu* speaks of "underneath" as "the ultimate depth of life, that being the absolute reality." That the Bodhisattvas of the Earth dwell underneath means that they dwell in the truth.

Fire burns, water cleanses, wind blows away dust and dirt, and the earth supports plants—all these natural functions correspond to the functions of the Bodhisattvas of the Earth.

What is the significance of the functions of the Bodhisattvas of the Earth in terms of our daily life? To fight for happiness, consuming our own life force; to carry on the movement to purify others' lives as well as our own; to clear away the ugliness in society just as the wind blows away dust; to become an indestructible pillar in which any-one can place full confidence—all of these are the natural functions of the Bodhisattvas of the Earth.

The Bodhisattvas of the Earth need never to be told to do anything by anyone. They work spontaneously for the benefit of the people and society, upholding the philosophy of the Mystic Law. It is a natural duty, which they sense within their own lives. Where does that sense of mission come from? Where in our hearts do the Bodhisattvas of the Earth dwell? Nichiren Daishonin explains this by quoting T'ien-t'ai's words—that they dwell in "the ultimate depth of life, that being the absolute reality." In other words, the Bodhisattvas of the Earth dwell in Nam-myoho-renge-kyo, the entity which reigns over all the spiritual functions in man. By chanting Nam-myoho-renge-kyo, we bring its life force from within ourselves. We manifest the ultimate entity of our life and use our inner life force to improve our lives and society as we carry out our mission as Bodhisattvas of the Earth. In the final analysis, the functions of the Bodhisattvas of the Earth are those of Myoho-renge-kyo. So, when we manifest ourselves as the entities of Nam-myoho-renge-kyo, we become by our actions Bodhisattvas of the Earth, and we join the ranks of people who continue this unparalleled odyssey in the eternal current of life.

Mission as a Great Bodhisattva

This discussion reminds me of two episodes which Josei Toda personally experienced in prison, especially the second. On New Year's Day, 1944, he began alternately to chant daimoku and read the Lotus Sutra, visualizing the Dai-Gohonzon enshrined at the Head Temple, Taiseki-ji. At the beginning of March, he was reading the first chapter, *Toku-gyō-hon*, of the Sutra of Infinite Meaning, the sutra introductory to the Lotus Sutra itself. When he came to a twelve-line verse consisting of thirty-four negative descriptions of the Buddha's entity, he suddenly became enlightened to the truth that the Buddha is life itself. He could not repress the profound emotion which kept welling up within him. This was the first episode.

Spring went by, then the summer, and autumn was turning into winter. In the freezing cell, emaciated and weak, my master was a bag of skin and bones, but he continued his intense meditation. One day in mid-November he was going over a passage in the *Yujutsu* (fifteenth) chapter of the Lotus Sutra: ". . . All these bodhisattvas, hearing the voice of Shakyamuni Buddha preaching, sprang forth from below. Each one of these bodhisattvas was the commander of a great host, leading a retinue as numerous as the sands in sixty thousand Ganges Rivers; moreover, others led retinues as numerous as the sands in fifty thousand, forty thousand, thirty thousand, twenty thousand, ten thousand Ganges; moreover. . . ."

Before he knew what had happened, he was floating in the air. He found himself among a multitude, his palms joined together, praying to the magnificent Dai-Gohonzon. He clearly witnessed the solemn ceremony which revealed the eternity of life, and he himself was a participant. In the light of the morning sun streaming through the window into the small, wretched cell, he sat stupefied with utmost joy, oblivious of the hot tears rolling down his cheeks. "I *am* a Bodhisattva of the Earth!" No words could have expressed the profound and intense joy he experienced then. He had awakened to his mission as a Bodhisattva of the Earth. "Now I know the objective of my life," he thought resolutely to himself. "I will never forget this day. I will dedicate the rest of my life to propagating the Supreme Law."

About the same time, Mr. Toda's master, Tsunesaburo Makiguchi, breathed his last in another cell in the same prison. He was seventy-three. In spite of his advanced age, Mr. Makiguchi had never ceased fighting the suppression by the military authorities, never yielding an inch. Finally, on November 18, 1944, he died a martyr to his belief. Mr. Makiguchi died at the same time that Mr. Toda awakened to his lifelong mission.

In some cases this awakening is called second president

Toda's enlightenment. It means, however, that he attained a great awakening to his mission as Nichiren Daishonin's disciple. The prewar Soka Gakkai could also conceive of some movement for *kōsen-rufu*, but its awakening to the mission of *kōsen-rufu* was so weak that it collapsed in the face of suppression by the military authorities. Visualizing the Gohonzon in the most severe circumstances of prison, Mr. Toda chanted daimoku and awakened to his mission as a Bodhisattva of the Earth. With joy, gratitude and realization, he cried out from prison for the attainment of *kōsen-rufu*. Herein lies the profound significance of his declaration. His awakening was a single-minded devotion to *kōsen-rufu*, which would never waver in any of the storms of life. Whatever the case, this was the starting point for the Soka Gakkai's remarkable development as the organization for the propagation of true Buddhism.

In his essay, "The History and Conviction of the Soka Gakkai," my master wrote: "About the time of Mr. Makiguchi's death the number of my daimoku was approaching two million. It was then, with the mercy of the original Buddha, that I experienced a mystic state of life. From that time on I spent every day being interrogated and chanting daimoku, overjoyed that now I could understand the Lotus Sutra, whereas I had been unable to before."

It was this single, decisive moment which destined the Soka Gakkai to become the center of a multitude of bodhisattvas who would spring forth, filled with energy and potential, one after another. Mr. Toda was then forty-five. Confucius once said, "At the age of forty I was free of delusion. At the age of fifty I knew heaven's will." My master exclaimed, "It took me five years longer to dispel my delusion, but five years shorter to know heaven's will." Mr. Toda's awakening to his mission was what destined the Soka Gakkai to become the great organization following the way of the Bodhisattvas of the Earth.

In the following year, standing among the ruins of war-ravaged Tokyo, Mr. Toda took his first step in the reconstruction of the Soka Gakkai. His master had left the prison in death; the disciple left it alive. Life and death—these are the mysterious workings of life essence. President Toda's heart must have been filled with a thousand emotions, but the profundity and abundance of those feelings became the source for the growth which the Soka Gakkai has now achieved. On July 3, 1945, the day he was released from prison, the single disciple, Josei Toda, firmly pledged to his master, Tsunesaburo Makiguchi: "Our lives are really eternal, without beginning or end. I now know that we were born in this world with the great mission of spreading the seven-character Lotus Sutra in the Latter Day of the Law. What are we, then? In the final analysis, we are bodhisattvas of the essential teaching, Bodhisattvas of the Earth."

Mr. Toda's awakening that he, and his master, were Bodhisattvas of the Earth gradually found its way into the lives of individual Soka Gakkai members until they, too, awakened to the fact that they were also. However, it had not yet caused the rebirth of the organization as a whole. It was not until May 3, 1951, when Mr. Toda was inaugurated as second president, that the great awakening spread through the whole Soka Gakkai. The declaration he made in his inaugural speech was what became the core principle of the organization:

> According to the Lotus Sutra or in terms of our functions, we are Bodhisattvas of the Earth. However, from the inner viewpoint of our faith, we are kindred souls and disciples of Nichiren Daishonin. Whether we stand in the presence of all the Buddhas and bodhisattvas or in the depths of hell, we chant the Lotus Sutra of seven characters to the Dai-Gohonzon and have one thing we can be proud of—the Dai-Gohonzon within our hearts.

With that declaration Nichiren Shoshu Soka Gakkai's march

began, carrying it toward its subsequent development, a growth that has been unprecedented in the annals of Buddhism.

Life-to-Life Communication

The Lotus Sutra says that Bodhisattva Jōgyō should now appear to propagate this teaching in the Latter Day of the Law, but has this actually happened? Whether or not Bodhisattva Jōgyō has already appeared in this world, Nichiren has at least made a start in propagating this teaching.

Nichiren Daishonin knew that outwardly his behavior and practice were those of the incarnation of Bodhisattva Jōgyō. However, his inner enlightenment and his ultimate identity were those of the original Buddha. In the majority of his writings he speaks in a very roundabout way even of his outward appearance as Bodhisattva Jōgyō. He says that he was "the first to propagate," "the first to spread," and so on, without specifically identifying himself as Bodhisattva Jōgyō. According to the Lotus Sutra, the multitude of bodhisattvas of the essential teaching, who sprang forth from the earth, were so magnificent in appearance that they even eclipsed the Buddha, who was preaching the essential teaching. Among them, the leader, Bodhisattva Jōgyō, looked the most dignified of all. The Daishonin, in contrast, looked no better than a common priest. If he had claimed to be Jōgyō, the people might have become unnecessarily suspicious and create the evil cause of slandering him. This probably made him avoid a straightforward statement.

However, "Nichiren has at least made a start in propagating this teaching" clearly states that he is Bodhisattva Jōgyō himself. Consider the purposes for which Shakyamuni expounded the Lotus Sutra. One of them was to summon the bodhisattvas of the essential teaching from underneath

the earth and entrust them with propagation in the Latter
Day after his passing. Therefore, as soon as the transfer was
completed with the *Jinriki* and *Zokurui* chapters, all the
Buddhas returned to their respective lands, the Treasure
Tower vanished, and the solemn assembly returned from
the air to Eagle Peak.

Thus we are made to understand the extent Shakyamuni
went to in order to entrust the Law to the Bodhisattvas of
the Earth, especially to their leader, Jōgyō. In the Latter
Day, Nichiren Daishonin was spreading the Law which
Jōgyō should propagate. If the Daishonin were not Jōgyō
but some other person, then the ceremony of the Lotus
Sutra would have been entirely meaningless. The appearance of Tahō Buddha and all the other Buddhas throughout
the universe would have lost its significance. First, that is
impossible. Neither would the Daishonin have allowed
such a situation. It is evident, therefore, that outwardly he
was acting as Bodhisattva Jōgyō but his inner enlightenment
was that of the Buddha who established a Law powerful
enough to illuminate darkness on into eternity.

**Be resolved to summon forth the great power of
your faith, and chant Nam-myoho-renge-kyo with
the prayer that your faith will be steadfast and correct
at the moment of your death. Never seek any other
way to inherit the ultimate law and manifest it in your
life. Only then will you realize that earthly desires
are enlightenment and the sufferings of life and death
are nirvana. Without the lifeblood of faith, it would
be useless to embrace the Lotus Sutra.**

**I am always ready to clear up any further questions
you may have.**

"Be resolved" indicates the tremendous importance of the
guidance which follows. At that time Sairenbō found himself in the worst hardship imaginable, at a crucial juncture

which would determine whether he would attain enlightenment or not. The phrase "be resolved" carries with it the Daishonin's fervent wish for him to somehow inherit true Buddhism's lifeblood. The heritage of the ultimate law flows only in the lives of those who summon forth the great power of their faith and chant Nam-myoho-renge-kyo. "Summon forth the great power of your faith" is the way the Daishonin, with his entire being, encouraged the faith of this one person.

For faith to "be steadfast and correct at the moment of your death," you must have an undisturbed faith in the Mystic Law at that final moment, feel the greatest joy to have been able to embrace the Law, and end your life with the deepest satisfaction that you have nothing whatsoever to regret. Therefore, the passage as a whole urges us to pray sincerely now, while we are alive, so that everything within us centers completely on Nam-myoho-renge-kyo at the moment of our death. It also teaches us to pray with the awareness that each moment is the last moment of our life.

When we pray with such awareness, the Mystic Law will well forth from the depths of our life and merge with the Mystic Law pervading the entire universe. In this bond the ultimate law flows ceaselessly. I want you to know that there is no other way to inherit and manifest the ultimate law in your life. Only then can you, even though common mortals, be able to reveal yourselves as entities of the Mystic Law who transform earthly desires into enlightenment and change the sufferings of life and death into nirvana.

The heritage of Buddhism flows within the faith of individuals—the belief of those who chant Nam-myoho-renge-kyo with the prayer that their faith will be firm and true at the moment of their death. In Buddhism the Law is the foundation of everything. However, the Law cannot produce any value by itself. There must be people who embrace the Law and make the truth it contains part of their lives. It takes people to discover the Law, and people to convey it to others. That is why the emphasis in Buddhism on how to transmit the Law from one person to another is so strong, and that is why people are given the highest value.

Hyaku-rokka Shō (The One Hundred and Six Comparisons) states, "The Law does not spread by itself; because people propagate it, both the people and the Law are worthy of respect." *On Taking Faith in the Lotus Sutra* reads, "All the teachings of the Buddha are propagated by people. Hence T'ien-t'ai's statement, 'A person represented the Law even during the Buddha's lifetime. How, then, is it possible in the Latter Day for the Law to be worthy of respect if the person who spreads it is not?' If the Law is supreme, so is the person who embraces it. To slander that person, therefore, is to slander the Law." Here we can see the great value the Daishonin attached to people, as individuals and together.

Only one life can activate another life. The spirit of Buddhism flows in life-to-life communication, in the course of mutual help and guidance among or between people. Earlier we studied the phrase, "Thus I heard," in *The True Entity of Life*.* "I" in the phrase is Ananda, one of Shakyamuni's ten major disciples who listened to more of his master's teachings than any other disciple. In another sense, "I" denotes life. Otherwise, T'ien-t'ai would not have stated that "I heard" indicates a person who upholds the True Law. "I heard" in no way signifies the simple act of listening with one's ears. It means to accept, believe and practice the Buddha's teaching with one's entire being.

Faith's Lifeblood

In conclusion, I would like to briefly retrace the development of this Gosho to see how painstakingly the Daishonin

*See pp. 81–82.

expounded the true heritage of the lifeblood to Sairenbō. Nichiren Daishonin states at the beginning, "To reply, the ultimate law of life and death as transmitted from the Buddha to all living beings is Myoho-renge-kyo. The five characters of Myoho-renge-kyo were transferred from the two Buddhas inside the Treasure Tower, Shakyamuni and Tahō, to Bodhisattva Jōgyō, carrying on a heritage unbroken since the infinite past." Here he declares conclusively that the Law—the Gohonzon—is itself the heritage of the ultimate law.

This is the Law which flows in the depths of the people's lives. Those who chant Nam-myoho-renge-kyo are themselves the living heritage of the ultimate law. The Daishonin declares this in the statement, "Shakyamuni who attained enlightenment countless aeons ago, the Lotus Sutra which leads all people to Buddhahood, and we ordinary human beings are in no way different or separate from each other. Therefore, to chant Myoho-renge-kyo with this realization is to inherit the ultimate law of life and death."

In terms of time, the lifeblood—the mystic relationship between the Law and the lives of the people—continues eternally throughout past, present and future. "The heritage of the Lotus Sutra flows within the lives of those who never forsake it in any lifetime whatsoever—whether in the past, the present or the future." In terms of space, the heritage of the ultimate law flows within the lives of the Daishonin's disciples who, in perfect unity, chant Nam-myoho-renge-kyo and advance together toward *kōsen-rufu*. He says, "All disciples and believers of Nichiren should chant Nam-myoho-renge-kyo with one mind (*itai dōshin*), transcending all differences among themselves to become as inseparable as fish and the water in which they swim. This spiritual bond is the basis for the universal transmission of the ultimate law of life and death."

In a word, the heritage of the ultimate law flows forever

within the people's lives, from the infinite past to the eternal future. It lives vibrantly in the fusion between the Law—the Gohonzon—and the people's lives, and in the mutual recognition and encouragement of those who uphold the Law. Thus the lifeblood of Buddhism is always focused on the people, and this is the heart of Nichiren Daishonin's very being and of Buddhism for the people. It embodies a depth of compassion, therefore, which only the original Buddha could bring into being. I believe that no one, before or since, has taught anything greater.

However, whether we can inherit the lifeblood of the Daishonin's Buddhism or not depends entirely on our faith. This is why he warns us in the Gosho's conclusion: "Without the lifeblood of faith, it would be useless to embrace the Lotus Sutra." Everything depends on faith. Without faith, the heritage of the ultimate law, which was taught in such length from four viewpoints as outlined earlier, would prove to be totally false. On the other hand, *with* faith, everything the Daishonin says *can* be achieved. "Without the lifeblood of faith, it would be useless to embrace the Lotus Sutra." We cannot attain true enlightenment by the Law—the Lotus Sutra—alone. We must have the lifeblood of faith, faith which is directly handed down from the Daishonin, who knew the Lotus Sutra with his entire being and manifested the oneness of the Person and the Law. Without this faith, which establishes the living connection between the Person and the Law, it is useless to embrace the Lotus Sutra. The sentence, "Without the lifeblood of faith, it would be useless . . . ," also tells us that only through faith can we bring forth the Gohonzon's powers of Buddha and Law.

The Japanese title of *The True Object of Worship* is *Kanjin no Honzon Shō*, which means "the object of worship for attaining Buddhahood." The twenty-sixth High Priest, Nichikan Shonin, put particular emphasis on the phrase, "for attaining Buddhahood." According to the records of his lecture on this subject written by his disciples, he stated, "Engrave this phrase in your hearts as a will from me." Why did Nichikan Shonin go so far as to say that it was his will? This is because to embrace the Gohonzon is itself to attain Buddhahood, and therefore the most important practice of all. What Nichikan Shonin wanted to convey was that embracing the Gohonzon is faith. "The object of worship for attaining Buddhahood" can also be called "the object of worship for continuing one's faith."

A well-known passage in *The Real Aspect of the Gohonzon* goes, "Never seek this Gohonzon outside yourself. The Gohonzon exists only within the mortal flesh of us ordinary people who embrace the Lotus Sutra and chant Nam-myoho-renge-kyo. . . . The Gohonzon is found in faith alone." This is the Daishonin's declaration that the Gohonzon is contained only in faith. In his *Exegesis on The True Object of Worship*, Nichikan Shonin states, "If we believe and embrace this Gohonzon and chant Nam-myoho-renge-kyo, our flesh and blood is the Gohonzon of *ichinen sanzen*, the life of the original Buddha, Nichiren Daishonin." He concludes by saying, "Therefore, aspire solely to the power of the Buddha and the power of the Law, and devote yourselves to faith and practice. Do not pass your entire life in idleness and regret it for all eternity."

Thus, the sentence, "Without the lifeblood of faith, it would be useless to embrace the Lotus Sutra," is a stern reminder. Without faith and practice, we can bring forth neither the power of the Buddha nor the power of the Law, let alone manifest the object of worship of *ichinen sanzen* within ourselves. Everything boils down to the fact that the heritage is faith itself.

The ninth High Priest, Nichiu Shonin, speaks on the heritage of faith in his *Kegi Shō* (On the Formalities of Nichiren Shoshu):

Faith, heritage and the water of the Law are [ultimately] one and the same. . . . If we do not depart from the faith upheld since Nichiren Daishonin's day, our mind and body will become Myoho-renge-kyo itself. If we act contrary to it, our mind and body will remain those of an ordinary person. If we remain so, it is impossible to receive the lifeblood which enables us to attain Buddhahood in the flesh.

In his *Commentary on the Kegi Shō*, the fifty-ninth High Priest, Nichikō Hori, explains the above passage as follows:

In the final analysis, faith, heritage and the water of the Law are one and the same. Through faith the believer receives the water of the Law from the original Buddha. The water of the Law thus received flows within the believer's life, just as blood circulates within the human body. For this reason, to convey the water of the Law through faith is to transmit the heritage. Therefore, faith should never be disturbed or shaken. If it is disturbed, the water of the Law will cease to flow. Or, even if it continues to run, it will become defiled and irregular, thus cutting off the flow of Buddhism itself. As long as faith remains unshaken, the pure and immaculate heritage of Buddhism will continue to flow with vigor, no matter how many ages may pass.

Nichikō Shonin solemnly states:

Ours is the faith which has been upheld since the day of the supreme teacher of Buddhism, Nichiren Daishonin, and the founder of the Head Temple, Nikkō Shonin. Although we are disciples far removed from their time, if we follow this faith truly, our defiled minds and bodies are purified, becoming the mind and body of Myoho-renge-kyo. The two essentials of pure faith and devoted practice change our entire being. If we ignore these two and disobey the Buddha's will by following heretical or blind belief, the river of the Law will become blocked, and we will be pushed back, in mind and body, to the state of benightedness that we were in before. We will lose our right to the lifeblood which enables us to attain Buddhahood in the flesh. How pitiful that would be!

As is clear from this, the lifeblood of faith is transmitted only within the faith which has been upheld since the day of Nichiren Daishonin and Nikkō Shonin. Herein lies the vital position of the successive high priests, as the envoys of the original Buddha, who have inherited the ultimate law of life. As Nichikō Shonin stated, "the pure and immaculate heritage of Buddhism will continue to flow with vigor," the sacred life of Nichiren Daishonin flows through the lives of us, the Bodhisattvas of the Earth, as long as we maintain the correct faith and carry out activities for *kōsen-rufu*, the goal given by Nichiren Daishonin. If we lose sight of this goal, not only will the Daishonin's Buddhism be reduced to formalism, but his teachings will prove to be false.

In any event, the Gohonzon is the fundamental object of worship, the basis of everything. If one forgets that and gives more veneration to something or someone else, he is committing serious slander. It is impossible to bring the powers of Buddha and the Law forth from the Gohonzon without the lifeblood of faith. In President Toda's day there were members who overly prided themselves on having received the Gohonzon. Mr. Toda would say to them, "Without faith it is but a useless treasure. . . . You must try very hard to bind your faith directly to the Gohonzon. Otherwise you will only invite great misery." Just as he had warned, quite a few of those members were later very sorry that they had not had stronger faith.

Nichikō Shonin implies that we should learn about faith through the spirit of Nichiren Daishonin and Nikkō Shonin. We of the Soka Gakkai study the Daishonin's Gosho, engrave Nikkō Shonin's *Twenty-six Precepts* in our hearts, and work to attain *kōsen-rufu* under the guidance of the High Priest, never begrudging even our lives. Only within such faith can the lifeblood of the original Buddha flow strongly.

The Original Buddha's Conviction

With my deep respect,
Nichiren, the *Shramana* of Japan
The eleventh day of the second month in the ninth
year of Bun'ei (1272)

I want to say a few words about the date on which the Daishonin wrote this Gosho. On the same day, as if by coincidence, internal strife broke out. He had predicted this and warned the government about it in the *Risshō Ankoku Ron* (On Securing the Peace of the Land through the Propagation of True Buddhism) in 1260, and again during the Tatsunokuchi Persecution on September 12, 1271. The prophecy came true, as the Daishonin states in the *Letter from Sado* written on March 20 the same year:

> Now, twenty-six years since the battle of Hōji, the Kamakura government is again plagued by internal strife. Rebellions have already broken out twice on the eleventh and the seventeenth day of the second month of this year.... The current rebellion is what the *Yakushi* Sutra means by "the disaster of internal strife." The *Ninnō* Sutra states, "When the sage departs, the seven types of calamity will invariably arise.".... Nichiren is the pillar, sun, moon, mirror and eyes of the ruling clan of Kanto. On the twelfth day of the ninth month of last year when I was arrested, I boldly declared that if the country should lose Nichiren, the seven disasters would occur without fail. Didn't this prophecy come true just sixty and then one hundred fifty days later?

The rebellion was engineered by Hōjō Tokisuke against his half-brother, Regent Hōjō Tokimune. Tokisuke headed the Rokuhara government in Kyoto, an agency of the Kamakura shogunate. He attempted to usurp the regency from his brother, but Tokimune discovered the plot beforehand. Taking the initiative, the regent sent troops and killed

Noritoki, Morinao and the other suspected plotters. Mortal combat continued between the members of the same clan until Tokisuke's faction was totally annihilated. The incident is called the February Disturbance.

The Daishonin had sensed that internal strife was imminent about a month before the incident. Immediately after the Tsukahara Debate on January 16, he pointed this out to Honma Rokurōzaemon and warned him about it. Therefore the Daishonin, while writing this Gosho, must have had a premonition that the whole country was being jolted by the terrible strife. Nevertheless, looking out over the future, he calmly wrote this Gosho in order to leave his heritage for the perpetuation of the Law. His deed also demonstrates that the more agitated the world is, the more important it becomes to establish an unshakable foundation.

Shramana is a Sanskrit word meaning a humble seeker of the Way or one who masters the true law and denounces evil laws. Thus, it means a person who leaves his family to practice Buddhism. When the Daishonin wrote *The True Object of Worship* in April 1273, he signed it, "Nichiren, the *Shramana* of this country." At the end of *On the Buddha's Prophecy*, written in intercalary May 1273, he wrote, "Written by Nichiren, the *Shramana* of Japan."

"The *Shramana* of this country" stands in contrast to "*Shramana* of T'ien-t'ai,*" which the monks of the Tendai sect in Japan called themselves. It expresses the Daishonin's conviction and indicates that Japan was the country in which the original Buddha made his advent to save mankind for all eternity. The original Buddha was Nichiren Daishonin himself, for he mastered the Law of supreme righteousness in the Latter Day, and dedicated himself to refuting all evil laws. The *Shramana* of Japan, as he called himself, is synonymous with the Buddha of the Latter Day, as he states in the *Ongi Kuden*, "The Buddha of the Latter Day is the common mortal, the common priest. . . . He is called a

Buddha, and he is called a common priest."

I close here. But my eternal friends, have faith and know that what our organization is doing, each hour, each day, each decade, and the activities of all members toward the goal of *kōsen-rufu* are together the heritage of the ultimate law of life and death. Always with this conviction, let us move forward together along the path of faith toward the glorious twenty-first century.

THREE

The True Object of Worship

Gosho Text

Question: You have not yet fully answered my question about the mutual possession of the Ten Worlds.

Answer: The *Muryōgi* Sutra states: "[If you embrace this sutra,] you will naturally receive the benefits of the six *paramitas* without having to practice them." The *Hōben* chapter of the Lotus Sutra says: "They wish to hear the teaching of perfect endowment." The Nirvana Sutra states: "*Sad* indicates perfect endowment." Bodhisattva Nagarjuna comments: "*Sad* signifies six." The *Daijō Shiron Gengi Ki* (Annotation of the Four Mahayana Theses) states: "*Sad* connotes six. In India the number six implies perfect endowment." In his annotation of the Lotus Sutra, Chia-hsiang writes, "*Sad* means perfect endowment." The Great Teacher T'ien-t'ai remarks: "*Sad* is a Sanskrit word, which is translated as *myō*." An arbitrary interpretation of these quotations may distort their meaning, but in essence they mean that Shakyamuni's practices and the virtues he consequently attained are all contained within the single phrase, Myoho-renge-kyo. If we believe in that phrase, we shall naturally be granted the same benefits as he was.

With full understanding of Shakyamuni's teachings, the four great men of Learning said: "We have gained the supreme cluster of jewels when we least expected it." They represent the world of Learning that is within ourselves. The *Hōben* chapter states: "At the start I pledged to make all people perfectly equal to me, without any distinction between us. By now the original vows that I made have already been fulfilled. I have led all the people onto the path of Buddhahood." The enlightened life of Shakyamuni Buddha is our own flesh and blood. His practices and resulting virtues are our bones and marrow. Chapter Eleven of the Lotus Sutra says: "Those who choose to protect this sutra serve Tahō Buddha and me. . . . They also serve all the other Buddhas present who dignify and glorify all the worlds." Shakyamuni, Tahō, and all the other Buddhas in the ten directions represent the world of Buddhahood within ourselves. By searching them out within us, we can receive the benefits of Shakyamuni, Tahō, and all the other Buddhas. This is what is meant by the following passage in Chapter Ten: "If one hears the Law for even a single moment, he will be able to attain perfect enlightenment."

The *Juryō* chapter reads: "The time is limitless and boundless—a hundred, thousand, ten thousand, hundred thousand nayuta aeons—since I in fact attained Buddhahood." Present within our lives is the Lord Shakyamuni who obtained the three enlightened properties of life before *gohyaku-jintengō*, the original Buddha since time without beginning. The *Juryō* chapter states: "Once I also practiced the bodhisattva austerities and the life which I then acquired has yet to be exhausted. My life will last yet twice as many aeons from now." He was speaking of the world of Bodhisattva within ourselves. The Bodhisattvas of the Earth are the followers of Lord Shakyamuni in our lives. They follow the Buddha just as T'ai-kung and Tan, the Duke of Chou, served as ministers to King Wu of the Chou dynasty and later assisted his son and successor, the infant King Ch'eng; or just as Takeshiuchi served Empress Jingū and later her grandson Crown Prince Nintoku as a highly valued minister. Bodhisattvas Jōgyō, Muhengyō, Jyōgyō and Anryūgyō represent the world of Bodhisattva within our lives. The Great Teacher Miao-lo declares: "You should realize that our life and its environment are the entity of *ichinen sanzen*. When we attain Buddhahood, according to this principle, our life pervades the entire universe both physically and spiritually."

Lecture

Prime Point of Faith

Throughout the world, members of the Soka Gakkai observe 1978 as the second "Year of Study." It seems especially suitable to begin the year by studying together a passage from *Kanjin no Honzon Shō* (The True Object of Worship). As he made clear in this treatise, Nichiren Daishonin inscribed the Gohonzon (the object of worship) to save all people in the Latter Day of the Law. This is an article of faith for us, and a doctrinal pillar of our belief. I give this lecture in the light of guidance received from High Priest Nittatsu, who alone carries the heritage of Nichiren Shoshu.

By way of introduction, let me expand upon the meaning of *kanjin no honzon*, which might be literally rendered as "the object of worship for the observation of one's mind." In this, or any, discussion, we must never lose sight of our single most important truth: the ultimate principle of Buddhism is Nam-myoho-renge-kyo of the Three Great Secret Laws, and Nichiren Daishonin embodied it as the object of worship so that all succeeding generations could attain Buddhahood. The prime point of our faith and practice is that object of worship, and throughout the Latter Day of the Law, no other principle can lead us to Buddhahood.

Honzon, or object of worship, means something which one reveres above all, something to which one devotes one's life. The Daishonin expounded in the *Ongi Kuden* (his oral teachings of the Lotus Sutra, compiled by Nikkō Shonin): "*Nam* derives from Sanskrit and signifies devotion. There are two objects of devotion: the Person, which is Shakyamuni, and the Law, which is the Lotus Sutra." The Daishonin used "Shakyamuni" and "Buddha" to mean exactly the same thing whenever he talked about the Lotus Sutra from the viewpoint of his own enlightenment. In the above quotation "Shakyamuni" indicates not Gautama Buddha of India, but the original Buddha who revealed the supreme teaching of Nam-myoho-renge-kyo as hidden within the *Juryō* chapter of the Lotus Sutra. If the original Buddha appeared in the Latter Day of the Law as Nichiren Daishonin, then what is the Lotus Sutra referred to in the passage above? It is not the twenty-eight-chapter Lotus Sutra expounded by Gautama Buddha, for the Daishonin wrote in *Reply to Lord Ueno*, "Now in the Latter Day of the Law neither the Lotus Sutra nor the other sutras are valid. Nam-myoho-renge-kyo alone is valid." Whenever the Daishonin speaks of spreading the Lotus Sutra in the Latter Day, he means the essence of the sutra, Nam-myoho-renge-kyo. Thus, "devotion to Shakyamuni and the Lotus Sutra" means "devotion to Nichiren Daishonin and Nam-myoho-renge-kyo."

As you read through the Gosho you will find that, depending on the situation, the Daishonin sometimes explains the object of worship in terms of the Person and at other times in terms of the Law. The following passages speak of the object of worship in terms of the Person: "The object of worship in the *Juryō* chapter is Shakyamuni, the Buddha appearing in this world who has possessed the three enlightened properties of life* since time without beginning" (from *On the Three Great Secret Laws*); "Throughout the world as

*The property of the Law (*hosshin*), the property of wisdom (*hōshin*) and the property of action (*ōjin*). *Hosshin* is the truth of a Buddha's life; *hōshin*

well as in Japan all people should revere Shakyamuni of true Buddhism as the object of worship" (from *Requital for the Buddha's Favor*).

On the other hand, *Debates on the Object of Worship* discusses the object of worship in terms of the Law. It reads, "Question: What should common mortals in the evil-filled Latter Day of the Law take as their object of worship? Answer: They should make the daimoku of the Lotus Sutra their object of worship." By "the daimoku of the Lotus Sutra" the Daishonin means the Law of Nam-myoho-renge-kyo.

The Daishonin describes the object of worship alternately as the Person and the Law in order to clearly establish that the Person and the Law are united in the Gohonzon; or, the Person is the Law, and the Law is the Person. Nam-myoho-renge-kyo is the life of Nichiren Daishonin, and he embodied it in the form of a mandala. That is the Gohonzon. The *Ongi Kuden* passage quoted above assumes the oneness of the Person and the Law, as the Daishonin declares elsewhere in the same Gosho: "The supreme title of the Buddha who is originally endowed with the three enlightened properties of life is Nam-myoho-renge-kyo."

With regard to the unity of the Person and the Law embodied in the Gohonzon, the Daishonin states in *The Real Aspect of the Gohonzon*: "The Great Teacher Dengyō wrote, 'The entity of *ichinen sanzen* is the Buddha who obtained enlightenment for himself, and that Buddha assumes no august attributes.' Therefore this Gohonzon is the supreme mandala never before known, for it has not appeared until more than twenty-two hundred and twenty years after the Buddha's death." "*Ichinen sanzen*" represents the Law, and the "Buddha," enlightened to the Law,

---

is the wisdom to perceive the truth; while *ōjin* is the merciful actions of a Buddha to save people and the physical body which manifests the Buddha's life in this world for that purpose.

represents the Person—the Buddha is one with the Law.

Here we can conclude that Nichiren Daishonin realized that he himself was the Buddha who embodied the Mystic Law. He was also the Buddha endowed with the three enlightened properties of life. In the *Ongi Kuden*, he identified that Buddha, as the votary of the Lotus Sutra in the Latter Day of the Law, to be himself. The Daishonin embodied his enlightened life in the form of the Gohonzon.

Reply to Kyō'ō, which was sent to Shijō Kingo and his wife, reads: "I, Nichiren, have inscribed my life in *sumi*, so believe in the Gohonzon with your whole heart. The Buddha's will is the Lotus Sutra, but the soul of Nichiren is nothing other than Nam-myoho-renge-kyo."

Believing wholeheartedly in the teaching contained in these passages, we worship the Gohonzon as the manifestation of Nichiren Daishonin's life. With this conviction, it is possible to say that Nichiren Daishonin resides even today within the Grand Main Temple at Taiseki-ji—as the Dai-Gohonzon of the High Sanctuary. The successive high priests of the Head Temple are entitled to transcribe the Dai-Gohonzon so that the Gohonzon is enshrined at temples, community centers and individual homes throughout the world. There is no need to lament not being alive during the lifetime of Nichiren Daishonin, nor should anyone regret not living near the place where the Daishonin made his advent and where the Dai-Gohonzon exists. More importantly, I would like you to be assured that no matter the place or age in which you live, so long as you embrace the Gohonzon and pray to it, you are in the eternal land of the Buddha. Be convinced that you rise with the Buddha every morning and you spend all day, every day, together with the Buddha.

If the Gohonzon is Nichiren Daishonin's life, and if the Gohonzon embodies the oneness of Person and Law, then the Daishonin embodied the same fusion within himself.

Hence, the Gohonzon is the entity of *ichinen sanzen*. As Dengyō stated, "The entity of *ichinen sanzen* is the Buddha who obtained enlightenment for himself," and Nichiren Daishonin is that Buddha.

It is extremely difficult for an ordinary person to try and fathom the Daishonin's spirit and behavior, but I would venture to guess that the life-or-death struggle he fought—and won—over twenty years, from the time of his declaration of true Buddhism until the Tatsunokuchi Persecution and the Sado Exile, confirmed to himself his identity as the object of worship in the form of the Person. By confronting and overcoming terrible, continuing persecutions, the Daishonin lived out all the predictions in the Lotus Sutra of the trials that those who propagate the Mystic Law in the Latter Day are destined to meet.

In the *Hosshi* (10th) chapter of the Lotus Sutra we read, "Since hatred and jealousy abound even during the lifetime of the Buddha, how much worse will it be in the world after his passing?" The *Hōtō* (11th) chapter mentions "the six difficult and nine easy acts," and the *Kanji* (13th) chapter contains a twenty-line verse which describes the three powerful enemies.* To have actually lived the sutra's words during his activities as its votary reconfirmed the Daishonin's realization that both the originally enlightened Buddha indicated in the sutra and the entity of *ichinen sanzen* revealed during the ceremony in the air† are his own life.

A passage in *The Opening of the Eyes* says, "Although Nichiren's knowledge of the Lotus Sutra is ten million times less than that of either T'ien-t'ai or Dengyō, his perseverance and supreme compassion are awe-inspiring." Because of his supreme compassion to save all people from their suffering, the Daishonin endured the worst sort of adversity for more than twenty years. Persecutions began

*See page 54.
†See page 29.

from the moment he engaged in the propagation of the Mystic Law. In Buddhism, opposition by those in power is traditionally considered the most severe and unpredictable of the "three powerful enemies." The Daishonin incurred the wrath of that enemy when he first remonstrated with the government, submitting his treatise, *Risshō Ankoku Ron* (On Securing the Peace of the Land through the Propagation of True Buddhism). Problems might never have arisen had the Daishonin not translated his boundless compassion into action. As he later wrote in the Gosho, "My present exile is not because of any crime." He did not incur the anger of the government for breach of law or custom, but because he expressed his compassion through his actions. The government's fear of him only reflected the magnitude of the actions he took.

Observing One's Mind

We, his disciples who live true Buddhism throughout the world, are heir to his great compassion, and so we, too, will inevitably encounter some opposition. We must encourage each other to grow strong with the conviction that the validity of our Buddhist faith and practice will be borne out only when we unflinchingly persevere through all circumstances.

By surviving the Tatsunokuchi Persecution and the Sado Exile, Nichiren Daishonin fulfilled all the predictions of the Lotus Sutra as Bodhisattva Jōgyō, and then he revealed his identity as the original Buddha. It was after Tatsunokuchi and before Sado that he inscribed the first Gohonzon.

The invincible life-condition of the original Buddha was already within the depths of his being. The late president Josei Toda, in a lecture on a passage of *Letter to the Priests of Seichō-ji*, stated that when the Daishonin, as an acolyte at that temple, prayed to Bodhisattva Kokūzō to become the wisest man in Japan, he already realized that he was the original Buddha.

Actually, the Daishonin could not have declared the beginning of true Buddhism at the age of thirty-two had he not attained the necessary life-condition. He knew all too well that the age of the Latter Day of the Law had already come, when prophecy foretold a decline in the power of Shakyamuni's Buddhism; he knew it would have been entirely inappropriate to bring back Shakyamuni's Buddhism as a new set of beliefs. He was able to bring to the people a totally new kind of Buddhism because he was convinced of his identity and his mission to save all people of the Latter Day of the Law. Still, the Daishonin manifested himself as the original Buddha only after living to the letter the predictions in the Lotus Sutra for a period of some twenty years. After the incident at Tatsunokuchi and banishment to Sado, he cast off the transient identity as an envoy of the Buddha and actually declared his true identity as the original Buddha.

Nichiren Daishonin inscribed the Gohonzon so that all generations born in the Latter Day could attain Buddhahood. His own contemporaries were personally able to experience his greatness, and because he was naturally bound to die, he inscribed his own life in the form of the Gohonzon for posterity. We often think of the Gohonzon as a physical representation of the Law, but it is actually the embodiment of both the Person and the Law. "Nam-myoho-renge-kyo, Nichiren" is boldly inscribed down the center of the Gohonzon; "Nam-myoho-renge-kyo" is the Law, and "Nichiren" is the Person.

The Daishonin considered the fundamental quality of the Gohonzon to be the oneness of Person and Law. But how should we, who worship the Gohonzon, consider it? According to the Daishonin we should take the viewpoint of *kanjin*, literally, to see one's mind; hence the title of this work on the Gohonzon, *Kanjin no Honzon Shō.*

What is the meaning of *kanjin*? A passage from this Gosho says, "*Kanjin* means to observe one's own mind and to find the Ten Worlds within it." The Daishonin added that just as a person cannot see his own face without a mirror, one cannot see the Ten Worlds in his own mind without the mirror of Buddhism. Another passage in the same Gosho reads, ". . . various sutras make reference here and there to the six paths and the four noble worlds [that constitute the Ten Worlds], but only in the clear mirror of the Lotus Sutra and T'ien-t'ai's *Maka Shikan* (Great Concentration and Insight) can one see his own three thousand conditions— the Ten Worlds, their mutual possession, and the thousand factors."

As is clear from this passage, *kanjin* means to see *ichinen sanzen*, three thousand potential states, in a momentary existence of life. Yet, *ichinen sanzen* is the truth of one's life, confined to the realm of theory. The Daishonin concludes that Nam-myoho-renge-kyo is the concrete entity of *ichinen sanzen*, the ultimate reality containing three thousand potential states of life. Therefore, "to observe one's own mind and to find the Ten Worlds within it" means perceiving one's life to be the entity of Nam-myoho-renge-kyo.

A human being in any one of the Ten Worlds has the ultimate entity, Nam-myoho-renge-kyo, in the depths of his life. The theoretical teaching of the Lotus Sutra tells us, in fact, that each individual human being is originally an entity of the Mystic Law. In the core of the theoretical teaching, the *Hōben* chapter, is the phrase, "all phenomena reveal the true entity." Nichiren Daishonin construes that phrase as expressing the ultimate truth. That is why he brings it into *The True Entity of Life*, in the following way: "All beings and their environments in any of the Ten Worlds, from Hell at the lowest to Buddhahood at the highest, are, without exception, the manifestations of Myoho-renge-kyo. . . . All phenomena are themselves manifestations of Myoho-renge-kyo. This is the meaning of 'all phenomena reveal the true entity.'"

The existing fact that every individual person is inherently the entity of the Mystic Law is not the same as the actual attainment of Buddhahood. If it meant Buddhahood, then there would be no difference between the Buddha and the common man, nor would there be any need for Buddhist faith and practice. The question is whether or not each individual awakens to the realization that he or she is an entity of the Mystic Law. The *Kanjin no Honzon Shō* describes the attainment of the supreme state of Buddhahood in one's own life. When people awaken to their true entity, they attain Buddhahood; one who does not remains an ordinary mortal. This is, as you know, what the Daishonin means in *The True Entity of Life*: "There is a clear distinction between a Buddha and a common mortal, in that a common mortal is deluded while a Buddha is enlightened. The common mortal fails to realize that he himself possesses both the entity and the function of the Buddha's three properties."

A passage occurs in *On Attaining Buddhahood*: "If you wish to free yourself from the sufferings of birth and death you have endured through eternity and attain supreme enlightenment in this lifetime, you must awaken to the mystic truth which has always been within your life. This truth is Myoho-renge-kyo. Chanting Myoho-renge-kyo will therefore enable you to grasp the mystic truth within you."

To "awaken to the mystic truth which has always been within your life," and to realize that you have always been Nam-myoho-renge-kyo, is to attain supreme enlightenment. Awakening to the fact that you are the entity of the Mystic Law is to observe your own mind (*kanjin*). *Kanjin*, then, ultimately means attaining Buddhahood.

Thus, the object of worship "for the observation of one's mind" exists so that the people in any of the Ten Worlds can see themselves as the entity of the Mystic Law and attain Buddhahood. No matter what one's life-condition is, the Gohonzon enables anyone and everyone to equally attain Buddhahood, or enlightenment. This became possible for the first time when Nichiren Daishonin established the object of worship.

Faith Means Embracing

You may perhaps know that when the twenty-sixth High Priest, Nichikan Shonin, explained how to read the title, he said, "Consider the word *for* your inheritance from me." His definition was, of course, intended to refute misinterpretations, such as "observing the object of worship *in* one's mind" or "observing one's mind *through the treatise on* the object of worship."

More important, he declared that the Gohonzon is "the object of worship *for* observing one's mind," not "the object of worship as a theoretical truth." The latter title relates to theoretical revelation of *ichinen sanzen*, the surface realization gleaned from the Lotus Sutra, or "Buddhism of the harvest." Shakyamuni's Buddhism of the harvest means that he expounded his enlightenment as an effect, while the Daishonin's philosophy, Buddhism of the seed, teaches the cause of enlightenment and instructs the common mortal in his quest for the ultimate state of life. In contrast, Shakyamuni's object of worship is expounded in the literal interpretation of the Lotus Sutra. "The object of worship for observing one's mind" is the actual embodiment of *ichinen sanzen*, or Buddhism of the seed, which was revealed in the depths of the Lotus Sutra.

The vital point here is that the inscription by Nichiren Daishonin of the object of worship is the embodiment of *ichinen sanzen*, as he himself revealed in order to sow the seeds of enlightenment. Shakyamuni Buddha's object of worship is theoretical *ichinen sanzen*, expounded so that others might reap the harvest of enlightenment.

This is a vast subject, actually. All religions have objects of worship that are usually expressions or symbols of some supernatural or external power governing life and human destiny. People have a subservient attitude in prayer when asking for salvation, forgiveness and compassion, or in some cases, try by subservience to satisfy those powers and avoid their wrath. Such attitudes have contributed to creating the special position of the clergy as intermediaries between man and his object of worship. The pursuit of external objects symbolizing the supernatural inevitably leads to the formation of a strict hierarchy in the religious world. This extended to the secular world, where the aristocracy, especially chieftains and kings, were often said to be sanctioned by the divine grace, which led to rigid social stratification as well. That is why so many religious groups developed negative, inhumane ideas about human dignity and equality.

The "theoretical *ichinen sanzen*" revealed in Shakyamuni's Buddhism of the harvest is completely different from those established religions. However, since Shakyamuni expounded his enlightenment as an effect, his object of worship became separated from common mortals still suffering in delusion. The enlightened were inevitably regarded as special and ideal, much removed from the lives of ordinary people. Consequently, this type of view drives people into the same pitfalls encountered in other religions. T'ien-t'ai's Buddhism provides a good example of this. It was based on the Buddhism of the harvest and became a religion of the privileged class. It was inevitable that it would appeal only to emperors, nobles and distinguished individuals, and alienate the common people.

In contrast, "the object of worship for observing one's mind" is the life of *ichinen sanzen*, the source of enlightenment. According to Nichikan Shonin, the "observation of one's mind" in this context is the *kanjin* of the ordinary people. "The object of worship for observing one's mind," therefore, does not exist outside our lives; it is identical to the Mystic Law which has always dwelt in the lives of all people. That is why the Daishonin declares that there is no distance between the object of worship and people. A person need only chant daimoku to the Gohonzon morning and evening to awaken in his being the entity of the Mystic Law.

Such awakening needs sufficient wisdom, however. The Lotus Sutra tells us that "faith is the key to wisdom." One must "use faith instead of one's limited understanding" and "gain entrance through faith." Nichiren Daishonin redefines "faith" in concrete terms as "embracing" the Gohonzon. To "embrace" the Gohonzon is to observe one's own mind, that is, to awaken to the fact that you yourself embody the Mystic Law. This is what we call *juji soku kanjin*, embracing the Gohonzon is in itself enlightenment.

Finally, I want to discuss *kanjin no honzon* in relation to the Three Great Secret Laws. Three comprise the Gohonzon which is the object of worship of the supreme teaching; chanting daimoku with firm faith in the Gohonzon; and *kaidan*, the sanctuary of the supreme teaching, which is the place where the Gohonzon resides. In essence, however, all three are contained in the One Great Secret Law: the Gohonzon—the object of worship for observing one's mind. The object of worship of the supreme teaching is the life of the Buddha of absolute freedom who is in perfect harmony with the universe. The daimoku of the supreme teaching is Nam-myoho-renge-kyo—the name of the original Buddha enlightened in the three properties of life. That is why Nichiren Daishonin stated in the *Debates on the Object of Worship*: "They should make the daimoku of the Lotus Sutra the object of worship."

Similarly, *dan* of *kaidan* (literally, sanctuary for ordination) is the Chinese translation of the Sanskrit *mandala*, and essentially it means that the Gohonzon is the "sanctuary." The idea of sanctuary has its origin in ancient India, from the altar that was set up as a place where priests received precepts. It is said that the Four Heavenly Kings* were positioned at the four corners of the sanctuary to ward off demons, and a statue of the Buddha was enshrined in the center to dignify the ceremony for priests taking vows.

Various people flanked the Buddha to indicate his status. As the Daishonin stated in *The True Object of Worship*, the Buddha who preached the Hinayana sutras was flanked by Mahakashyapa and Ananda; when expounding provisional Mahayana and the theoretical teaching of the Lotus Sutra, he was flanked by Bodhisattva Monju and Bodhisattva Fugen.

The object of worship, to which the original Buddha is central, is flanked by Shakyamuni Buddha and Tahō Buddha, who are again flanked by the Four Great Bodhisattvas. Unknown in the Former and Middle Days of the Law, this object of worship is the Gohonzon which Nichiren Daishonin established to enable all people to see the truth of their lives. As High Priest Nittatsu has declared, this Gohonzon *is* the High Sanctuary. Therefore the Dai-Gohonzon is called "the Gohonzon of the Three Great Secret Laws" and, again, that is why all three can be identified with the One Great Secret Law.

Clearly, then, the Gohonzon of the Three Great Secret Laws is the Dai-Gohonzon of the High Sanctuary that Nichiren Daishonin inscribed on October 12, 1279. As he revealed in *On Persecutions Befalling the Buddha*, that was the

---

*Jikokuten (Skt., Dhritarashtra), Kōmokuten (Virupaksha), Bishamonten (Vaishravana) and Zōchōten (Virudhaka), lords of the four heavens, said to live halfway down the four slopes of Mt. Sumeru. Their respective functions are to protect the world, to discern evil and punish those who commit evil, to listen to the sutras and protect the place of practice, and to relieve people of their sufferings. In the *Darani* (26th) chapter of the Lotus Sutra, they pledged to protect those who embrace the sutra.

purpose of the Daishonin's advent. With the inscription of the Dai-Gohonzon, the great law was established to save all mankind throughout all time.

Nichikan Shonin made the following statement about the greatness of the Dai-Gohonzon:

> This is the origin of all Buddhas and sutras and the place to which they return. The blessings of the myriads of Buddhas and sutras throughout space and time, without a single exception, all return to this Gohonzon, which provides the seed of Buddhahood and is hidden in the sutra, just as the tree's hundreds and thousands of branches and leaves all return to the same root. This Gohonzon provides great and boundless benefits. Its mystic functions are vast and profound. So if you take faith in this Gohonzon and chant Nam-myoho-renge-kyo even for a while, no prayer will go unanswered, no sin will remain unforgiven, all good fortune will be bestowed, and all righteousness proven.

Let us all know only the greatest joy in being able to see the Dai-Gohonzon, and never faltering, let us practice our faith all the more intensely until we realize with invincible conviction that to embrace the Gohonzon is to attain Buddhahood. Let us strive to propagate the great law wherever it is in our power to do so, and thus achieve utmost fulfillment in our lives. Deepening our faith this year, let us study harder than ever before and work courageously in our activities for *shakubuku* so that this year will be one of pride and confidence.

Attitude toward Study

This is one of the most important passages of this treatise, centering on the principle that "embracing the Gohonzon is attaining Buddhahood." First, I urge you to learn the attitude you should take toward reading and studying this writing. Nichiren Daishonin himself discussed this in his cover letter dated April 26, 1273—one day after he wrote *The True Object of Worship*. I would like to look especially at those passages which relate to this subject.

In the beginning of his letter the Daishonin expressed his thanks for gifts—summer kimono, *sumi* inksticks, writing brushes—and stated: "I have written down some of my thoughts concerning the true object of worship and I am sending the treatise to you [Toki], Ōta, Soya and the others." Because he deliberately said "*some* of my thoughts," one may get the impression that this treatise is relatively insignificant. It is his modesty, however, that made him speak so casually of one of his most vitally important teachings, into which he poured his heart and soul. "It concerns a very important matter, the purpose of my advent. Only those who are strong in faith and open-minded should be allowed to read it." He warns that the content of the treatise demands serious reading, because it is a statement of his own enlightened life-condition.

He knew that Toki, Ōta, Soya and the others mentioned in the letter were strong in faith, and therefore he allowed them to read the treatise. Nichiren Daishonin strictly warned them to allow "only those who are strong in faith and open-minded" to share it—those who thoroughly believe in the Daishonin and persist in faith throughout their lives without faltering, no matter what happens to them.

Let me stress two relevant points in your study: (1) Strengthen your faith so that you can carry it out throughout your life, and (2) sharing the great life force and compassion of the original Buddha, Nichiren Daishonin, develop an unquenchable passion for propagation in this age.

The cover letter also states, "The treatise contains much criticism and few answers. What it reveals, however, has never been heard of before, and it is bound to startle those who read or hear of it. Even if you show it to others, never let three or four persons read it together at a time."

In the history of Buddhism the ultimate truth, the ultimate order, was considered to "beggar all description and defy all imagination," lying beyond the reach of human words and intellect. Even less conceivable was the possibility that it might materialize in a tangible form. But Nichiren Daishonin embodied it as the Gohonzon so that all people could comprehend the truth by chanting daimoku to it. That the Gohonzon actually did become a material reality is so difficult to believe or understand that neither existing knowledge nor human reasoning can explain it. Nichiren Daishonin knew that something so incredible would only create suspicion, and that might develop into disbelief and slander, eventually dooming many to the pit of hell. That is why he warns: "Never let three or four persons read it together at a time."

Saying, "Only those who are strong in faith and open-minded should be allowed to read it," the Daishonin stressed that only believers who can discuss it together frankly should be allowed to do so. When Nichikan Shonin lectured on *The True Object of Worship*, he began by confirming the real meaning of the Daishonin's strict warning. Then he said, sensing the bond among his listeners that united them in the same goal and strong, seeking faith, "I feel as if all of you, more than forty people, were one person."

The same is true of ourselves. We are a body of believers who have single-minded faith in the Gohonzon, and united we are working to achieve the noble goal of *kōsen-rufu*. Moreover, I am convinced that Nichiren Daishonin would feel tremendous joy in knowing that such a great number of people, who have pure faith and unity, read and study a work that reveals his innermost enlightenment.

Nichiren Daishonin closed the letter by saying: "In the twenty-two hundred and twenty odd years since the Buddha's passing, the ideas contained in the heart of this treatise have never been revealed before. Despite all the official persecutions befalling me, I expound it now at the beginning of the fifth half-millennium, when the time is ripe for its propagation. I hope those who read it will remain firm in their faith so that both master and disciples can climb Eagle Peak together to pay their respects to Shakyamuni, Tahō, and all the other Buddhas in the universe."

The great compassion in this work, the Daishonin's indomitable efforts to leave this letter to posterity even in the face of such severe trials as a government exile to Sado Island, never fails to move me when I read it. He wrote it even while day and night he was hounded by followers of heretical sects, such as Nembutsu, trying to take his life. The quality of the paper of the original text, which consists of seventeen pages, differs between the first and second halves, and the Daishonin had to use both sides of the paper, testifying to destitution so severe he could not even obtain the necessary brushes and paper. No difficulty was too much, however; he encouraged anyone who read the letter to carry out his faith and attain Buddhahood no matter what, since he was emerging into the very core of Buddhism.

The so-called "three Buddhas"—Shakyamuni Buddha, Tahō Buddha and all the other Buddhas in the universe— also stand for the three properties of the Buddha—the property of the Law, the property of wisdom, and the property of action. They also represent the Buddha with the three enlightened properties of life. "To pay their respects to the three Buddhas" means to awaken to the truth that you are the Buddha with the three enlightened properties, that is, to attain Buddhahood. To "climb Eagle Peak" means that by attaining Buddhahood, our environment also becomes the Buddha's land, clearly signifying the oneness between human life and its environment.

The text we are studying now is just a part of the whole treatise, *Kanjin no Honzon Shō*, or *The True Object of*

Worship, but because it is the most essential, we can discover the essence of the entire writing by studying it. It is important to be aware that Nichiren Daishonin wrote this treatise during his exile to Sado Island. The Daishonin revealed the object of worship amidst great persecution, and in so doing he taught us the principle of Buddhism: difficulties or obstacles lead us to enlightenment. To me, the profound meaning contained in the treatise comes through powerfully when I consider the period in his life from the time of this writing to the inscription of the Dai-Gohonzon.

The Gohonzon we revere embodies the original Buddha's life-condition, exalted far above any persecution resulting from the devilish nature hidden in the government authority. When we pray to the Gohonzon, therefore, we are taking our difficulties and making them the cause for human revolution. Studying *The True Object of Worship* has taught me how inexorably true that is, and that is why I urge you to study it also, and preserve your faith and keep it always strong, no matter what the circumstances, so that you can fill the pages of your life with satisfaction and meaning.

The Seed of Wisdom

Question: You have not yet fully answered my question about the mutual possession of the Ten Worlds.

"Embracing the Gohonzon is attaining Buddhahood" is the central principle of true Buddhism, as well as the most important teaching in *The True Object of Worship*. Nichiren Daishonin uses questions and answers to bring out the meaning of this teaching. In the section that precedes the question quoted above, he posed another question: it is difficult to believe and understand that the sacred life of a Buddha exists within all ordinary people. In summary, the Buddha's benefit, power, wisdom and dignity are so magnificent, vast and profound that it is inconceivable for us, ordinary mortals, to possess the same supreme condition of life.

In answer to this question, Nichiren Daishonin quotes passages from sutras. A passage from the *Muryōgi* Sutra, which opens the Lotus Sutra, states that the king of all Buddhas and the queen of the Lotus Sutra join together to give birth to a bodhisattva. The *Fugen* Sutra, which closes the Lotus Sutra, states: "This Mahayana sutra is the treasure, the eye and the seed of life for all Buddhas in the universe throughout the past, present and future." They are saying that the fortune and virtue of the Buddha are boundless, his wisdom fathomless, and his power vast, but there is some seed, or cause, which has given birth to them all.

According to the pre-Lotus Sutra teachings, attaining each of the Buddha's attributes—fortune, virtue, power, wisdom— requires its own corresponding Buddhist austerity. One had to be born over and over again for an unimaginably long period of time to carry out these austerities. This process is like the growth of a tree. Whereas the provisional sutras attempt to analyze each leaf and branch, the Lotus Sutra looks at the seed, the origin of the branches and the leaves. The statement in the *Muryōgi* Sutra, "Infinite meaning derives from the one Law," is the declaration that the one Law produces infinite fortune and wisdom. The *Fugen* Sutra states that the fortune, virtue and wisdom of all Buddhas are derived from the one original law, but it is the Lotus Sutra that makes the definitive statement. Further- more, what the sutra has revealed as the Law, that is, the original seed, is the title of the sutra—Myoho-renge-kyo, or ultimately Nam-myoho-renge-kyo.

To embrace Myoho-renge-kyo is to embrace the seed of all Buddhas. If Nam-myoho-renge-kyo is planted in the life of a common mortal, he will be endowed with all the fortune, virtue and wisdom of the Buddha; and when it is nurtured with care he will eventually reap the fruit of the benefits and wisdom of Buddhahood. This is the meaning of *juji soku kanjin*: embracing the Gohonzon, the embodiment of Nam-myoho-renge-kyo, is attaining Buddhahood. In any case, the above-quoted passage, "Question: You have not yet . . . ," seeks a definitive answer to the preceding doubt about the possibility of Buddhahood inherent in all people. The questioner demands a full explanation, so that he can dispel all his doubts about the mutual possession of the Ten Worlds.

Human Attributes

Answer: The *Muryōgi* Sutra states: "[If you embrace this sutra,] you will naturally receive the benefits of the six *paramitas* without having to practice them."

The sentence quoted in the answer appears in the explanation of the seventh of the ten "mystic powers of benefit contained in this sutra" mentioned in the *Muryōgi* Sutra. Needless to say, because the *Muryōgi* Sutra is an introduction to the Lotus Sutra, "this sutra" means the Lotus Sutra, specifically its title, Myoho-renge-kyo. The passage that includes the quoted sentence reads as follows:

> If good people, men and women alike, hearing this sutra either during the Buddha's lifetime or after his departure, rejoice, believe and develop a seeking spirit; if they embrace, read, recite, copy, preach and practice its teaching; if they aspire to Buddhahood, manifest all the good properties of life and foster a spirit of great compassion; and if they wish to save all people from suffering, they will naturally receive the benefits of the six *paramitas* without having to practice them; they will awaken to the law of eternity in themselves; all their delusions of life and death and earthly desires will be immediately destroyed, and they will rise to the seventh stage of bodhisattva practice.

If you carry out faith for others as well as for yourself with joy, seeking spirit and gratitude, you will naturally develop and manifest the benefits of the six *paramitas*, even though you do not practice all those that are essential to the bodhisattva austerities. This is because "this sutra" or Myoho-renge-kyo contains the treasures of all the Buddhas.

Let me elaborate on the six *paramitas*. They are six different kinds of practice which the bodhisattvas of Mahayana Buddhism were required to carry out in order to attain Buddhahood. There is even a whole sutra that specifically deals with them alone, and they have been the essential practice in Mahayana Buddhism since ancient times. *Paramita* is a transliteration of the Sanskrit and stands for "salvation" or "reaching the other shore." "This shore" is the human life-condition, ridden by suffering and illusion, whereas the other shore is nirvana, or the life-condition of enlightenment. Each of the six *paramitas* must be practiced in order to cross over to the other shore of enlightenment. Do not overlook this point: this passage of the *Muryōgi* Sutra teaches us that those who embrace the Mystic Law do not have to practice the six *paramitas* as austerities, but that they will naturally acquire all the benefits which would follow from their practice.

Then, what do the six *paramitas* stand for? Frankly, I think we can say that they represent the attributes which make human beings truly "human." Throughout the ages men have pondered human attributes, and the pursuit of the truth of humanity has spurred men to think, to probe, to write, and countless minds have groped for answers. I think the six *paramitas* are, in a sense, a systematic answer to their vital quest. They are also the sure guideline for our movement toward human revolution, toward the reformation and completion of an individual self. In short, they provide us with the goals of our human revolution.

The first of the six *paramitas* is almsgiving. There are

three kinds of almsgiving: the almsgiving of treasure, which means material offerings; the almsgiving of the Law, which means preaching and teaching of the Law; and the almsgiving of fearlessness, which means to remove fear and give peace of mind. I will not go into detail, but let me simply remind you that material offerings are not the only means of giving alms. Buddhists place greater emphasis on preaching and teaching of the Law, or removing fear and giving peace of mind.

Material offerings limit salvation to a short period of time. Since material things are limited, they cannot offer complete salvation. Take a famished person, for example. If you give him bread, he can survive only another day. Instead, if you teach him practical skills, he can work and survive throughout his life without being hungry. This is, in a general sense, the almsgiving of the Law. For those who sink into despair so deep that they lose the will to live even when they can earn a living, it is necessary to give alms in the form of fearlessness, since it removes fear and anxiety and gives them hope and peace of mind.

In Beethoven's remarks about "joy through suffering," we can be uplifted. His words become, in effect, the almsgiving of fearlessness. The almsgiving of treasure causes a person to rely on another and tends to deprive him of his spirit of independence, whereas the almsgiving of the Law and of fearlessness brings the spirit and ability of independence. Remember that in Buddhism the almsgiving of the Law and of fearlessness is of utmost importance. As we practice our faith, *shakubuku*, lectures and guidance to introduce and explain Buddhism to others are the almsgiving of the Law, which includes the almsgiving of fearlessness.

Once you embrace the Mystic Law, the practice of almsgiving requires courage. Of course, the spirit of Buddhism is basically compassion, but the late president Toda used to say, "We are common mortals. Even though you talk about practicing compassion, it is easier said than done. Courage goes hand in hand with compassion. Courage leads to compassion." Your courageous and imperturbable work for propagation, in the face of the rough waves which may assail you, is itself the practice of compassion. Keep in your mind the Daishonin's words, "You cannot be cowards and still be Nichiren's disciples," and advance fearlessly in propagation.

The second of the six *paramitas* is the keeping of precepts. In Buddhism "precept" is construed as "to stem injustice and to stop evil," meaning to extirpate evil karma created by thought, word and deed, and to interdict Buddhists from all vices. Precepts were originally laid down as norms for those who practiced Buddhism. But since priests who renounced the secular life represented those who practiced Buddhism in its early days, precepts were actually laid down as rules to regulate their collective life. That is why they are generally complicated and cover all aspects of life. As the ages passed and situations changed, people began to find it impossible to carry out the precepts. In fact, they gradually became more harmful to human nature than beneficial. This is why Hinayana Buddhism, which is mainly predicated on precepts, passed into oblivion in the Middle and Latter Days of the Law in China and Japan.

This simply explains the fallacy in thinking that precepts postulated under certain circumstances in a certain society can be applied without revision to people in different circumstances. According to the original purpose of precepts, on the contrary, different precepts should be laid down to fit new circumstances.

As the principle of the mutual possession of the Ten Worlds shows, the human mind contains both vice and virtue. A passage of *Treatment of Illness* reads:

Good and evil have coexisted in human life since time immemorial. According to the provisional teachings and

the sects based on them, both good and evil remain in
one's life through all the grades of the bodhisattva practice
up to the stage of *tōgaku*, the one just below Buddhahood.
Then only the people at and below *tōgaku* have some faults
or other. In contrast, the Hokke sect based on the Lotus
Sutra reveals the principle of *ichinen sanzen* and shows that
both good and evil are inherent even in those at the highest
stage of *myōkaku*, or enlightenment. The fundamental
nature of enlightenment manifests itself as Bonten and
Taishaku, whereas the fundamental darkness manifests itself
as the Devil of the Sixth Heaven.*

The Daishonin says that even a Buddha has all of the Ten
Worlds and is the entity of *ichinen sanzen*. The Buddha
possesses the life-conditions of Hell, Hunger, Animality and
Anger. Much more so in the case of ordinary people. These
evil natures are always trying to manifest themselves. They
are linked with the basic instincts of material existence, the
fundamental motivation for human survival, and therefore
their workings are most likely to dominate. Learning,
Realization and Bodhisattva, on the contrary, which represent the good side of life, work to transcend ugly characteristics deeply embedded in our life, and thus they have to
work against the instinctive human tendency toward evil.
It is like trying to counteract the law of gravitation.

Constant effort and precaution are necessary therefore to
prevent yourself from gravitating toward your evil nature,
like walking on the edge of a cliff. To keep the precepts
is like steering a car safely through on a dangerous road.

Generally speaking, duties which one imposes on himself
of his own will can be considered precepts. The French
writer Romain Rolland wrote in his *Vie de Beethoven*:
"Often he spoke of the duty which he imposed on himself

*Most powerful of the devils, who dwells in the highest of the six
realms of the world of desire. He works to prevent believers from practicing Buddhism and delights in dominating people at his will.

to act by means of his art 'for poor humanity, for humanity to come,' to help humanity, to restore human courage, and to shake people off from their sleep and cowardice. He wrote to his nephew, 'Our time needs mighty spirits to lash into action these wretched, beggarly human souls.' "* The duty Beethoven imposed on himself was a precept for his own life. In modern terms, a precept is self-restraint or self-control, and in that sense it is a vital requisite of man.

The third of the six *paramitas* is perseverance. If you try to scale the highest summit of the human life-condition called Buddhahood, you should naturally be prepared for thorny roads on the way. A proverb says, "It is easy to overcome a robber in the mountains, but difficult to subdue one in the heart." Indeed, the sutras contain innumerable stories about how those who practiced Buddhism had to persevere through great hardships and overcome huge obstacles. The difficulty in perseverance comes out sharply in the story of Shariputra. In his past existence he gave up practicing his faith when he could not bear seeing one of his eyes being thrown away after he had given it to a Brahman as alms.

Shakyamuni Buddha faced and persevered through horrendous persecutions, which are known as "the Nine Great Persecutions." A passage of *On Zenmui Sanzō* states: "The Buddha, as he made his advent in this world, was named Shakyamuni, which means perseverance. He did not censure but forbore the slanders of all the people." In the Gosho, *On Four Kinds of Gratitude*, is the passage: "This world is called *saha* which means 'enduring.' This is why the Buddha [born in this world] is named Shakyamuni [perseverance]." Nichiren Daishonin stressed forbearance as one of Shakyamuni's most important characteristics.

Nichiren Daishonin, the Buddha of the Latter Day

*Translated from *Vie de Beethoven* (Paris: Librairie Hachette, 1920), p. 72.

of the Law, more than anyone else truly and completely epitomized perseverance as he lived through persecutions even greater than anything that befell Shakyamuni Buddha. He made his advent in this evil Latter Day to save the people who slander true Buddhism. Hence the prediction of the Lotus Sutra, "Since hatred and jealousy abound even during the lifetime of the Buddha, how much worse will it be in the world after his passing?"

What I have been talking about so far is the discussion of perseverance in relation to the Buddhist austerities and practice. Broadly speaking, life in this world as a human being is always accompanied by experiences which are undesirable, laborious and painful. But how pitiful are those who take their own lives when they find life unbearable!

We must work together to remove the sources of pain and suffering from our society so that people can be happy in life, and much more, we must try to eliminate the stupidity of fighting and abusing each other. Nonetheless, you must realize that despite your efforts, unavoidable suffering will follow you throughout life. It is vital that man persevere through his suffering, and to bear all hardship and pain in order to live the justice he espouses. This vital requirement is what the third of the six *paramitas* teaches us.

The fourth of the six *paramitas* is assiduity. It means to give utmost effort, both physical and spiritual, in practicing ceaselessly the five *paramitas*, including the following two, meditation and wisdom. Assiduity here means to practice ceaselessly.

I would like to expand on this subject in terms of the way we live. Since we are heir to joy, anger, sorrow and pleasure, all of us are naturally imperfect. A true religion does not suppress and mold these subtle human emotions into a fixed pattern, but cherishes each emotion as it sends the courage and vitality to live directly into the heart, the mother of emotions. Imperfection can even be a positive attribute. Since the human being is imperfect, he needs a progressive spirit, and progress gives meaning to existence. If human beings do not make efforts to advance, human society will be plagued by Animality and Anger. That is why assiduity is so crucial. A top can stand on its tip because it spins rapidly; a bicycle maintains balance when it moves ahead. The same is true of human beings. Have you ever noticed the vibrant voice and fresh, glowing complexion of those who are trying to advance and progress?

The fifth of the six *paramitas* is meditation, implying concentration on the contemplation of truth. Shakyamuni Buddha gives us a typical example of this *paramita* of meditation or mental concentration. Abandoning severe ascetic practices, bathing in the Nairanjana River and having gruel offered by Sujata, Shakyamuni was purified both physically and spiritually and entered meditation under the Bodhi tree. Later on, the Great Teacher T'ien-t'ai of China established the idea of *isshin sangan* (the wisdom to see the Three Truths in view of the momentary existence of life) and *ichinen sanzen* (three thousand conditions in a momentary existence of life), stressing specifically the practice of meditation. That is why his teachings are generally referred to as "the Buddhism of the meditation of the mind and the Law."

As has been stated so far, meditation is a vital form of practice which is the final stage of Buddhist austerities. It is also one of the vital requirements for human existence. What is meditation? In a broad sense it is having goals and ideals to achieve, something fundamental to use as a guide for life. Without clear goals and a secure foundation, both the "perseverance" and "assiduity" will eventually be frustrated. Even if "perseverance" survives frustration, a person will eventually end up feeling a sense of aimlessness and futility. First President Tsunesaburo Makiguchi maintained imperturbable mental and spiritual calm even when he was in prison. His exalted life-condition shines through a passage in a letter he sent to his family from prison:

> Unlike the time when I was in the custody of the Metropolitan Police Department, I now live alone in a three-*tatami*-mat room, and as long as I can read, I feel comfortable and satisfied. Please keep our home secure without worrying about me. . . . In this solitary prison cell, which I feel is for the better, I am able to dedicate myself to contemplation. I strictly observe morning and evening gongyo, and I never neglect making a special prayer. . . . Faith is first and foremost for both you and me. Even though this is an ordeal it pales into insignificance before Nichiren Daishonin's. Forge your faith all the more strongly. I think it totally inappropriate to lament the present hardship, for we live bathed in vast and boundless blessings. As the sutras and the Gosho teach us, we will certainly see later on through experience that "poison never fails to turn into medicine."

President Makiguchi's clear mind and sublime attitude are a good example of the meditative spirit that comes of living the cause of Buddhism, despite persecution.

People's minds are unstable, and vulnerable to changing situations and groundless rumors, because of their lack of the fundamental guidelines—the composure of "meditation." As a result, entire societies lose sight of the humanistic way of life and end up hurting and killing one another. The history of humankind has demonstrated the deplorable propensities of man, confirming my belief that we can best contribute to lasting peace through propagation of true Buddhism, the only faith that gives human beings a fundamental support from within.

The last of the six *paramitas* is wisdom, wisdom which enables one to master all the laws, remove deluded views and perceive truth as it is. The ultimate goal of Buddhist practice is to achieve Buddhahood. Buddha means an awakened or enlightened one, that is, a person who has awakened and attained wisdom. This is made clear by the original Sanskrit word *Buddha* which derives from *budh*, meaning enlightenment or perfect wisdom. Hence, another title of the Buddha is the Enlightened One.

Enlightenment or wisdom in contemporary language is often used to mean specific knowledge in physics, economics, mathematics, or any other field. In contrast to that kind of wisdom, which differs according to the field, the ultimate wisdom that is the source of and embraces them all, is the wisdom the Buddha possesses. That is why the Buddha's wisdom is called *anuttara-samyak-sambodhi* in Sanskrit. *Anuttara* means to be supreme, the highest; *samyak* stands for equity and impartiality as well as purity and all-inclusiveness, and *sambodhi* connotes full awakening or unsurpassed wisdom. The Sanskrit phrase as a whole means "the supreme and all-inclusive wisdom and the supreme and impartial awakening."

Wisdom, as the last of the six *paramitas*, means then the ultimate awakening or wisdom in Buddhism. Generally applied to ways of living, however, wisdom has also been considered a fundamental attribute for man in all times and places. In the contemporary Western world, human beings are categorized as *Homo sapiens*, to distinguish them from the earlier *Pithecanthropus* and *Homo erectus*. While *Homo sapiens* means one who has sagacity, intelligence and wisdom, in ancient India people called human beings *manusha* or "thinking human," for they regarded wisdom as the characteristic of man.

By means of wisdom human beings have been able to grasp myriads of phenomena and have understood the law of causality which governs them. This understanding has enabled them to foresee what will ensue from a given phenomenon and how to prepare for it. Thus, wisdom has enabled human beings to gain the power necessary to protect themselves from the menaces of nature and to harness those forces for constructive purposes. In fact, biologically speaking, human beings, feeble and fragile as they are, have continued to survive until the present age by virtue of their wisdom.

On the other hand, man, who has conquered all other living beings with his powerful intellect, now sets about to destroy nature and even jeopardize his own existence. At this crucial point our lives depend on controlling and reorienting the destructive power of knowledge by the wisdom of the internal self, which springs from the depths of life. It is Buddhism which gives us the wisdom of the innermost self. That is why I cannot overstress the need to recognize that Buddhist wisdom is the highest requirement for contemporary mankind.

To Embrace Is to Attain

We have seen so far that the six *paramitas* deal specifically with the requirements necessary for human beings to live as "humans." Other philosophies and religions have merely preached them separately, but the six *paramitas* must be expounded as a whole. Stressing only one or two of them will lead to an impasse, or to partiality and dogmatism. Following only the *paramita* of almsgiving or altruism, most people, since they live in the realities of life, will give in to resignation. The practice of keeping precepts alone will kill a progressive spirit, lead to stagnation and spiritual distortion. The attachment to forbearance alone will open the way to evil and vice, and assiduity alone will lead one to trample on others. Meditation alone will remove one from the realities of life and might lead to self-righteousness. Similarly, wisdom independent of the other *paramitas* will allow a person to grow crafty and sly.

In order for human beings to live as "humans," therefore, these requirements must be fulfilled at the right time and in the right place. In this sense, the fact that the six *paramitas* were given together is truly significant; but what is vitally important is the phrase of the *Muryōgi* Sutra, ". . . you will naturally receive the benefits of the six *paramitas*." To paraphrase that, when you embrace the Mystic Law, you will naturally receive the benefits of the six *paramitas* in their entirety. And Myoho-renge-kyo is the entity which harmoniously manifests all the requirements revealed in the six *paramitas*.

The six *paramitas* as taught in this context originally mean the practice of bodhisattvas who aspire for Buddhahood, but more fundamentally, they mean that the Ten Worlds and the three thousand conditions are all contained in the single law of Myoho-renge-kyo, and that each of them manifests itself in the right place and time. Anyone can experience all of the Ten Worlds and the three thousand conditions, and in order for human beings to live in the ideal human condition, every one of them is necessary. When the integration of the Ten Worlds breaks down, one's existence becomes restrictive and discordant, giving rise to sorrow and pain.

Nam-myoho-renge-kyo is the power that contains and integrates all things. A passage of this *True Object of Worship* states:

> The true object of worship is described in the ceremony of the transmission as follows: "In the air above the *saha* world [which the Buddha of the essential teaching identified as the pure and eternal land], Nam-myoho-renge-kyo appears in the center of the Treasure Tower with Shakyamuni and Tahō Buddhas seated to the right and left, and the Four Bodhisattvas of the Earth, led by Jōgyō, flank them. . . ."

Without Nam-myoho-renge-kyo, every one of the Ten Worlds, which originally possesses the Ten Worlds within itself, becomes disintegrated from the others, causing people to suffer from pain and solitude. As described above, however, once it is predicated on the Law of Nam-myoho-renge-kyo, all the workings of human life, from Hell to Buddhahood, are oriented so they can manifest their original qualities and naturally work for the well-being of humanity. That is why Nam-myoho-renge-kyo is called "the perfect and full teaching."

When you base your life on the Gohonzon, your life will be neither frustrated nor led into an impasse, and you will naturally receive all the benefits which would ensue from the practice of the six *paramitas*. A human life which becomes one with the Mystic Law through chanting also simultaneously comes into perfect harmony with the great cosmic life, and this invigorated life will turn all obstacles into springboards for growth and dynamically change negative situations into positive ones.

All our behaviors are oriented in the right direction so that they can manifest themselves as the intrinsic workings of our essential life—Nam-myoho-renge-kyo. A passage of the Gosho reads: "Nam-myoho-renge-kyo is like the roar of a lion. What sickness can therefore be an obstacle? . . . Wherever your daughter may frolic or play, no harm will come to her; she will be free from fear like the lion king." This passage implies the life-condition of the original Buddha, but even we ordinary people will eventually be able to attain the same state of mind if we continue to practice faith on the basis of the Gohonzon. This is what is meant by "you will naturally receive the benefits of the six *paramitas*."

The late president Josei Toda said, "In order to help people achieve the unrestricted state of mind that will allow them to live as they wish in the great ocean of benefits, I will fight, donning the robe of forbearance and wielding the sword of compassion." I pray that you will all construct your lives so that you can derive great benefits and deep satisfaction.

The Teaching of Perfect Endowment

The *Hōben* chapter of the Lotus Sutra says: "They wish to hear the teaching of perfect endowment." The Nirvana Sutra states: "*Sad* indicates perfect endowment." Bodhisattva Nagarjuna comments: "*Sad* signifies six." The *Daijō Shiron Gengi Ki* (Annotation of the Four Mahayana Theses) states: "*Sad* connotes six. In India the number six implies perfect endowment." In his annotation of the Lotus Sutra, Chia-hsiang writes, "*Sad* means perfect endowment." The Great Teacher T'ien-t'ai remarks: "*Sad* is a Sanskrit word, which is translated as *myō*."

In this passage Nichiren Daishonin expands on the preceding sentence quoted from the *Muryōgi* Sutra. Here he refers to sentences from sutras, treatises and annotations to demonstrate how the Gohonzon, the embodiment of Nammyoho-renge-kyo, possesses in itself all practices and their resulting virtuous effects.

The quotation from the Lotus Sutra refers to the question which Shariputra, representing the audience, asked the Buddha. In answer, the Buddha explained the purpose of a Buddha's advent in this world—to open and reveal the Buddha-wisdom, for the sake of all people, and then to let them realize that wisdom and enter the state of Buddhahood. This means precisely to let people attain the law of the supreme vehicle. The Lotus Sutra in its entirety reveals this law, which is Myoho-renge-kyo. The entity of "the teaching of perfect endowment" Shariputra asked about is, therefore, Myoho-renge-kyo.

The Daishonin devotes the rest of the passage to the Sanskrit word *sad*, translated as *myō* of Myoho-renge-kyo, meaning endowment and the number six. The title of the Lotus Sutra reads *Saddharma-pundarika-sutra* in Sanskrit, and

Kumarajiva translated it as Myoho-renge-kyo. Nichiren Daishonin interprets Nam-myoho-renge-kyo in his *Ongi Kuden*: "In Sanskrit it reads *Saddharma-pundarika-sutra*, which is translated here as Myoho-renge-kyo. *Sad* is myo, *dharma* ho, *pundarika* renge, and *sutra* kyo."

The annotation, rendered by the Chinese Buddhist scholar Hui-chun, explains why the same Sanskrit word *sad* assumes the dual meaning of "endowment" in the Nirvana Sutra, and "six" by Bodhisattva Nagarjuna. In ancient India the number six was considered synonymous with perfect endowment. This was probably because the people in ancient India used the number six as the basis of their numerical notation. Even now many numerical systems throughout the world are based on the senary system, including the duodecimal demarcation of the day, the twenty-four hours of the day, the twelve months of the year, the three hundred and sixty degrees of the circle, the zodiac, the dozen and so forth. The enduring prevalence of these traditions testifies to the profound significance of the number six.

The Mystic Law is inherent in all things because it embodies the law of life present in all phenomena of the universe. The Gosho, *On the Mongol Emissary*, reads: "The texts of non-Buddhist philosophies and the Hinayana or provisional Mahayana scriptures of Buddhism explain but parts of the law of life. They do not elucidate it as does the Lotus Sutra." The Lotus Sutra brings out "life" in its totality, while the other sutras and non-Buddhist scriptures explain life only in its individual aspects. All philosophies, whatever their sources may be, are explanations of some part of the Mystic Law, and they are therefore infused with new life when their practice is based on the Mystic Law. The six *paramitas* symbolize the causes and the beneficial effects of Shakyamuni's Buddhism. They are incorporated into Myoho-renge-kyo, which establishes the totality of life, of which nothing is independent.

Boundless Benefits of the Gohonzon

An arbitrary interpretation of these quotations may distort their meaning, but in essence they mean that Shakyamuni's practices and the virtues he consequently attained are all contained within the single phrase, Myoho-renge-kyo.   If we believe in that phrase, we shall naturally be granted the same benefits as he was.

Here the Daishonin concludes that embracing Myoho-renge-kyo is attaining Buddhahood.   This is by far the most important part of this treatise.   He was reserved in his personal interpretation and gave priority to sutras, treatises and annotations.   This passage tells us the ultimate truth of Buddhism, the way by which all human beings can attain Buddhahood in this lifetime.   Thus he lets us see the vast powers and virtues of the Gohonzon which we worship every morning and evening.   That is why Nichikan Shonin, the twenty-sixth High Priest, explains the Gohonzon in *The Exegesis of The True Object of Worship*:

> This Gohonzon provides great and boundless benefits. Its mystic functions are vast and profound.   So if you take faith in this Gohonzon and chant Nam-myoho-renge-kyo even for a while, no prayer will go unanswered, no sin will remain unforgiven, all good fortune will be bestowed, and all righteousness proven.

President Josei Toda quoted this passage at every opportunity to give encouragement to those who struggled with sickness and poverty.

"An arbitrary interpretation of these quotations may distort their meaning" applies, more than anyone else, to me, for I am lecturing on the treatise.   If I ineptly interpret it, I might incur the Daishonin's rebuke.   I sincerely hope you will burn this passage into your hearts and that you will repay Nichiren Daishonin for his great compassion in embodying Myoho-renge-kyo as the Gohonzon for us to worship.

This passage has profound significance, but first let me explain it literally. It means that all the virtues Shakyamuni Buddha attained through practices in past existences and all the benefits he acquired through his efforts to save people after attaining Buddhahood in this life are contained in Myoho-renge-kyo. By embracing this Mystic Law, therefore, we will naturally receive all his virtues and benefits.

"Shakyamuni" and "his practices and the virtues he consequently attained" in the above-quoted passage can both be interpreted in many ways and contain various meanings, however. Nichikan Shonin classifies them into six categories in *The Exegesis of The True Object of Worship*. "Shakyamuni" here refers to the six types of the Buddha. Shakyamuni Buddha revealed himself in different ways according to the depth of his teachings, as he expounded *zōkyō* (Hinayana teachings), *tsūgyō* (lower provisional Mahayana teachings), *bekkyō* (higher provisional Mahayana teachings) and *engyō* (true Mahayana). *Engyō* indicates the Lotus Sutra which consists of the theoretical and the essential teachings. The Buddha's five appearances in the *zōkyō*, *tsūgyō*, *bekkyō* and the two halves of the Lotus Sutra fall under the category of Shakyamuni's Buddhism, while Nichiren Daishonin reveals his identity as the Buddha of the Latter Day who expounds Nam-myoho-renge-kyo— the ultimate law of life hidden in the depths of the *Juryō* (sixteenth) chapter of the Lotus Sutra. In this connection, the Daishonin is also called "Shakyamuni," expounded in the in-depth interpretation of the Lotus Sutra.

"Shakyamuni's practices and the virtues he consequently attained" in the Gosho text not only refers to the aspects of Shakyamuni mentioned above, but also any other Buddha.

That is why Nichikan Shonin states in his *Exegesis of The True Object of Worship*:

> The practices of all Buddhas and all their resultant virtues are contained in the five characters of the Mystic Law. The benefits of the Gohonzon are therefore vast and boundless. Its mystic functions are vast and profound. Any mention of Shakyamuni in the passage therefore represents all Buddhas and the virtues they attained.

The Gohonzon, then, is the treasure into which the practices and virtues of all Buddhas throughout space and time are condensed. Its mystic function envelops the universe.

How Shakyamuni Buddha practiced Buddhism and how he attained Buddhahood is explained in the question posed in the passage preceding the text. Though Shakyamuni is thought to have attained enlightenment in India at the age of thirty, his practice of Buddhism spanned the period of *sanzen-jintengō*, during which he practiced Buddhism as Prince Nōse, Bodhisattva Judō, King Shibi and Prince Satta, and made offerings to many other Buddhas. The joy he felt after he attained enlightenment under the Bodhi tree defies description.

In the essential teaching of the Lotus Sutra, the Buddha said that his enlightenment occurred during the time of *gohyaku-jintengō*, proving that he practiced the bodhisattva austerities before that time. The virtues he attained are incomparably greater than those he enjoyed after attaining Buddhahood in his life in India, as he describes: "Appearing in the worlds throughout space, I expounded all of the sacred teachings and enlightened myriads of people." Even in the capacity of the Buddha who attained Buddhahood in this life, his past practices were extremely severe, as are shown in the examples of Sessen Dōji* and Gyōbō Bonji.

*See pp. 177–79.

I would like to say something about Makasatta (Prince Satta), who is mentioned elsewhere in this Gosho. An unimaginably long time ago there lived a king named Makarada, who had three princes, Makahanara, Makadaiba and Makasatta. One day the king took them to the countryside, and while walking in a great bamboo grove they met an injured tigress. She seemed seriously hurt and unable to hunt, though famished. Seven baby tigers, about a week old, surrounded her. Makahanara said, "The tigress bore seven babies and is now so hungry that she will probably even devour her babies before long." Whereupon Makadaiba grew sad, saying, "The poor tigress will die. I wonder if we could do anything to save her." Listening to his elders, Makasatta thought, "My flesh and blood is destined to perish, even though it is reborn a hundred and thousand times. It will simply perish without benefiting anything. Therefore I will discard my life this moment."

After his father and elder brothers left, he took off his clothes and threw himself before the famished tigress. Undoubtedly frightened by his bold attitude, the tigress did nothing but growl. Then, he climbed up to the top of a nearby cliff and again he threw himself down before the tigress. But the tigress was too emaciated to prey upon him. Finally he used his last ounce of energy to stab a decayed bamboo stalk into his carotid artery. Sucking the fresh blood which gushed out, the famished tigress quickly regained her vitality and devoured the prince, leaving nothing but his bones.

Telling the story to his disciple Ananda, Shakyamuni Buddha identified the prince as himself in a past existence dedicated to the Buddhist practice of almsgiving. The story is known as "Discarding Life for the Tiger." The *Konkōmyō* Sutra describes the scene as the prince gave up his life at that moment:

All of a sudden the earth jolted in six different ways, rising and falling like waters fanned by a gale; the sun lost its brilliance as if in a total eclipse; the heaven showered all kinds of flowers and fragrances, which, falling in mixture, filled the forest, and the heavenly beings all extolled him in chorus.

This is one of the stories which testify to the extreme severity of practice Shakyamuni carried out before he attained enlightenment. All these practices, however, constitute only a part of the vast and boundless benefit of the Mystic Law.

The benefit Shakyamuni attained through his practices shows clearly the working of the law of cause and effect expounded in his Buddhism, and how the present effect is always the result of a past cause. President Toda often drew an analogy to the Jōhari Mirror when he talked about this subject. The mirror hung in the palace of King Emma, and was also called the Mirror of Karma. When King Emma interviewed the deceased he said, "You have done this much wrong while you were alive, haven't you?" But the deceased tried to deny it, "I have done nothing of the sort, I can assure you, sir." The king retorted, saying, "Take a look in the Mirror of Karma over there!" Much to his surprise, the deceased could see all the evils he committed when he was alive in the mirror.

This story is not a mere moral; by drawing an analogy it teaches us that the law of cause and effect which governs life is totally immutable. President Toda said: "In this *saha* world it is our physical existences and situations which constitute the Mirror of Karma. The karma we created in our past existences causes us to feel karmic retribution, both physically and spiritually, in this world."

This is the real nature of human life, from which no one can escape. Any attempt to avoid it is fruitless. That is why Shakyamuni Buddha preached the importance of dedicating ourselves to Buddhist practice, lifetime after lifetime, in order to expiate all the sins and vices we committed.

So far, our discussion has been focussed on the literal meaning of the passage of the Gosho text. Let us take the same passage and apply it to Nichiren Daishonin. We know from *The One Hundred and Six Comparisons* that he is the eternal Buddha who originally possesses boundless benefits including all the virtues which result from the practices of all Buddhas as "the master of the True Cause and True Effect." When Nichikan Shonin explains that Shakyamuni, as he appears in the Gosho text, stands for all Buddhas and the virtues they attained, he is telling us that Nichiren Daishonin possesses the endowments of all Buddhas. The Daishonin combined all the benefits of his virtuous deeds into the Gohonzon of the Three Great Secret Laws. He declares in the Gosho, "I, Nichiren, have inscribed my life in *sumi*, so believe in the Gohonzon with your whole heart. The Buddha's will is the Lotus Sutra, but the soul of Nichiren is nothing other than Nam-myoho-renge-kyo." This declaration substantiates the Gohonzon, identifying it with his life itself. As he ushered in the rising sun of a new Buddhism, the moonlight of Shakyamuni's Buddhism faded, giving way to an epoch-making event in both the history of Buddhism and the history of mankind.

I would like to talk about the law of causality working within life, in terms of the True Cause and the True Effect, which, as I pointed out in my lecture on *The One Hundred and Six Comparisons*, provides a valuable vantage point from which to expand on the profound significance of the Gohonzon. I will not go into the original meaning of the True Cause and the True Effect now, but elaborate on them as two different ways to view human life.

Life exists in a moment. The moment flashes by like an arrow and becomes the past. The future becomes the present in the same moment. Thus, life exists only in succession of moments, and even eternity is no more than the continuation of moments. In any given moment we can feel happiness, misery, hope or despair.

The law of cause and effect governs life at each moment, and the karma created by all deeds up to the present is the total accumulation of the past; it defines the present which is manifested in a single moment. The workings of life in that moment form a cause for the future effect. Neither past nor future can exist apart from the present.

Past-oriented Attitude

Life at present contains life which has continued since time without beginning. It also defines life which continues from the present moment on to eternity. The major difference between the Buddhism of the True Cause and that of the True Effect hinges upon the interpretation of the true nature of the moment, which, endlessly succeeding itself, is the manifestation of what we call life. Buddhism of the True Effect refers to the past-oriented attitude which defines the present only as the result of the past, adhering to the results, whereas Buddhism of the True Cause is the belief that the present changes into a cause for the future.

The law of cause and effect governs life, and one's present existence is always the effect of the past. Nichiren Daishonin says in the *Letter from Sado*:

> One who climbs a high mountain must eventually descend. One who slights another will in turn be despised. One who deprecates those of handsome appearance will be born ugly. One who robs another of food and clothing is sure to fall into the world of Hunger. One who mocks noble men or anyone who observes the precepts will be born to a poor family. One who slanders a family that embraces the True Law will be born to a heretical family. One who laughs at those who cherish the precepts will be born a commoner and

meet with persecution from his sovereign. This is the general law of cause and effect.

The original passage quoted appears in the *Hatsunaion* Sutra, but the Daishonin expressed it in his own words to exemplify the continual transmigration of cause and effect. As he says, "the general law of cause and effect" is always actually working in the realities of life. That is why we must live now, embodying karmic retribution both physically and spiritually. As long as we remain chained by this cycle of cause and effect, we have only a slim possibility of rechanneling our present karma-bound life into a bright new path.

Think of someone in the world of Hunger. Even if he traces the cause of his present agony to his past life and discovers that he robbed others of clothing and food, he can only feel a deep sense of regret. He will not know why he did such a thing, nor will he be able to recover his past life to change the cause. To fulfill his dream for a happy life in the future he must sever the chains of his karma one by one in this life, and the next, and the next. Even though he tries to make good causes, he will find it very difficult to do so because his past is such a heavy burden. Out of despair some people live a life of self-abandonment or even commit suicide in despair.

To illustrate the past-oriented attitude, let me quote from a famous Japanese novel written by Sōseki Natsume (1867–1916). Entitled *Kokoro* (Heart), the story centers around a man called "Sensei" who struggles with egoism as he regrets what he has done to his friend K when they were both university students in the same boarding house. Quietly, Sensei came to love the pretty girl in the family. Much to his surprise, his friend K suddenly confides his own agonized love for the girl. Sensei is startled, since K seemed to have been completely immersed in study, and to have no time for love. From that time on Sensei has mixed emotions, but he deceives his friend and continues to court the girl until he secures informal consent for marriage. When K learns of this development he is so desperate that he commits suicide. All he leaves behind is a simple note to Sensei saying that he was too weak a person to have any hope for the future, and there was no other way out.

Sōseki describes how Sensei felt that night when he discovered that his friend K had committed suicide:

> I experienced almost the same sensation then as I did when K first told me of his love for Ojōsan [the daughter]. I stood still, transfixed by the scene I beheld. My eyes stared unbelievingly, as though they were made of glass. But the initial shock was like a sudden gust of wind, and was gone in a moment. My first thought was, "It's too late!" It was then that the great shadow that would for ever darken the course of my life spread before my mind's eye. And from somewhere in the shadow a voice seemed to be whispering: "It's too late... It's too late..." My whole body began to tremble.*

From that moment on Sensei's mind became slave to guilt. Shortly after graduation Sensei married the daughter, but even in their newly married life he could not drive "the dark shadow" away from him. His attempt to mitigate his guilt with liquor failed and the shadow loomed larger than ever. Finally, Sensei decided to live as if he were dead. He described his state of mind as follows:

> Though I had resolved to live as if I were dead, my heart would at times respond to the activity of the outside world, and seem almost to dance with pent-up energy. But as soon as I tried to break my way through the cloud that surrounded me, a frighteningly powerful force would rush upon me from I know not where, and grip my heart tight, until I

*Sōseki Natsume, *Kokoro* (Tokyo: Charles E. Tuttle Company, Inc., 1969), p. 229.

could not move. A voice would say to me: "You have no
right to do anything. Stay where you are." Whatever
desire I might have had for action would suddenly leave me.
After a moment, the desire would come back, and I would
once more try to break through. Again, I would be restrained. In fury and grief I would cry out: "Why do you
stop me?" With a cruel laugh, the voice would answer:
"You know very well why." Then I would bow in hopeless
surrender.*

Sensei finally takes his own life, leaving his wife to live
on alone. The story vividly depicts how heavy a burden it is
for a human being to go on living with a sense of sinfulness.
Though Sōseki makes no mention of Buddhism in the story,
the life Sensei had to live is reminiscent of the life of True
Effect. In his case, however, he was bound by the chain of
causality which he himself could clearly perceive. Even
causality in this life is grave enough to drive man into death.
The burden of karma we have accumulated from time
without beginning is heavy beyond imagination. If people
have to obliterate such karmic retributions one by one, they
will mostly be driven into despair.

This type of action, centering on True Effect, underlies
the teachings of Shakyamuni Buddha. The law of cause and
effect in this case defines the present life-condition only as
the result of the past karmic cause. Naturally, belief based
on that kind of Buddhism fails to inspire hope and joy for
the future. Though Shakyamuni's Buddhism gives ideas on
how life has transmigrated so far and how it continues on
into the future, it never clarifies the source of power for
developing life in the future. In other words, it preaches
what will become of life but never defines the self-motivat-
ing, positive force capable of reforming life. That is why
Shakyamuni's Buddhism is called the Buddhism of the True
Effect.

*Ibid., p. 243.

Breaking the Chain of Karma

Only through the Buddhism of the True Cause, which probes the depths of the momentary existence of life and discovers the Mystic Law there—the origin of everything—can people find the means of lightening their troubled lives. This is because the Buddhism of the True Cause is rooted in the depths of life, whereas the Buddhism of the True Effect is based on the ever-changing phenomena of life. The difference between the two is directly stated in the following quote referring to the law of cause and effect from the same *Letter from Sado*: "Nichiren's sufferings, however, are not ascribable to this causal law."

Nichiren Daishonin breaks through the realm of immediate cause and effect and enters into the depths of the life-moment, the entity of the fundamental causality which penetrates eternity. This entity is Nam-myoho-renge-kyo, which has neither beginning nor end. It is the entity of life which flows on, interweaving with the causality of the Ten Worlds, and it is also the fundamental force that governs the entire universe. That is what "Shakyamuni's practices and the virtues he consequently attained" means according to Buddhism of the seed inherent in the *Juryō* chapter of the Lotus Sutra.

Putting his own life as the Buddha who embodies Nam-myoho-renge-kyo into the inscription of the Mystic Law, he bestows it upon the people of the Latter Day, just as he said in the Gosho: "If we believe in that phrase, we shall naturally be granted the same benefits as he was." I can see unequaled compassion in his words "be granted." Life without beginning is more than ordinary people can fathom because it is the ultimate state of life, most difficult to believe and most difficult to understand. Even then, the advent of Nichiren Daishonin seven centuries ago made it possible for us to perceive it. He himself assumed the appearance of an ordinary person as he said in the Gosho, "Nichiren, who in this life was born poor and lowly to a *chandala** family," and through his behavior showed us the meaning of "Shakyamuni's practices and the virtues." What is more, he has left us the great power and boundless benefits in the form of the Gohonzon so that all future generations can prosper.

President Toda said about the Gohonzon's beneficial power in his lecture, "The Causality throughout Three Existences":

> Devoting oneself to the Gohonzon and chanting Nammyoho-renge-kyo is the way to change one's destiny for the better. All the causes and effects in between disappear, and a common mortal since time without beginning emerges.

These words convey his profound insight. Awe-inspiring as it may sound, the life of Nichiren Daishonin, who is the absolutely free, eternal Buddha, dwells within our strong spirit to dedicate ourselves to the Gohonzon. When we sit upright facing the Gohonzon, a common mortal since time without beginning and the Buddha since time without beginning sit facing one another. That moment of relation provides a sublime seat where you join your palms together to become one with the true entity of all phenomena. It contains the overflowing power to embrace, integrate and motivate all existences. This is what is meant by "all the causes and effects in between disappear, and a common mortal since time without beginning emerges." The emergence of the common mortal in itself forms the cause to produce the effect of benefits for all eternity.

Shakyamuni Buddha preached concepts of unimaginably long spans of time—*sanzen-jintengō* and *gohyaku-jintengō.*

---

*The lowest class, lower than the caste system, in India, comprised of those whose profession required them to kill living creatures. The Daishonin was born to a family of fishermen.

In contrast, Nichiren Daishonin expounds the most profound concept of time called *kuon ganjo*, with neither beginning nor end. He has established the original law of the universe which breaks all the chains of causality in Shakyamuni's Buddhism, probing into life so deeply as to identify man with the universe. "All the causes and effects in between disappear" is like the stars and the moon illuminating the heavens which disappear once the sun rises. But the heavenly bodies have not actually disappeared; they are simply outshone by the radiant beams of the sun. In like manner, the Buddhism of the True Cause, which embraces all the lights of the Buddhas throughout space and time, including Shakyamuni, casts its glorious light universally. The advent of true Buddhism lets people think of Shakyamuni's Buddhism in a totally new perspective.

"A common mortal since time without beginning emerges" is a monumental idea in the life philosophy—the present moment is all that counts. If we try to interpret Shakyamuni's Buddhism in terms of the Daishonin's Buddhism, we may be able to redefine it as the culmination of wisdom great enough to approach the original law of Nam-myoho-renge-kyo. At the very moment we chant to the Gohonzon, however, we manifest the original law, and by so doing we manifest the power of Myoho-renge-kyo in society, embodying it both physically and spiritually in ourselves. Shakyamuni's Buddhism exhorts us to strenuous practices to reach the Mystic Law, just as hundreds and thousands of leaves and branches are traced to one root. In contrast, Nichiren Daishonin's Buddhism reveals the Mystic Law itself, which enables one who embraces it to expand it through our activities onto hundreds and thousands of leaves and branches of society. The bright light of the Mystic Law has now begun to illuminate the world.

All kinds of institutions, ideologies and religions tower before us as an inevitable result, and they continue to bind people tight with their chains. Mankind is forced into subservience to heavy pressures he himself has created, suffocating under their weight. The Buddhism of the True Cause corrects the distorted relation between master and subject and gives direction to what it should be. This philosophy sends its hopeful light into the century to come as it restores supremacy to the dignity of life—the idea that a single life-entity is heavier than the earth. Our movement for fundamental reformation will encounter hardships, and rough waves are certain to rise against it. No matter what may happen to you in the course of your life and on the way to worldwide propagation, I ask all of you to endure the trials and proudly live up to the words of the Daishonin: "Indubitably, as the three obstacles and four devils* arise, the wise will rejoice, yet the foolish will cower."

Every person has his own troubles and dreams for the future. The sick wish to be in good health; one who has no house to live in wants to have a home and peaceful family life; one tries desperately to subdue the instinctive urge toward anger and greed which can take over and dominate, both physically and spiritually. Having hopes but knowing no way or means to attain them, people often end up in frustration. Once he embraces the Buddhism of the True Cause, however, any individual can create a bright future, for the very moment the individual's desire becomes one with his eternal being, the desire is simultaneously achieved in the depths of his life. At that very moment karma changes and an immeasurable eternal treasure gathers to become manifest in the future, just as a totally dark room is illuminated the moment you turn on the light.

This is solely because the Gohonzon contains the practices of all Buddhas throughout space and time and their resulting virtues, and because the power of the Buddha and the power of the Law within the Gohonzon are vast and boundless.

*See page 60.

Then you no longer have to continue your practice lifetime after lifetime to eliminate your past evil karma, as is thought in the Buddhism of the True Effect. Even if you have accumulated little good fortune in the past, all the Buddha's practices are contained in devoted faith in the Gohonzon and the resulting virtues flow naturally into a bright course for the future.

That is why the Daishonin said on Sado Island where he was an exile: "At this moment I, Nichiren, am the richest man in all of Japan," and "I feel immeasurable delight even though I am now an exile."

All in all, the inscription of the Gohonzon gives all people in the Latter Day a direct link with the life of the original Buddha and a way to become one with it. The purpose of the original Buddha, Nichiren Daishonin, was to allow all people to become as exalted as the Buddha of the "beginningless time." He said in his oral teachings, the *Ongi Kuden*, "The *Juryō* chapter states that we common mortals are endowed with the three enlightened properties of the Buddha. This indicates Nichiren and his disciples who chant Nam-myoho-renge-kyo." Elsewhere in the same Gosho he also said, "The Nam-myoho-renge-kyo I, Nichiren, now chant enables people to attain Buddhahood for as long as the ten thousand years of the Latter Day. This is what is meant by 'I have now fulfilled the pledge I made in the past.'"

Indisputably, what matters is faith in the Gohonzon. What is more, the key to enlightenment is how long you will continue your faith and how much you will deepen your faith. As the Daishonin says, "To accept is easy; to continue is difficult. But Buddhahood lies in continuing faith." He also urges us to sustain our faith, saying, "Arouse deep faith and polish your mirror night and day. How should you polish it? Only by chanting Nam-myoho-renge-kyo." I ask you to do gongyo in the morning and evening regularly so that you can carry your faith onward like the never-ending flow of a stream.

Supreme Jewel beyond Imagination

With full understanding of Shakyamuni's teachings, the four great men of Learning said: "We have gained the supreme cluster of jewels when we least expected it." They represent the world of Learning that is within ourselves.

The sentence quoted occurs in the fourth chapter of the Lotus Sutra. Here four great men of Learning—Mahakashyapa, Katyayana, Subhuti and Maudgalyayana—express their joy at having understood the Buddha's intent after hearing the Parable of the Three Carts and the Burning House. They have gained something they least expected—the all-embracing Mystic Law, the core of the Buddha's teachings that contains all the deeds and resulting virtues of Shakyamuni Buddha. Here they are thanking the Buddha for preaching the Mystic Law to them. Usually one attains the Law only when he sincerely seeks it. The Buddha's profound compassion, however, enabled the men of Learning to attain the Law without seeking it. That is why they rejoiced with such profound gratitude.

It was not that these disciples of Learning did not seek after anything. As the Parable of the Three Carts and the Burning House explains, they had been seeking something. The parable goes like this. There was once a millionaire who had dozens of children. They had always wanted three kinds of carts: carts pulled by sheep, by deer and by oxen. One day the millionaire's mansion caught fire, and he desperately shouted for his children to come out of the house, but to no avail. Then, remembering their wish, he called to them, saying that the carts they wanted so badly were right outside the gate. The children raced out of the house to get the carts. When they ran out of the mansion, however, the millionaire instead gave each of them a huge cart pulled by a magnificent white ox, which was far better than the carts they had desired.

The three carts indicate the teachings of the three vehicles —Learning, Realization and Bodhisattva—and the children's desire for them was so strong that they immediately came out of the house. The white ox cart the father actually gave his children means the supreme vehicle of the Mystic Law.

The teaching of the supreme vehicle concerns the state of Buddhahood, a state too lofty for the disciples of Learning to imagine. It is therefore no wonder that they did not actively seek it. The disciples pursued far less valuable jewels—the teachings of the three vehicles. But the Buddha gave them the supreme treasure of the Mystic Law by finally preaching the Lotus Sutra, something far greater than they had ever expected to obtain.

The parable can also be applied to those who believe in the Gohonzon now, in the Latter Day of the Law. The immediate motives which led us to receive the Gohonzon were, in most cases, probably minor, trifling desires arising out of daily life. There are very few of us who took faith in the Gohonzon because we envisioned and yearned for the ideal state of Buddhahood. But as we take faith in the Gohonzon and study Buddhism more and more deeply, we come to understand that a Buddha means an entity of human life filled with wisdom, good fortune and vital force. Further, we finally realize that the Gohonzon is not something merely to fulfill our trifling desires, but that it embodies the life of the Buddha. It is a priceless treasure that enables common individuals to become as noble as the Buddha. The jubilant life force the four great men of Learning manifested when they gained the supreme vehicle also dwells within the lives of us who embrace the Gohonzon.

Let me expand on *jitoku* (self-attained). The verse portion of the *Juryō* chapter begins with *ji ga toku butsu rai* (since I attained Buddhahood), which refers to Shakyamuni's attainment of Buddhahood at *gohyaku-jintengō*. According to the Daishonin's Buddhism, there is an even deeper meaning here. The Daishonin explains that Buddhahood is not attained at a certain point in time, like *gohyaku-jintengō*, but is indwelling for all eternity. According to the Daishonin's Buddhism, the sentence quoted above is shown to mean, "Obtaining *ga butsu rai* by oneself." Nichiren Daishonin explains this in the *Ongi Kuden*: "*Ga* (self) indicates the property of the Law, *butsu* (the Buddha) the property of wisdom, and *rai* (becoming) means the property of action. These three properties of the Buddha, who has neither beginning nor end, become one's own. From this, consider the meaning of gaining the supreme cluster of jewels without seeking it."

Ga is the Buddha's life existing throughout past, present and future, which is the enlightened property of the Law. *Butsu* signifies the wisdom that develops out of the great life force of the original Buddha, and enables one to fathom past, present and future existences, and to expound Buddhism freely among all people to save them and to create value at every moment. This is the function of the enlightened property of wisdom. *Rai* indicates the totally unrestricted activities of the original Buddha to save troubled people. It is therefore the enlightened property of action. Nichiren Daishonin is the original Buddha who holds all three enlightened properties of life, and the Gohonzon embodies his life. *Ji ga toku butsu rai* means that the three enlightened properties are obtained from oneself; they are not given by anyone or anything else.

The ultimate teaching of Shakyamuni's Buddhism was the revelation of the unimaginably long span of the Buddha's life, called *gohyaku-jintengō*. But even that is not infinite. It has a particular referent in the past. As long as the concept of Buddhahood remains within a finite, temporal framework, it is something to be attained, and that leads to a fundamental distinction between the Buddha and people. Actually, Shakyamuni himself attained Buddhahood in *gohyaku-jintengo* only after he had practiced bodhisattva austerities in an even more distant past.

In Nichiren Daishonin's Buddhism, however, *kuon*—which is often interpreted to mean the infinite past—actually does not mean the past at all. It means eternity, or the aggregate of every single moment of time. Once you realize that *kuon* exists in every moment, it is no longer correct to say that one becomes a Buddha, but that one awakens to the fact of being a Buddha to begin with. Because it means to manifest what is inherent in human life, it is called *jitoku* or "self-attained." Nichiren Daishonin is the completely unrestricted, original Buddha with the three enlightened properties of life. In general, however, believers in the Mystic Law also naturally possess the three enlightened properties of life. "Obtaining the supreme cluster of jewels without seeking it" applies not only to the men of Learning but to everyone else as well. That is why Nichiren Daishonin said in the *Ongi Kuden*: "Nichiren and his disciples who now chant Nam-myoho-renge-kyo are the votaries of self-attained Buddhahood."

Treasure Too Close to See

The quote says, "We have gained the supreme cluster of jewels when we least expected it." Let us think about the idea of "something coming into one's possession unsought" in context of our daily life. "Unsought" means that ordinary people can hardly know something as sublime as the Mystic Law. We possess the Gohonzon before we know that it is the supreme cluster of jewels. Some people receive the

Gohonzon without prior knowledge of faith, and others accept faith in the Gohonzon at the encouragement of their friends or upon being awakened by their bad karma, even though they may have scorned religious faith. Once you embrace the Gohonzon, however, you honestly realize that it is the very thing you have been most wanting to find. Many priceless things exist around us, but they are usually hard to recognize. The air around us, for example, goes unnoticed; it is often used as a metaphor for amorphousness or insignificance, as in the phrase, "vanishing into thin air." Though we rarely think about it, when traveling in a spaceship or submarine nothing is more vital than air.

In the same way, we are so accustomed to life and living that we rarely contemplate its deep meaning. Since one can live without ever having to think about it, he may get lost in daily routine. Nichiren Daishonin's Buddhism, however, teaches us that an incomparably valuable jewel is hidden in our daily life. We are shown the supreme value in human life—something which we are in intimate contact with every day. Therefore, when people come to know true Buddhism, they finally understand how far they neglected this supreme jewel, and they find invaluable joy in their discovery.

Let me go over *jitoku* once again. It means to realize something in oneself, by oneself and to do so according to one's own will. The great life force of Buddhahood becomes manifest only in the strenuous, dedicated efforts to fuse oneself with the Gohonzon, and therefore *jitoku*, in a word, means faith. *Ga butsu rai* means the Buddha of the three enlightened properties of life or the Gohonzon, whereas *jitoku* equals *kanjin* (to observe one's own mind and find the three enlightened properties in it). *Ji ga toku butsu rai* as a unified concept means that to embrace the Gohonzon is to attain enlightenment. The Gohonzon is an absolute objective reality, without which there can be neither enlightenment nor human revolution. Simultaneously, the

Gohonzon's power does not become manifest unless one carries out the assiduous practice of one's faith.

Since the jewel one seeks is the Buddhahood within one's life, it is impossible to manifest it without achieving oneness with the Gohonzon. Were Buddhahood a jewel existing outside oneself, one could simply receive it from someone. But because Buddhahood exists within oneself, only the courageous practice of faith can call it forth. Essentially, man acquires power through his own training. Machines, facilities and advice from others are all only external aids, which help him develop his potential. A world record in sports is made with the help of excellent facilities, scientific research and well-trained, experienced coaches. But the athlete himself has to achieve the record. This is much more true in faith. One can never gain the great life force of Buddhahood from the outside, and science and technology are no help at all. In this sense Buddhism teaches the strictness of a cause-and-effect relationship and lets us understand the three thousand conditions in every entity of life.

Conversely, when one develops his life from within, he opens up a brand-new world. Unless we lay the foundation by developing our life, any castle we make will be built upon sand. If a tree has shallow roots, it will topple over in a gale. The treasure tower of life rooted in the ground of eternity stands in all its nobility, unperturbed by the winds and waves of life. An environment, no matter how nice, can only grow worse unless it is built with one's own strenuous efforts. Even people in the world of Rapture are subject to the five types of decay.* On the other hand, the

*The five signs of decline which appear when the life of a heavenly being comes to an end. (1) His clothes become dirty. (2) The flowers on his head wither. (This implies that he gradually loses his mental faculties.) (3) His body becomes dirty. (4) He sweats under the arms. (This implies that he worries, fears or suffers.) (5) He cannot feel happy anywhere. (This implies that he loses his conviction.) These five indicate that pleasure in the state of Rapture fades away very easily.

world we construct with our own efforts to achieve our human revolution is indestructible. Living in this way, we can perceive a vast, promising future stretching before us.

When we establish a firm inner self by courageously challenging ourselves and changing our earthly desires into the great wish to save mankind, we can develop a truly humanistic civilization and usher in the "century of life." Incidentally, *shōmon* (men of Learning) can literally be translated as "those who hear," i.e., those with seeking minds to hear the Buddha's teachings, for a seeking mind always pushes on to development and growth, and never allows satisfaction with the present situation. Only when you actively strive to grow and progress can you truly comprehend the greatness of Buddhism.

Strive among the People

Concerning the people of Learning, the fourth chapter of the Lotus Sutra reads, "We have gained the supreme cluster of jewels when we least expected it." The *shōmon*, understanding what the Buddha meant, changed themselves into true *shōmon* by breaking through their inherent egoism. The chapter describes the scene: "We now are true *shōmon*, listening to the voice of the Buddha's Way and causing all to hear it. We now are true arhats, and are entitled to receive offerings from the heavens, men, demons, and deities in every world."

The men of Learning, who had listened to Shakyamuni Buddha only for their own enlightenment, changed radically into people who led others to listen to the Buddha's teachings. In other words, *shōmon* here means not only to hear the (Buddha's) voice, but to let all others hear it. Yet these people, who so reformed their lives, are the same who were refuted by the Buddha in the pre-Lotus Sutra teachings, as the Daishonin describes in *The Opening of the Eyes*: "The men of Learning and Realization, who thought that they had understood Buddhism and attained Buddhahood . . . were instead ingrates since they guided their fathers and mothers to a path which would never lead to Buddhahood."

Trapped in a world of solitude and encrusted with arrogance and egocentricity, the men of Learning were not only severely refuted by the Buddha in the pre-Lotus Sutra teachings, they were even despised by the commoners they themselves had looked down on. The Buddha rebuked the *shōmon* with the intention of training them as the true disciples who would propagate Buddhism unrestrictedly, and in order to propagate Buddhism they could not be arrogant and egocentric. In the Lotus Sutra, however, they unexpectedly gained the supreme jewel of Buddhahood, and from then on struck out bravely among the common people to let them hear the Buddha's teachings. That is why they were finally able to attain Buddhahood.

The men of Learning had endured the Buddha's rebukes for a long period, so they were more than overjoyed when they heard the Lotus Sutra which allowed them to attain Buddhahood, and they pledged to devote themselves to its propagation. The fourth chapter describes how they "danced for joy!" The true mission of the men of Learning was revealed for the first time, and without it, their aeons-long austerities would have been to no avail. Indeed, their attainment of Buddhahood in the Lotus Sutra is the supreme principle. Talking about those who became true *shōmon*, Nichiren Daishonin said, "They represent the world of Learning that is within ourselves." He urges us also to develop the same benevolence so that we can lead others to listen to the Buddha's teachings, just as they did.

In the *Ongi Kuden*, Nichiren Daishonin amplifies the above-quoted chapter of the Lotus Sutra, ". . . listening to the voice of the Buddha's Way and causing all to hear it":

Thus, Shariputra expressed his understanding of the Law by

saying in this [third] chapter, "listening to this voice."
"Listening" means to take faith in the Lotus Sutra, and "the
voice" indicates the voice and sound (i.e., the rhythm) of
all phenomena, which signifies the Mystic Law. . . . Regard-
ing this voice, the fourth chapter says, "listening to the
voice of the Buddha's Way and causing all to hear it."
"All" means human beings living in the phenomenal world,
and "the voice" means Nam-myoho-renge-kyo.

"The voice of the Buddha's Way," therefore, means
Nam-myoho-renge-kyo, and "all" indicates all human
beings. The Mystic Law is the force which causes Buddhahood to become manifest from within the lives of all people.
Elsewhere in the *Ongi Kuden* Nichiren Daishonin says,
". . . voices do the Buddha's work." Indeed, the voice
derived from the Mystic Law penetrates human hearts.

You become true disciples and men of Learning when,
while you yourself listen to Nam-myoho-renge-kyo and live
it, you cause people wandering through the three evil paths
or the six lower worlds to hear Nam-myoho-renge-kyo.
The Bodhisattvas of the Earth who devotedly propagate
the Mystic Law as common mortals in this polluted world
are the true men of Learning.

A Japanese scholar once made a profound statement:
"Voice is life. It is emitted from the depths of life. It
resonates throughout the universe." The sonorous voice we
utter while doing gongyo and chanting daimoku is just such a
voice, and it causes the universe and the life within it to
resonate more profoundly than any great music. Sent with
a spirit of altruism to all fields of human endeavor, the voice
of profound sincerity can break through the shells of greed,
anger and stupidity that smother human hearts. That is the
meaning of the statement of the Nirvana Sutra, "If he takes
the slanderer severely to task, drives him off or punishes
him, then he is my disciple and one who truly understands
my teachings."

The Buddha's Life Is Our Own Body

The *Hōben* chapter states: "At the start I pledged to make all people perfectly equal to me, without any distinction between us. By now the original vows that I made have already been fulfilled. I have led all the people onto the path to Buddhahood." The enlightened life of Shakyamuni Buddha is our own flesh and blood. His practices and resulting virtues are our bones and marrow.

The subject in this passage from the Lotus Sutra is Shakyamuni, who attained Buddhahood in this life. In terms of his in-depth interpretation, however, Nichiren Daishonin uses the quote to indicate the original Buddha. Nichikan Shonin therefore takes this passage to imply the Buddha of absolute freedom since time without beginning. Nichiren Daishonin himself explains this passage from the *Hōben* chapter in the *Ongi Kuden*: " 'I' means Shakyamuni who is the Buddha since time without beginning. He is the teacher of true Buddhism, which is actually we, common mortals. . . . The *Juryō* chapter says that we are the Buddha with the three enlightened properties of life."

In a nutshell, the subject of the sentence is Nichiren Daishonin, the Buddha of the Latter Day of the Law. He states that when an ordinary person embraces the Gohonzon and sincerely chants daimoku, he becomes the Buddha with the three enlightened properties of life just like Nichiren Daishonin. That is also why he wrote, "The enlightened life of Shakyamuni Buddha is our own flesh and blood." This means that the enlightened life of the Buddha, the three properties inherent in it, exists within the lives of common mortals. Thus, the Daishonin shows again that anyone can become a Buddha just as he is.

The last sentence in the passage relates to something I

have discussed many times—that the practices and resulting virtues of the Buddha are all contained in our lives. Let me expand on the "practices and resulting virtues" in terms of cause and effect. The practices are the cause—the nine worlds of life in which common people enjoy all kinds of happiness. However, the happiness of the nine worlds is all relative happiness. The resulting virtues are the effect—Buddhahood. That is the world of absolute happiness in the depths of enlightened life.

When we embrace the Gohonzon of the Three Great Secret Laws, we see that "the enlightened life of Shakyamuni Buddha is our own flesh and blood." In his own words, Nichikan Shonin says, "If we believe and embrace this Gohonzon and chant Nam-myoho-renge-kyo, our flesh and blood is the Gohonzon of *ichinen sanzen*, the life of the original Buddha, Nichiren Daishonin." Since the Gohonzon embodies the life of Nichiren Daishonin who is the original Buddha, we manifest the same entity when we believe and embrace the Gohonzon and chant Nam-myoho-renge-kyo. Then, Nichiren Daishonin as our master is the Buddha, and as his disciples we are also Buddhas—that is, we realize the oneness of master and disciple. That is why Nichikan Shonin interprets this passage as a statement of the oneness of master and disciple.

Religions in all ages have systematized theologies that center on some kind of absolute being transcending human existence. The Judeo-Christian religions create such a gap between God and human beings that all their believers can do is to throw themselves upon God's grace. Buddhism, however, assures us that all people are essentially Buddhas, and as such, the most sublime possible existence. The Daishonin's egalitarian declaration, therefore, completely departs from religions that place human beings in a position inferior to the deity. At the same time, his lofty, humanistic declaration fundamentally supports modern declarations of human rights which have tried to restore human dignity and take absolute power out of the hands of authorities supposedly representing the absolute being.

There is profound significance in the fact that Nichiren Daishonin compares "the enlightened life of Shakyamuni Buddha" to "flesh and blood," and "practices and resulting virtues" to "bones and marrow." Talking about himself, the Daishonin said in the *Letter from Sado*:

> In my heart I cherish some faith in the Lotus Sutra, but my body, while outwardly human, is fundamentally that of an animal, which once subsisted on fish and fowl and was conceived of the male and female fluids. My spirit dwells in this body like the moon reflected in a muddy pond or gold wrapped in a filthy bag.

The physical and spiritual entity of a human being is more elevated than any other existence—it reflects the "moon" of Buddhahood and encloses the "gold" of Buddhahood. It is easy to think of the deep compassion Nichiren Daishonin gave each individual desperately struggling to survive through the three calamities and seven disasters.* My heart resounds to his voice in *The True Entity of Life*, "I, Nichiren, do not cry, but my tears flow ceaselessly," as if I were actually hearing it.

All in all, the significance of our activities lies in how well we can attune ourselves to the vibrant life of the original Buddha. One person opens the treasure tower of another, who, in turn, opens the treasure tower of a third, thus extending the reach of our activities. Our steady work to bring human life in tune with the vibrant chords of the

---

*Calamities described in various sutras. There are two categories of three calamities—minor and major. The minor ones are inflation (especially when caused by famine), war, and pestilence. The major ones are disasters caused by fire, wind and water. The seven disasters differ according to the sutras. The *Yakushi* Sutra defines them as pestilence, foreign invasion, internal strife, extraordinary changes in the heavens, solar and lunar eclipses, unseasonable storms and typhoons, and unseasonable droughts.

Gohonzon will extend to more and more people as it continues. The Indian poet Rabindranath Tagore (1861–1941) once said:

> The meaning of the living words that come out of the experiences of great hearts can never be exhausted by any one system of logical interpretation. They have to be endlessly explained by the commentaries of individual lives, and they gain an added mystery in each new revelation.*

We do not study the Gosho merely to understand its literal meaning. Rather, we etch each word into our lives. Buddhism actually exists in the heart of each individual, just as Nichiren Daishonin teaches, "The eighty-four thousand teachings are the diary of my own being." The teachings of the Gosho draw from the depths of our own being an indestructible will to live, as opposed to the use of the power of authority to teach and instruct human beings from above. This is why those teachings vibrate in our daily actions and why they are called the Buddhism for real life, not just theorizing.

One human heart moves another. Nichiren Daishonin teaches us this as a living principle. In order to save all ordinary people, he himself was born as one of us and shared our human joys and sorrows. He united himself indivisibly with our hearts. His life-condition is that of absolute happiness, which is described in the Gosho as the "treasures of the heart." Because it contains an indomitable sense of fulfillment, it far surpasses any "treasures in a storehouse" or "treasures of the body," which fall into the category of relative happiness. In this regard, President Toda once said, "Belief in this great faith keeps the rhythm of life in tune with the universe, so that one can feel the joy of living to his heart's content. A life force filled with joy is

---

*Rabindranath Tagore, *Sādhanā* (Madras: The Macmillan Co. of India Limited, 1972), p. viii.

the very source of happiness." To take the goal of attaining Buddhahood in this life means to attain the joy of living. Be firmly convinced that this is the only way we can become enveloped by the great compassion of the original Buddha, who "pledged to make all people perfectly equal to me, without any distinction," and advance together unperturbed by any obstacles.

The Spirit to Protect

Chapter Eleven of the Lotus Sutra says: "Those who choose to protect this sutra serve Tahō Buddha and me. . . . They also serve all the other Buddhas present who dignify and glorify all the worlds." Shakyamuni, Tahō, and all the other Buddhas in the ten directions represent the world of Buddhahood within ourselves. By searching them out within us, we can receive the benefits of Shakyamuni, Tahō, and all the other Buddhas. This is what is meant by the following passage in Chapter Ten: "If one hears the Law for even a single moment, he will be able to attain perfect enlightenment."

This passage discusses the oneness of parent and child in terms of the three enlightened properties of life. "Me" in the quotation refers to Shakyamuni and means the enlightened property of wisdom. "Tahō" stands for the enlightened property of the Law, and "all the other Buddhas" are the Buddhas who came to participate in the ceremony of the Lotus Sutra from the worlds in the ten directions of the universe. Since they appeared in those worlds as emanations of Shakyamuni Buddha, they collectively mean the enlightened property of action. Shakyamuni, Tahō and all the other Buddhas symbolize the three enlightened properties of life. "Those who choose to protect this sutra (the

Gohonzon)" succeed those Buddhas and manifest the three enlightened properties of life, just as children succeed their parents. By protecting the Gohonzon they receive the same benefits as they would receive for serving the Buddha with the three enlightened properties of life. That is why Shakyamuni, Tahō and other Buddhas represent the world of Buddhahood within ourselves.

The point I would like to make here is the meaning of "protect." In various sutras, the Buddha urged people to protect his teachings. "Protect" may sound conservative, but it is not a passive act. In order to let the flow of Buddhism continue, one must positively transmit it to others and make it prosper. The true spirit of Buddhism flows within the actions of propagation to save those who are unhappy. Let me also draw your attention to the word "choose" in the above quotation. Clearly, it suggests not a passive but a positive attitude; it means to practice Buddhism with your thoughts, words and actions.

Protection is to maintain one's faith in the Gohonzon from beginning to end. By doing so, one guards the supreme life-condition of Buddhahood within oneself. To protect the Gohonzon is to protect one's own life, as the Daishonin teaches us in the Gosho, *On the Treasure Tower*: "You may think you offered gifts to the Treasure Tower of Tahō Buddha, but that is not so. You offered them to yourself." As is inscribed on the Gohonzon, the condition of Buddhahood within us exists in the midst of the three thousand constantly shifting conditions of life. Such life-conditions as Hell, Hunger, Animality and Anger are all inherent in practical life, as are Learning, Realization and Bodhisattva, and all the other life-conditions.

If you slacken in your efforts even a moment, the life-condition of Buddhahood goes behind the thick clouds of the nine worlds. We must always embrace and protect the Gohonzon to the limits of our power so that the Mystic Law within us, which always shines brilliantly, may not be covered by the cloud of obstacles and devils. Water becomes foul unless it flows ceaselessly, and so does human life. Carry out your morning and evening gongyo and challenge a new goal every day, as Nichiren Daishonin urges us in the Gosho: "Strengthen your faith day by day and month after month. Should you slacken even a bit, demons will take advantage."

Next, I ask you to protect the children of the Buddha just as you protect the Gohonzon. To protect the children of the Buddha is to protect the sutra and teachings. The Daishonin stresses in *On the Buddha's Prophecy*, ". . . there was no one there to whom these sutras could be taught. Their efforts were as meaningless as trying to teach Buddhism to wooden or stone statues garbed in priests' robes and carrying mendicants' bowls." He also said in *On Taking Faith in the Lotus Sutra*, "If the Law is supreme, so is the person who embraces it. To slander that person, therefore, is to slander the Law. To disrespect the child is to disrespect the parents." Therefore we must protect the children of the Buddha. They are your brothers and sisters unified in the profound bond of Buddhism. They are Bodhisattvas of the Earth, endowed with an irreplaceable mission. I ask you to "arise and greet him from afar, and respect him in the same way as you do the Buddha," just as the Lotus Sutra describes.

Thirdly, it is important to firmly protect the precious organization of Buddhists wherein you encourage and teach each other. Nichiren Daishonin states in *The Three Priests' Prayers for Rain*: "There is no better way to attain Buddhahood than to have good friends (*zenchishiki*). What good will one's own wisdom do? If one has sense enough to distinguish between hot and cold, he should treasure his good friends. However, the most difficult thing of all is to meet a good friend." In order for us common mortals to attain Buddhahood, there is no way but to meet good friends, and the Daishonin therefore urges us to seek them out.

I want you to understand that each one of you is a good friend to everyone else. The Nichiren Shoshu Soka Gakkai consists of individuals gathered to encourage and polish each other under the common goal of attaining Buddhahood and *kōsen-rufu*. We must treasure and respect our Buddhist association and our Buddhist friends, for they are part of the most valuable treasure we have. To protect them is to protect the sutra.

Our association still has a long way to go toward worldwide propagation. But the dignity of the original Buddha running deeply within it will brighten the future of mankind in the decades to come. My conviction comes from an unshakable belief in the Daishonin's words in *The True Entity of Life*: "Only I, Nichiren, at first chanted Nammyoho-renge-kyo, but then two, three and a hundred followed, chanting and teaching others. Likewise, propagation will unfold this way in the future. Doesn't this signify 'emerging from the earth'?" To protect yourself and your Buddhist organization dedicated to justice is to protect the future of all mankind.

To Hear the Sutra Is to Live It

To "hear" in the quote from Chapter Ten means to embrace the Gohonzon. In the *Ongi Kuden*, Nichiren Daishonin interprets "hearing" in terms of faith and practice. The section concerning "Thus I heard" reads, ". . . according to T'ien-t'ai, 'I heard' symbolizes those who strongly embrace the sutra. . . . People who do not believe in the sutra never hear the sutra in this sense. Those who practice the Lotus Sutra hear the essence of this phrase."

"To hear the Law for even a single moment" means that even if you only embrace the Gohonzon and practice for a moment, you are able to manifest the supreme enlightenment of the Buddha at that moment. Every moment that we believe in the Gohonzon and chant daimoku, the life-condition of Buddhahood wells up from within us. If you begin the day with a sincere recitation of gongyo, praying to achieve your goals, and conclude it with evening gongyo, chanting daimoku with gratitude to the Gohonzon, you will attain Buddhahood in this lifetime, and in all future existences.

Let me quote a relevant passage from T'ien-t'ai's *Hokke Mongu* (Words and Phrases of the Lotus Sutra) which clarifies the meaning of "Thus I heard." "Question: You should say, 'My ears hear.' Why do you instead say, 'I hear'? Answer: 'I' indicates the master of the ears. It receives all perceptions. This is how the world is understood." The true meaning of "hearing" is not merely the auditory function but perception with all the power of one's life itself. In other words, all human perceptions, including consciousness, work collectively at the same time. "I" thus signifies life in its totality.

Elsewhere in the same work, T'ien-t'ai quotes Bodhisattva Nagarjuna's *Treatise on the Mahaprajnaparamita Sutra* which reads, "There are three kinds of self in common mortals: the deluded self, the arrogant self and the original self." "Self" can be interpreted in many ways, but it is vital to grasp the nature of self. If it is a deluded or arrogant self, then the true spirit of Buddhism cannot enter into one's life. To be exact, "I" of "Thus I heard" is Ananda, one of the ten major disciples of Shakyamuni Buddha, and the treatise says about him, "Ananda is a man of pursuing spirit who, free from his deluded self, firmly subdued his arrogant self. Thus he well deserves to be called a man of the original self." When you eliminate arrogance and illusion and seek Buddhism with a pure seeking spirit, you can, like him, say that you "hear" Buddhism in the deepest sense of the word.

T'ien-t'ai also says, "To expand on the meaning of

'hearing,' Ananda was born the very night the Buddha attained enlightenment. He served the Buddha for more than twenty years, but he did not 'hear' the Buddha's teachings before he served the Buddha." T'ien-t'ai meant that to "serve" the Buddha is to "hear" the teachings. "Hearing" in this context is not merely listening to words; it means a life-to-life interchange. *Onshitsu* (hatred and jealousy) critically impedes this life-to-life contact of faith. To define *onshitsu*, Nichiren Daishonin quotes Miao-lo in the Gosho: "*On* indicates having ill feelings, and *shitsu* means unwillingness to listen [to the Buddha's teaching]."

Think hard about what he means by "unwillingness to listen." "Good advice sounds harsh to ears" and "Good medicine tastes bitter" are common proverbs. Common mortals remain common mortals exactly because they do not like hearing what is disagreeable and painful. On the contrary, they are all too easily swayed by flattery and adulation. As long as you take the line of least resistance, you cannot expect to grow. Worse, you are creating the cause for your own ruin, since you surround yourself with people who do not help build inner strength, but rather, serve to tear it down.

In a story from *Taikōki* (The Life of Toyotomi Hideyoshi) by Eiji Yoshikawa, a character named Menju Iyeteru appears. He was mentor to the attendants of Shibata Katsuiye, one of the powerful feudal lords of sixteenth-century Japan. He was also a man of considerable insight, in spite of his youth. He felt that Shibata was behaving wildly, so one day he turned down a page in a book his lord wanted to borrow so he would notice it. Seeing the corner folded over, Shibata looked at that page and what he read there was an implicit remonstration against his behavior. Reading on, he felt displeasure sweep through him. From that time on the lord always kept Menju away from him.

Who was a faithful subject? Later on, when Shibata's

troops were almost wiped out by Toyotomi Hideyoshi at
the battle of Shizuga-take, it was Menju who saved Shibata's
life. As their forces began to retreat, Menju repeatedly
implored Shibata to hand over the banner that would
identify him as the leader. Shibata gave in, and no sooner
had Menju taken it than he turned his horse around and,
together with a small number of soldiers, rode straight back
into the enemy's ranks, dying a heroic death. At that,
Shibata realized immediately Menju's deep loyalty. He was
pierced by remorse that he had given the banner to him, but
it was too late. The victor, Toyotomi Hideyoshi, is said to
have reverently buried Menju's severed head and then sought
out his mother to give her his personal condolences. This
episode was originally written down to illustrate the loyalty
of a subject to his lord, vaunting the values of the age of
warring lords, but I think that we can glean another precious
lesson from it. Shibata Katsuiye was unwilling to listen to
Menju Iyeteru. His arrogance and negligence led him to
take the line of least resistance, which caused his defeat at
the battle, and ultimately, his death.

We must plunge in among our fellow members, speaking
and carefully listening to everything they have to say. The
horrible aspect about *onshitsu* is that it creates a wall between
the hearts of members, destroying the unity. Once fenced
off by these walls, our hearts become victim to the three
poisons of greed, anger and stupidity. Then we unconsciously destroy all of our own good fortune. This is why
individual guidance and sincere person-to-person encouragement are so significant. In the long run, an organization can
live up to its purpose only when it can nourish each individual
member. True, it requires tremendous life force to listen to
your troubled and grieved friends and it also takes tremendous
courage to open your hearts to those who are hard to get
along with. But the very difficulty involved is a valuable
thing in attaining your own human revolution and awaken-

ing souls that have long lain dormant in the lives of those friends. I urge you to muster up your courage, to move, listen and speak to them all. The Daishonin says in the Gosho, "When you split one joint in the bamboo, all the others follow." So, no matter how harsh your situation may be, when you face it directly and break through it, like splitting one joint in the bamboo, you can create a new, much better situation. Above all, pray to the Gohonzon with this conviction in your heart, for every prayer allows your inner, true self to shine.

All Buddhas and Bodhisattvas Within

The *Juryō* chapter reads: "The time is limitless and boundless—a hundred, thousand, ten thousand, hundred thousand nayuta aeons—since I in fact attained Buddhahood." Present within our lives is the Lord Shakyamuni who obtained the three enlightened properties of life before *gohyaku-jintengō*, the original Buddha since time without beginning. The *Juryō* chapter states: "Once I also practiced the bodhisattva austerities, and the life which I then acquired has yet to be exhausted. My life will last yet twice as many aeons from now." He was speaking of the world of Bodhisattva within ourselves. The Bodhisattvas of the Earth are the followers of Lord Shakyamuni in our lives. They follow the Buddha just as T'ai-kung and Tan, the Duke of Chou, served as ministers to King Wu of the Chou dynasty and later assisted his son and successor, the infant King Ch'eng; or just as Takeshiuchi served Empress Jingū and later her grandson Crown Prince Nintoku as a highly valued minister. Bodhisattvas Jōgyō, Muhengyō, Jyōgyō and Anryūgyō represent the world of Bodhisattva within our lives.

Nichikan Shonin states that this passage establishes the oneness of subject and lord in terms of *kuon ganjo*—time without beginning or end. In other words, the Buddha (lord) and bodhisattvas (subjects) are one in our single entity of life. Both the Buddha of *kuon ganjo* and the Bodhisattvas of the Earth exist within ourselves when we develop the inner life of *kuon ganjo*.

The first quote in the passage reveals the time of *gohyaku-jintengō* when Shakyamuni attained Buddhahood. The Daishonin refers to the Buddha of beginningless time who attained Buddhahood "before *gohyaku-jintengō*." The word "before" indicates that he is shifting time reference from the temporal framework of *gohyaku-jintengō* to that of *kuon ganjo*, time without beginning or end. Nichiren Daishonin said in *The Entity of the Mystic Law*, "Before *gohyaku-jintengō* Shakyamuni attained the entity of the Lotus Flower of the Mystic Law and then appeared in various worlds to show how to attain Buddhahood, revealing the ultimate principle to which the people are yet to be enlightened." This passage and the text given above point to the same frame—that of *kuon ganjo* or "before *gohyaku-jintengō*." According to *The Exegesis of The True Object of Worship* by Nichikan Shonin, *ga jitsu jōbutsu irai* (since I attained Buddhahood) refers to the three enlightened properties of life as an entirety: *ga* (self) signifies the enlightened property of the Law, *jōbutsu* (attaining enlightenment) the enlightened property of wisdom, and *irai* (the time since enlightenment) the enlightened property of action.

The second quote in the text reveals the practice through which Shakyamuni attained Buddhahood. The practice represents the True Cause, the nine worlds that have existed in our lives since time without beginning—*kuon ganjo*. The first quote refers to the True Effect which symbolizes the Buddhahood of *kuon ganjo*. The two quotes reveal that both the True Cause and the True Effect exist in our own lives.

Nichikan Shonin interprets the second quote in the text as "a natural flow," and as he puts it, "just as all rivers flow into the ocean," so all your activities based on true Buddhism will always lead to the ocean of resulting virtues (Buddhahood). This principle bears profound significance to our practice. In the ordinary world, in spite of all your efforts and pains you do not necessarily attain your objectives. In many cases you may end up a miserable failure. In real life the same causes do not necessarily bring about the same results, and efforts often turn out to be futile, or even become tragedies.

In Buddhism, however, no cause ever fails to produce its effect; all causes lead toward a greater effect. Dedication to the Gohonzon and efforts to teach it to others are never wasted, becoming the source of blessings. It is a stream which begins in the recesses of the mountain and at first is too small to notice, but it eventually finds its way onto the plains and finally reaches the ocean. Similarly, efforts in the world of Buddhism, no matter how inconspicuous, will inexorably flow into the great ocean of nirvana. This is what "a natural flow" means. Never forget that your painstaking efforts to propagate the Mystic Law will secure you benefits which last forever.

"The Bodhisattvas of the Earth are the followers of Lord Shakyamuni in our lives." The life-conditions of the nine worlds are represented by the Bodhisattvas of the Earth, who maintain support of the life-condition of Buddhahood and help to manifest it. They are the followers of the Buddha within ourselves. Thus, the Daishonin assures us that both the Buddha of *kuon ganjo* and the Bodhisattvas of the Earth exist within our lives. To make the relationship between these two life-conditions easier for his contemporaries to grasp, Nichiren Daishonin used the example of subjects and lords. Ordinarily, one thinks first of feudalistic customs when mention of subjects and lords comes up, but what the

Daishonin is stressing is the function of the Bodhisattvas of the Earth to help manifest the life of Buddhahood. He spoke of the oneness of subject and lord in terms of the internal development of human life.

Another important point is implied by the analogy drawn in the text. T'ai-kung was a historical figure in ancient China who was met and singled out by King Wen of the Chou dynasty as an indispensable minister. After the king's death he served his successor, King Wu. After King Wu passed away, T'ai-kung even served his successor, the infant King Ch'eng. Tan, the Duke of Chou, was one of King Wu's younger brothers and therefore an uncle of the infant king. He handled state affairs as regent until the young king reached adulthood. Similarly, in Japan Takeshiuchi no Sukune served the infant Crown Prince Nintoku. These mature and experienced ministers all served infant kings. The analogy is meant to show that though the life-condition of Buddhahood emerges when we first embrace the Gohonzon, it is still weak and underdeveloped. So what is necessary to make the Buddha's life-condition unshakable? The essential factor is the workings of the Bodhisattvas of the Earth. They are the single factor that can activate the life-condition of Buddhahood.

The Mission of Propagation

The Bodhisattvas of the Earth represent the life-condition that works to propagate the Mystic Law. They are all bodhisattvas who emerged from the ground in the ceremony of the Lotus Sutra to take on the mission to spread the True Law in the evil Latter Day of the Law. In other words, the Bodhisattvas of the Earth find their *raison d'être* in single-minded devotion to the propagation of true Buddhism. They attain their original life-condition when they carry out their mission. Nichiren Daishonin teaches us through this analogy that vigorous practice based on a profound awakening to our mission of *kōsen-rufu* is necessary, for without it we cannot support, protect and foster the life-condition of Buddhahood which exists in the depths of our lives.

In retrospect, the Soka Gakkai owes what it is today to the life-or-death struggle President Makiguchi and President Toda waged in prison to protect true Buddhism. President Josei Toda often told young men's division members: "A man should struggle with the harsh realities of life which confront him, no matter who or where he is, and no matter what task he may shoulder. When I was in prison I made the firm vow: 'Now I am in prison. So long as I am in prison, I will wage my battle right here.'" It was there that President Toda one day suddenly realized his profound mission and attained the supreme life-condition. Later on he said, "On the eve of the day I was released from prison I was able to pledge to the late president, Mr. Makiguchi, 'Our lives are eternal; they have neither beginning nor end. I have realized that we were born with the great mission to propagate the seven characters of the Lotus Sutra in the Latter Day of the Law. Judging our capacity from what I now understand, we are the Bodhisattvas of the Earth.'"

We can find our own original pledge and mission in the declaration of our revered teacher Toda, and his ceaseless efforts, supported by this conviction and carried out because of his realization, have brought about the unprecedented prosperity of true Buddhism we enjoy today. I ask you, therefore, to understand deeply that as a Bodhisattva of the Earth you can protect, develop and display the vigorous life force as the Daishonin teaches us, when you dedicate yourself to the activities for propagation and work courageously for your own growth.

The Daishonin said, "Bodhisattvas Jōgyō, Muhengyō, Jyōgyō and Anryūgyō represent the world of Bodhisattva within our lives." The Four Great Bodhisattvas appear in the *Yujutsu* (15th) chapter of the Lotus Sutra. As numerous as the sands of sixty thousand Ganges Rivers, bodhisattvas emerged rank after rank from the ground led by these four. Our lives contain all of their functions. The innumerable Bodhisattvas of the Earth, the Buddhas and bodhisattvas preached in other sutras, and the living beings in the Ten Worlds all exist within our own lives. That is why Chang-an wrote in his preface: "The *Maka Shikan* reveals the teaching that T'ien-t'ai himself practiced in the depths of his being." The Gohonzon, the object of worship for observing one's own mind, is the objective entity that allows the great life-condition existing in one's life to become manifest. "To observe one's own mind" (*kanjin*) means that embracing the Gohonzon makes that life-condition manifest.

Society fluctuates, and so do human minds. But the great pulsing rhythm that throbs between the universe and the innermost self remains steady with our firm faith in the Gohonzon. For this reason nothing can bolster your existence more strongly than unshakable faith in the Gohonzon, which is that ultimate reality. Those who live up to their belief at times face slander and criticism. As they go forward unperturbed, they may seem obtuse, but their spirit of forbearance is forged all the more strongly in the process. As Goethe said, "The hammer probably seems more active and devoted than an anvil. But it is the quiet anvil that endures endless pounding."

Who will eventually win the victory, a man of belief or those who drift along with the times like flotsam on the waves? Time will answer the question. Having faith provides the greatest and most enduring strength. I ask you to proudly advance in your mission and, as you do, to cherish the words of President Toda: "There are countless successes and failures in life, but for the final victory we must pray to the Buddha."

The oneness of master and disciple, the oneness of parent and child and the oneness of lord and subject, so deeply and clearly shown to us by Nichikan Shonin through the Gosho, also indicate the vital import of *The Opening of the Eyes*. This text reveals the object of worship in terms of the Person who embodies the three virtues of sovereign, teacher and parent. The life of Nichiren Daishonin, the original Buddha—the object of worship in terms of the Person in the Latter Day—is manifest in its entirety in the Gohonzon. Nichiren Daishonin is the Gohonzon, and the Gohonzon is the original Buddha with the virtues of sovereign, teacher and parent; to know this fact is to feel all the more profound gratitude for being able to worship the Gohonzon.

Life Pervades the Universe

The Great Teacher Miao-lo declares: "You should realize that our life and its environment are the entity of *ichinen sanzen*. When we attain Buddhahood, according to this principle, our life pervades the entire universe both physically and spiritually."

This is an excerpt from the *Guketsu* (Annotation of the *Maka Shikan*) by Miao-lo. I will conclude my lecture with some thoughts about this quote, for, while it is extremely difficult to understand, it is indispensable for understanding the life-condition of Buddhahood. I will, therefore, discuss it in considerable detail according to Nichikan Shonin's *Exegesis*.

First of all, "our life and its environment" means the life and environment of the original Buddha. The entity of *ichinen sanzen*, therefore, is the Gohonzon, which embodies the mutual possession of the Ten Worlds and the three thousand conditions of life. But *ichinen* of *ichinen sanzen* means single-minded faith, and so, when we take faith in the

Gohonzon, our life and its environment both become the entity of *ichinen sanzen*.

The last sentence in the quote, "When we attain Buddhahood . . . " describes the life-condition we manifest when we attain Buddhahood. "This principle" indicates the Mystic Law of *kuon ganjo*, the most difficult to comprehend. "Physically" here means the physical aspect of our life, the combination of the five elements—earth, water, fire, wind and *kū*. It is an objective truth to be realized. "Spiritually" refers to the subjective wisdom to realize that truth, the wisdom that comes from strong faith in the Gohonzon.

As a whole the above-quoted passage tells us that when we embrace the Gohonzon, our life manifests itself as the Buddha of *kuon ganjo*—that perfect union of objective reality and subjective wisdom. In other words, because the Gohonzon is the entity of *ichinen sanzen* embodying the oneness of life and its environment, when we take faith in it, our life becomes the same entity of *ichinen sanzen*. This is what is meant by *juji soku kanjin* (to embrace the Gohonzon is to attain Buddhahood).

The pervasiveness of life, both physical and spiritual, throughout the entire universe is a sign of the boundlessly vast life of Buddhahood and of the common people as well. It not only confirms that the world of humanity contains all the Ten Worlds, but also demonstrates how vast and sublime is the life of ordinary people. To me, this particular sentence also reveals true freedom.

To say that life pervades the entire universe may sound groundless and utterly inconceivable, but even natural science has come to recognize the potential of life through the gradual discovery of just what a highly complicated structure human life has. Take just the physical body. Each organ has its own highly sophisticated mechanism. The liver works to detoxify the body, and so far, over two hundred specific functions have been identified. According to some estimates, the liver may perform as many as a thousand functions in all. The chemical reactions the liver carries out, moreover, are highly complex, and not one so far has ever been successfully simulated in a laboratory. The liver is actually an enormous chemical plant. Not even a huge complex of factories would be sufficient to artificially duplicate all the chemical functions of the liver. Therefore, when the liver starts to malfunction, wide-ranging effects are experienced. One becomes spiritually disturbed, sometimes suddenly waking at night, or walking in his sleep.

Then again, look at the lungs. The total area of all the alveoli (air sacs) of the lungs is roughly the same as that of four large rooms. The lungs work to purify blood. The total length of all blood vessels in the body is 96,000 kilometers—enough to circle the earth twice. Our brain weighs just a little over one kilogram, yet it contains some twenty billion brain cells. Each of its nerve cells has an axon and branches, and intelligence develops as the axons interweave. Personality is determined by the particular pattern in which they interweave, but the total possible combinations of nerve axons are almost incalculable—they outnumber even the atoms in the island universe that surrounds our planet. That is why it is virtually inconceivable that any two personalities would be exactly alike.

A small calculator often works faster and more accurately than we do in simple calculations, and a large computer makes short work of even massive figures. But even the largest computer is no match for the tiny cells in our brain when it comes to such sophisticated functions as making judgments or creating something. At the present state of the art, an artificial brain built with a capacity even approaching that of the cerebrum would cover the entire surface of the earth. And even if the labor, technology and sheer

space needed were available, it is doubtful that it would
approximate the human brain. Not just the brain, but every
organ in this diminutive body of ours, performs operations
which, if artificially reproduced, would be global, or even
cosmic, in their magnitude. Seen in this perspective, a person uses only a fraction of his naturally-endowed abilities in
the course of his life.

Deeper Energies of the Mind

When it comes to human spiritual functions, the scale
expands hyperbolically. Our conscious spiritual activities
alone are infinitely complicated and diverse, expressing
themselves in the achievements of human civilization—in
the arts, humanities, social sciences and natural sciences. The
world of the unconscious, however, is another matter alto-
gether. It remains an almost untapped, vast reservoir of
power and ability whose dimensions we can only begin to
quantify through the work of psychoanalysts and, in the
past, the *a posteriori* testimony of mystics. The conscious
mind is the tip of the iceberg peeking above the waves,
while the huge bulk below is the unconscious. It is difficult
to counter the idea that in the long run, even though we
think we act from conscious motives, the unconscious is
universally dominant in man.

In *Seishin Bunseki Nyūmon* (Introduction to Psychoanaly-
sis), the Japanese psychologist Otoya Miyagi gives several
examples of how the force of the unconscious dictates the
workings of the conscious mind, and in turn controls our
physical actions. Even an action that appears to be mere
chance is, according to Miyagi, influenced by something in
the unconscious, of which we know next to nothing. A
person living in Zurich, for instance, is reported to have
pondered over whether to spend his holiday at home or

make a promised, but unsavored, visit to a friend who lived in Lucerne. He dallied over the matter, but finally decided to go on the trip and left home. On the way, he mechanically changed trains at a station while reading the morning paper. Only when the conductor came up to him a while later did he realize that he had changed to a train headed back to Zurich. Psychologists explain this as a case where the unconscious wish to spend the holiday at home was stronger than his sense of responsibility and conscious judgment, and that unconscious desire controlled his actions.

We sometimes quite casually forget a promise to do something or meet someone; but psychologically this is called "the oblivion of intention." In an interesting example of this type, a person was forced to invite one of his acquaintances to a particular function when he did not want to at all. He called and invited his acquaintance, but said that since he did not remember the exact date and time, he would send him a written invitation. Then he completely forgot, until the day after the function. In this case, too, the particular actions are explained by a dominant, unconscious urge. For most of us, actually, we are more likely to lose a letter with a bill in it than one containing a check, and will forget a dental appointment before we forget a party.

Experience and psychosomatic research have shown that the force of the unconscious always influences the body—the physical aspect of life. Professor Torijirō Ikemi at Kyushu University cites several cases in his book *Shinryō Naika* (Internal Medical Examination and Treatment), to testify that the force of the unconscious causes many illnesses in the human body. The first is the story of a middle-aged widow who is president of her own company. At some point, both legs became numb from the waist down, and she was unable to stand or walk without holding on to something. Ever since her husband was killed in the war shortly after their marriage, she had toiled to care for their child by herself. Some four years ago she was finally able to establish her own firm. Two years later, however, the company suffered a huge deficit when an assistant, whom she had deeply trusted, cheated on the accounts. Profoundly shocked, she lost all trust in other people. About the same time she noticed her legs becoming numb. She began a series of various treatments but her legs did not get any better. The cause of her affliction was the shock she suffered two years before and the unconscious dimension of her distrust in others, but she has never connected the two. Only by restoring her trust in other people will she get better. The profound spiritual shock also disabled her physically.

In another case, a white-collar worker suffered from hives and nausea for several months. The doctor made him keep a daily diary of his condition. It soon became clear that every Saturday he felt nothing wrong, but by Sunday afternoon hives began to appear, and he felt nausea on Wednesdays. Asked about the situation in his company, he answered that he was on bad terms with his boss. In addition, he could not do the kind of work he wanted to on his job. The situation had continued unchanged since he first entered the firm. Professor Ikemi indicated that his unconscious resistance and resentment had built up since he began to work there, and they brought on the illness. Mixed emotions deep down inside, frustrated hopes for the future and distrust of his own ability combined to cause his body to react with hives and nausea. The diary testified to the unconscious force; he was free from worry on Saturday and so there was nothing wrong with him, but on Sunday afternoon he became gloomy and restless, and he would break out all over again.

These phenomena offer impressive testimony to the power of the unconscious to disturb the physical property of life and eventually cause sickness, but they occur in a relatively shallow realm of human life. Human life extends to a stratum of the unconscious far deeper than we can imagine. Professor Hayao Kawai at Kyoto University, a Jungian psychologist, discusses the mind in *Muishiki no Kōzō* (The Structure of the Unconscious): "Judging from these examples, Jung considered that the stratum of the human unconscious could be divided into two, the personal unconscious related to the individual life, and the collective unconscious common to all human beings. They lie in such a deep stratum, however, that we are hardly ever aware of them in our daily lives." He also said about the collective unconscious, "It is not personally acquired but inherently endowed, and universal among all mankind."

The collective unconscious, which forms the deepest stratum of each human life, also forms a foundation common to all mankind. It is said that the entire spiritual heritage of man, gathered over two million years, flows within this deepest stratum. One of Jung's followers, C. S. Hall, analyzed man's fear of snakes and darkness, and concluded that such fears could not be fully explained by the experiences of a single lifetime. Personal experiences only seem to strengthen and reaffirm the inborn fear. We have inherited a fear of snakes and darkness from ancestors back in the unknown past. This is, then, a hereditary fear, according to Hall, which proves that ancestral experience is an engrained memory living in the deepest stratum of human life.

The unconscious contains not only all the experiences of our human ancestors; it also contains the experiences of our prehuman predecessors as well. The footprints of each change in the course of our development are etched into the deepest stratum of each human life, reflecting in some way the vicissitudes of the universe. I suspect that Jung conceived of some four billion human beings on the earth living as one being, and the great universe as a huge living existence. Each human being perhaps seemed like a cell which absorbs vital energy from the original force—universal life itself. This, I think, is the reality that Jung tried to articulate by his concept of the collective unconscious.

As Vast as the Universe

"Our life pervades the entire universe both physically and spiritually." This is the Buddhist intuitive conception of the vast expanse of one's life on a cosmic scale, which modern natural science has only just begun to recognize. Penetrating insights that arose out of Buddhist truths were thus able to uncover the boundless potential of human beings well before anyone could identify or quantify them scientifically. By now, natural science, too, has begun to find ways to identify the cosmic reach of the human potential, but the Buddhist approach to man allows for a still vaster expanse of life, reaching through the universe.

Jijuyūshin, the Buddha of unrestricted freedom, means the full manifestation of this cosmic potential in a single human life. It is the state one can obtain for himself. Nichiren Daishonin redefines it in the *Ongi Kuden*: " . . . the entity of life which one receives to do as he wishes." The Buddha of unrestricted freedom is the life force which manifests itself freely and moves even the macrocosm. Therefore, the principle of "the macrocosm is identical with the individual microcosm" is not some abstract idea but a solid reality for those who devote themselves to the salvation of the unhappy with Buddhahood established as the basis of their lives.

This principle makes it clear that our individual life is completely fused with the cosmic life and it has the same power as the life of the Buddha. How, then, can we bring forth the same life force as that of the original Buddha of *kuon ganjo*? For that purpose, Nichiren Daishonin inscribed his own life in the form of the true object of worship. "To embrace" is "to observe one's mind" and it is possible solely because the Daishonin inscribed the Gohonzon, the only power that enables us "to observe one's mind" and "to manifest the Buddha's enlightenment." Nichiren Daishonin waged a lifelong battle for the single purpose of inscribing the Gohonzon of the Three Great Secret Laws. That is why he declared that he had fulfilled the purpose of his advent when he inscribed the Dai-Gohonzon on October 12, 1279.

The persecutions which he confronted to fulfill his mission were of terrible magnitude. He did not inscribe the Dai-Gohonzon until exactly the right time. The peasants of Atsuhara, who represented all those with pure faith in the Latter Day, inspired Nichiren Daishonin to inscribe the Dai-Gohonzon when they persisted in their faith in the face of severe persecutions. The Dai-Gohonzon inscribed that October, seven hundred years ago, is the priceless entity joining the ultimate principle of Buddhism with the original Buddha's boundless compassion. It is the source of unified light which illuminates the darkness of mankind throughout the entire Latter Day.

Hundreds of years have passed since he inscribed it, and the compassionate light of the Dai-Gohonzon has brightened the lives of more than ten million in this country alone. It is now spreading on into the world, just as the Daishonin wrote, "If Nichiren's mercy is truly great, Nam-myoho-renge-kyo will spread for ten thousand years and more, for all eternity." Now, in the second "Year of Study," we approach the fiftieth anniversary of the founding of the Soka Gakkai (1980) and the seven hundredth memorial service for Nichiren Daishonin (1981).* I will close now, in the deep

---

*Since Nichiren Daishonin died on October 13, 1282, it may seem like the memorial service in 1981 should be called the 699th and not the 700th. According to Japanese tradition, however, the date of one's death is actually the first anniversary. In this light, it might be assumed that Nichiren Daishonin's second memorial was observed on October 13, 1283. Tradition confuses the issue, however, by calling this first-year service the "first

hope that you dedicate yourselves and your lives to the two ways of practice and study. I hope you will strengthen your faith to achieve your own enlightenment in this life and work for the happiness and prosperity of all mankind.

---

anniversary" rather than the second, as would be expected. On the second anniversary (for instance, on October 13, 1284, for Nichiren Daishonin), the service becomes the "third anniversary" and it adheres to strict numerical computation from there on. (There is no second anniversary.) So 1981 is the 700th anniversary, using this system.